THE ANSCHLUSS

THE
ANSCHLUSS

BY

GORDON BROOK-SHEPHERD

J. B. LIPPINCOTT COMPANY
PHILADELPHIA AND NEW YORK

This book is published in England under the title *Anschluss: The Rape of Austria.*

Copyright © Gordon Brook-Shepherd 1963

Printed in the United States of America
Library of Congress Catalog Card Number 63-15615

ACKNOWLEDGEMENTS

THE principal survivor of this episode is the Austrian Chancellor of the day, Kurt von Schuschnigg, and I am immensely grateful to him for frank and detailed answers to all my *questionnaires*, which followed up earlier meetings between us. Any criticism made here of his tactics is simply the historian's counsel of perfection. He did his honest best to play one of the worst hands that a statesman has ever had dealt to him, in one of the deadliest games against one of the most formidable opponents that history could have picked.

Many other officials in key positions at the time have also helped with new details or personal reminiscences. They include Theodor von Hornbostel, Political Director of the Austrian Foreign Office in 1938 ; Alois Vollgruber, Austrian Minister in Paris at the time ; and Prince Johannes Schwarzenberg, then serving at the Austrian Legation in Berlin and now Ambassador in London. Of the accounts given me by Western diplomats then active, I would like to single out that of M. Gabriel Puaux, French Minister in Vienna in 1938, and Schuschnigg's most trusted Western confidant there.

On the English side, I am grateful to Lord Avon (who as Mr. Anthony Eden resigned from the Foreign Office three weeks before the *Anschluss* crisis) for a useful reappraisal of Schuschnigg's dilemma as seen in London at the time. At Lord Avon's request, none of his remarks has been quoted, but the relevant volume of his memoirs, *Facing the Dictators*, was published in time to be consulted and used.

Among other British helpers, I want to thank particularly the Hon. Sir Harold Nicolson, whose private diary for the year 1938 provided me with a vivid glimpse of the mood and activities of that group of 'anti-appeasement' M.P.s who tried, with Eden, to stiffen Mr. Chamberlain's back.

Herr Karl Zrounek, Librarian of the Austrian Parliament, has given invaluable assistance in collecting archive material in Vienna, and in London I owe a special debt of gratitude to Fritz von Boschan, who placed his unique library on Austrian affairs entirely at my disposal.

The principal German actors in the drama are all dead (with the exception of von Papen, whose memoirs have been drawn on with due discretion), so that the German case, as stated here, is essentially that given by men like Göring and Ribbentrop before the Nuremberg Tribunals or in captured German Foreign Office and Nazi party records. The fullest use has been made of these sources, together with other documentary material, such as the Austrian 'Guido Schmidt Trial Protocols' and the files of the British Foreign Office for the period.

This was about as far as basic research could be taken, but it can never be far enough. I am only too well aware that some of the clues still missing might be provided tomorrow by an ex-member of the German or Austrian SS, an ex-Nazi diplomat or *Wehrmacht* staff officer who suddenly decided to break his silence.

Two points about arrangement, addressed mainly to the scholar. This is the first such detailed study to be written on the *Anschluss* crisis and, for that reason, I have given exhaustive source references throughout to the documents, books and special informants used. I apologize for any inconvenience caused by grouping them at the end of each chapter ; this was done deliberately, in order to leave the text uncluttered for the general reader.

Finally, in case there should be any criticism of the brevity of the historical introduction, I do realize that the background to the *Anschluss* question merits a book in itself. The trouble is that I have done this twice already (on a broad front in *The*

Acknowledgements

Austrian Odyssey and on a narrower front in *Dollfuss*), and I could not face even the remote possibility that, on these general issues, someone might be paying a third time for the same views. The Foreword has therefore been kept down to a sort of Prologue which gives the bare setting against which the detailed drama of February and March 1938 is unfolded.

GORDON BROOK-SHEPHERD

LONDON
  December 1962

CONTENTS

ILLUSTRATIONS

The Anschluss

FOREWORD

THIS is the story of Adolf Hitler's first foreign conquest — the seizure, twenty-five years ago, of his old homeland, Austria. It is, at the same time, the first chapter of the Second World War. The fall of Vienna in March 1938 dissolved the dream-world of the Versailles treaties, and began the long nightmare of the Nazi occupation of Europe. The *Anschluss*, as it was called, was the real beginning of Armageddon.

It has this meaning not simply because the invasion of Austria by Hitler's *Wehrmacht* destroyed both the general balance of continental power and the actual pattern of state boundaries as set up by the victorious Allies in 1918–19. More deadly than the blow itself was the way in which it was delivered.

During one week-end, Hitler and Göring together took over an independent country without a single shot being fired for or against them. The essential business, as we shall see, was done not on the battlefield but down the telephone ; the threat of naked force was merely the indispensable background to this bloodless conquest. Hitler's unopposed entry into Vienna served to show him that, in the face of Western irresolution, his bluster and blackmail could carry the day. So, from here on, he drew the same line through Prague and Warsaw — as straight on the map as it was in his mind.

Yet the murky riddle of how that mind worked is deepened rather than simplified by the *Anschluss* itself. The Austrians were Hitler's own people, a people who had rejected him in youth, and these were reasons enough why he could never see them except through a haze of love and hate combined.

However, there was more to it than that. Of all the Führer's triumphs, the rape of Austria displays most clearly that strange blend of fuzziness and clarity, of doubt and determination, in which his thoughts took shape.

It was at once the most inevitable of his conquests and the most accidental ; the best-planned, and the most improvised. This was largely because, though the grand strategy of the operation was his, both the tactics and the timing of it were decided by his victims. By the end of 1937, Hitler had determined on the execution of Austria at an early date ; it was Schuschnigg, the unhappy Chancellor of that unhappy country, who unwittingly fixed the exact day and put the noose around his own neck. This book, in short, will give comfort in roughly equal doses to those who believe Hitler had a precise time-table for aggression and those who believe he had none at all.

The idea behind the *Anschluss* — some form of fusion between the two German-speaking neighbour-states of Europe — was at least a century older than Hitler. In 1806, when Napoleon forced the Austrian Emperor Francis I to lay down the crown of the Holy Roman Empire, the historic framework of German political unity fell to the ground with it. Ever since, the same problem had nagged both Vienna and Berlin : could there any longer be a common German concept and a common German culture without a common German institution?

Bismarck tried to square the circle by separating the two. He sought to preserve Austro-Hungary as Europe's bastion against the Slav East, yet to exclude its ancient sprawling bulk from the compact body of his own new German Federation. The act of expulsion was performed in 1866 by the Prussian cannon at Königgrätz, when Austrians and Germans fought out their dilemma on the battlefield. Seventy years later, Hitler tried in turn to square this same circle by declaring both shapes to be identical. He simply equated race with state, and claimed the Austrians for his Reich because they spoke the same tongue.

There was rarely such clear-cut purpose to be found on the Austrian side. At least three different attitudes towards the Germans lived uneasily together during the last fifty years of the Empire's life. Some Austrians sought salvation in supremacy, and dreamed, even after Königgrätz, of restoring Vienna to her old splendours as the first capital of the German-speaking world. Others — followers of the so-called *Zusammenschluss* doctrines — saw salvation in an integrated partnership of the two peoples, a partnership that was indeed to find diplomatic and military expression in the Dual Alliance and the joint supreme command of the Central Powers in the First World War. Finally, some Austrians, already under the Empire, sought salvation by suicide, and strove to bring the Habsburg domains under the Wilhelminian crown.

We shall meet descendants of all three camps in the Austrian Republic of this story : on one side, the ultra-patriots, above all the Monarchists, who fought Hitler not merely because he was a Nazi but also because he sat in Berlin ; in the middle, the visionaries of a great Germanic partnership in which Austria would always be independent though never equal ; and, on the other wing, the hard core of the Austrian Nazi movement who, like Georg von Schönerer two generations before them, felt as Germans in their political loyalties as well as in their blood and speech. The three points to note about them respectively here are : first, that tradition was the only *natural* psychological weapon the Austrians could throw against Hitler ; second, that the advocates of partnership (depending on the terms envisaged) ranged from near-traitors to unquestioned patriots such as Schuschnigg himself ; and third, that even Austria's Nazi fanatics had a respectable historical lineage behind them.

What all this amounted to was that, by 1938, it was hard to find two Austrians for whom the word 'German' had exactly the same weight or meaning. It was through these mists of confusion that Hitler's tanks clattered so easily into Vienna.

The *Anschluss* philosophy itself went through violent ups-and-downs in the twenty years of the Austrian Republic's life. In November 1918, the $6\frac{1}{2}$ million German-speaking Austrians — impoverished heirs to the old multi-racial Empire of 50 millions which had been formally dismembered at Versailles — declared themselves outright to be an integral part of the new German Republic across their northern border. To the Austrian Socialists like Renner and Bauer who then headed the Vienna government, this was as much ideology as diplomacy : they wished to grasp hands with their fellow Social-Democrats in Germany and to link up two similar systems as well as two similar states.

But for the Austrian people as a whole (and the con-servative provinces of Tyrol and Salzburg who returned 90 per cent pro-*Anschluss* figures in unofficial plebiscites of their own certainly did not share Vienna's 'Austro-Marxism'), this post-war scramble for a union with Germany was less politics than sheer panic. The Empire they had administered for six and a half centuries had been transformed almost over-night into a ring of hostile 'succession states'. The rival pulls of dynasty and race had always torn at the Austrian's heart ; now, with the Habsburgs in exile and the skies mysteriously void of their double-headed eagles, the old Germanic blood-ties seemed the only safe things left in this insane new world.

It was the victorious Allies who stopped the infant Republic committing suicide in its cradle. (For the past 150 years, the Austrians have usually had their fate decided for them by out-siders: Napoleon, Bismarck, Clemenceau, Hitler, Khrushchev are the five big examples.) In 1919, the country was forced by the Saint-Germain Treaty to abandon its chosen name of 'German-Austria' and to call itself plain 'Austria' instead ; the same treaty reinforced the *Anschluss* veto already pro-

claimed at Versailles, and ordered the Republic to stay independent until and unless the League of Nations agreed
otherwise. Here is another strand in the tangled *Anschluss*
tapestry : union with Germany now became a doubly respectable idea precisely because the war victors had forbidden
it.

However, once planted reluctantly on its own feet by the
Allies, the First Austrian Republic discovered, rather to its
surprise, that it could walk alone. In the ten years after
Versailles, the *Anschluss* gradually became, even for the
Socialists, something to talk about rather than something to
achieve, though the abortive Customs Union negotiated with
Germany in 1931 showed the continued force of the idea,
particularly in the economic field. It was, of course, Hitler's
seizure of power in Germany in 1933 which revived the
philosophy as a political aim, and, at the same time, turned it
inside out. Henceforth it was Germany, not Austria, who
took the lead in pressing for a union ; and it was a vicious
dictatorship, not a weak fellow-Republic, that now opened
its arms across the border.

The result, like so much in this tale, was paradoxical.
For the first time since 1918, the *Anschluss* became practical
politics. Yet, also for the first time since 1918, it ceased to be
respectable politics. Union with Germany now meant union
with Nazism, and the Nazi creed was far too energetic,
humourless and intolerant ever to become a natural mass diet
for the Austrians. First the Right-Wing Christian-Social Party
and then their Social Democrat rivals struck all mention of the
Anschluss from their official programmes. Between these two,
the hard core of Austria's pan-Germans, at heart only the
advocates of 'partnership', were squeezed closer and closer
towards the outright Nazi rebels. In short, the fact that the
Anschluss became possible after 1933 only complicated the
arguments more. Hitler had committed the unforgivable sin
of demanding that the Austrians should make up their own

minds ; he had to end, five years later, by making it up for them.

This mental confusion with which Austria drifted into Hitler's grip can only be explained — apart from economic and diplomatic factors — by the country's total lack of internal unity or sense of national identity. To be sure, the Austrians had a hard enough start in 1918. They entered on statehood unprepared to think either as patriots or as democrats, since their centuries of service to a multi-national and autocratic Empire had stifled their development in both directions. And, after 1918, these two crying needs of the day unhappily became rivals instead of allies.

The Socialists succeeded in erecting a parliamentary Republic ; but trampled straight away on the nation's Imperial past. The Right Wing succeeded in preserving the nation's traditions ; only to trample in the end on the parliamentary Republic. A collision became inevitable when each side sought security in private para-military armies. The brief but bloody Austrian Civil War of February 1934 exploded this domestic dilemma without resolving it. Even after the terrible lesson of the February fighting, the patriots remained, broadly speaking, concentrated on the Right Wing of Austrian politics, while the democrats, who had been savagely defeated in the clash, licked their wounds in isolation on the Left.

One vain attempt had been made to build a common political structure under which the moderate men of both rival groups were supposed to work together. In 1933 the tiny peasant Chancellor Engelbert Dollfuss dissolved all Austrian parties (including his own Catholic Christian-Socials) and launched in their place the so-called 'Fatherland Front'. This was intended to be a new and dynamic political forum in which Austrians of all creeds and beliefs could rally behind their diminutive David in his struggle against the Nazi Goliath. Dollfuss was right in proclaiming that patriotism was the supreme need of the hour, but wrong in hoping that party strife in Austria could be buried by the simple process of burying the parties.

His 'Fatherland Front', for all its services in stimulating the sluggish pulse of Austrian nationhood, failed to heal the body politic as a whole. Its membership stayed essentially confined to that of the Right-Wing *bourgeoisie*, and the authoritarian régime of 'Austro-Fascism' which it supported remained anathema to the Socialists — not surprisingly, since it operated without either a Parliament or a trades union movement worthy of the name. To the workers, Dollfuss, even when brandishing his gallant anti-Hitler sling shot, still smelt too strongly of Catholic incense and of the gunpowder of the February battles. It was not until the last hours of the country's life, as Hitler's invasion army was actually massing along the Bavarian border, that the Right and the Left in Austria — still too slowly and far too late — began moving towards each other for protection.

Hitler himself, however, soon recognized the Dollfuss challenge for what it was : the first attempt to fire the young Republic with the proud spirit of the vanished Empire ; the first political programme to be based on the assertion of an Austrian nationhood, in flat defiance of his own racial creed of 'One people, One Reich'. (The contradiction seemed to lurk even in the calendar. 1933, chosen by Hitler to proclaim his 'Thousand-Year Reich' of the future from Berlin, was celebrated by Dollfuss in Vienna to mark the thousand years of Austria's past.)

The dynamic little Chancellor, the 'Millimetternich' of Nazi cartoons, had to be removed from the scene. An elaborate plot to overthrow him and his government and replace them with a puppet régime of crypto-Nazis was accordingly hatched out in Munich by four of the Führer's 'Austrian specialists', three of whom were Germans. On July 25, 1934, after one false start, the *putsch* was finally triggered off in Vienna. Most of the Ministers escaped capture and, with the Austrian Army remaining loyal, the revolt itself fizzled out by dusk. But Dollfuss had fallen — shot at close range in his Chancellory by two of the rebel 'task-force' and then allowed slowly to bleed to death as their prisoner. The one voice in Austria that Hitler feared had been silenced for ever. Like Henry II of England, the Führer had found henchmen to rid him of 'this insolent critic' ; though, as with Becket, we do not know whether the killing was ordered.

Kurt von Schuschnigg, who succeeded the murdered Dollfuss as Chancellor, had all of his predecessor's dedication and personal integrity, but little of his quicksilver instinct for politics, and even less of his popular magnetism. He also had none of Dollfuss's touchiness and proud *mystique* of office — which turned out to be a grave handicap when facing up to the Führer's bullying insults. Indeed, for all his unswerving loyalty to Austria, Schuschnigg could never quite escape himself from the magnetic pull of German loyalties. There was Bavarian, as well as Tyrolean, blood in his veins, and his education by the Jesuit priests of Vorarlberg — themselves largely exiles from the old German Reich — had left him with a lasting worship for the culture of Goethe and Beethoven and the political genius of Bismarck. There was little adaptability in his reserved, intellectual make-up, and he could never quite abandon the hope that Adolf Hitler — for all his monstrous vulgarity — might not one day calm down sufficiently to take his place, as an uncouth imitation of the 'Iron Chancellor', somewhere in this great line. '*Germania docet*' was, after all, what the priests had taught.

Thus there was a strong element of personal idealism, as well as down-to-earth political necessity, in the constant search for an accommodation with Hitler that Schuschnigg pursued during his four years of office. For his part, Hitler had been so appalled by the fiasco of the July 1934 *putsch* and the world-wide scandal of Dollfuss's assassination ('It's a second Sarajevo !' he had yelled in panic, on hearing the news) that, for a time, an accommodation seemed possible. The Führer used all his charms on von Papen, his forerunner as German Chancellor, to accept the post of Minister to Vienna and the mission of putting Austro-German relations back on a respectable footing. Papen, who at this point becomes a key figure in the action, agreed only after extracting from Hitler the solemn promise that violence would never again be used to 'solve the Austrian question'. As a result, from the autumn of 1934 to the spring of 1938, Vienna became subjected to two types of Nazi pressure, now conflicting, now merging : the 'evolutionary' tactics of Papen, seeking to drug her painlessly into surrender, and the 'revolutionary' tactics of the fanatics on both sides of the border, who still much preferred to blackjack her senseless and have done with it. Hitler dithered between the two approaches, and the end, as we shall see, was an odd mixture of both.

The half-way mark down the 'evolutionary' path to the *Anschluss* was the famous Austro-German Pact of July 1936. This agreement was the fruit of twelve months' patient negotiation by Papen, who was a formidable diplomatic adversary for the Austrians since he possessed all the charm of the Viennese and twice their astuteness. In it, Hitler solemnly recognized 'the full sovereignty of the Austrian Federal State', and agreed that internal political developments in the two countries, 'including the question of National Socialism in Austria', were domestic issues which should not be interfered with from outside.

As the Führer had not yet been proved a habitual liar, this pledge seemed, in the world of 1936, to give some comfort and even some measure of international protection. But to get it, Schuschnigg had to pay a heavy price. The Austrian side of the pact amounted to nothing less than a partial surrender of freedom, in both foreign and domestic affairs. Abroad, Austria undertook from now on to conduct her foreign policy 'in accordance with the fact that she recognized herself to be a German state'. At home, the Chancellor agreed, as part of a secret truce programme with the Nazis, to include at least two pan-Germans (members of the so-called 'National Opposition') in his Cabinet.

These men were duly appointed, and of both we shall hear a great deal later. One was Glaise-Horstenau, a war-time Imperial Austrian liaison officer to the German Army ; the other Guido Schmidt, a fellow-pupil of Schuschnigg's Jesuit College and a close personal friend of the Chancellor's. Glaise-Horstenau, as Minister without Portfolio, was charged with supervising the domestic truce with Hitler. Schmidt, as State Secretary at the Foreign Office, inherited Austria's newly-proclaimed 'German course' in diplomacy. Neither man was a Nazi, though the highly gifted and highly ambitious young Schmidt sometimes allowed people to think he was one. It really did not matter one way or the other. The essential point was that Schuschnigg had been forced to take into his government men who were considered acceptable to Hitler in the search for an accommodation with Germany. This was the fatal crack that Göring split wide open in March 1938.

The 1936 Pact thus publicly proclaimed and, at the same time, publicly mocked the sovereignty of Austria. Since there turned out to be only one gentleman involved in this 'Gentlemen's Agreement', the mockery proved the more important. For Schuschnigg, trying to cling to the strict letter of the agreement, it marked the end of Austria's concessions. For Hitler, interested only in its pan-German undertones, it was but the beginning.

The tug-of-war was hopelessly unequal. Throughout 1937 the Nazis, merely by insisting that the Chancellor should stand firmly on the ground marked out the year before, succeeded in dragging him step by step across the dividing line of sovereignty. Two important stages were Schuschnigg's agreement, in the spring of 1937, to incorporate a 'moderate' Nazi section into the central leadership of his non-party

'Fatherland Front', and the emergence, during that summer, of a lawyer called Artur Seyss-Inquart as the principal Austrian 'middleman' between Berlin and Vienna.

Seyss, like Schuschnigg, was a Catholic intellectual and a veteran of the Isonzo front, and politically the two men shared also many ideas about the historic need for an Austro-German 'partnership'. But their theories as to what share the German Nazi partner should be allotted always differed considerably and, in practice, the 'middleman' sold out the entire Austrian stake without a murmur when the crisis came in 1938. The name Seyss-Inquart, which is of Czech origin, will remain a sorry one in Austria's history, though treachery was the result of his actions rather than their motive. In due course, he was to destroy his Chancellor, his country and himself — all three with genuine reluctance.

In foreign policy, despite the 'German state' commitment of the 1936 Pact, Schuschnigg managed to retain some freedom of action to the end. He resisted constant pressure from Hitler to follow Germany's example by walking out of the League of Nations ; and, greatly to the displeasure of Berlin, he continued, throughout his last two years in office, to strive for some special relationship with that other threatened capital of Central Europe, Prague. This diplomatic independence rested, however shakily, on another legacy from the Dollfuss era, the Italian alliance, which must be mentioned in conclusion.

By the so-called 'Rome Protocols', signed in the Italian capital on March 17, 1934, Mussolini, Dollfuss and Gömbös, the Hungarian Prime Minister, had undertaken to co-ordinate their foreign policies and to 'consult together whenever at least one of them considered it desirable'. By this act Mussolini, who was then at the height of his power, declared himself the patron and protector of Austria and Hungary, and staked out Italy's long-term claims to influence in the Danube Basin, in the face of the rival pressures already exerted by France and Germany in that complex area.

For Vienna, this was a marriage of convenience, and of repugnance. The Italians were the traditional enemies of the Austrians, and there was practically no nation in Europe with whom an alliance seemed less natural. There was also no other with whom an effective pact against Hitler was possible. The two countries at least had a frontier in common, the Brenner, and they shared the same keen desire to keep Germany away from it. In 1934 Mussolini had both the will and the power to scare Hitler off this frontier, and he demonstrated both in July of that same year : as Dollfuss lay dying in his Chancellory during the abortive Nazi *putsch*, the Duce noisily moved his divisions right up to the Austrian border in an unmistakable gesture of warning to Berlin. The début of the new Italian alliance had been a brilliant success from Vienna's point of view. Unfortunately, this first demonstration of strength was also to be the last.

For a few months more all went well for Vienna. In April 1935, alarmed by Hitler's mounting provocations, the Duce met the British and French Prime Ministers at Stresa to discuss ways and means of containing the Nazi eruption. Out of this so-called 'Stresa Front' there emerged the only formal commitment the Western democracies ever made on Austria's behalf — an Anglo-French-Italian pledge to 'consult together' in the event of any threat to Austrian independence. As with the Rome Protocols, this Stresa undertaking fell far short of a defence guarantee. It was, however, the nearest Austria could get to security in an unstable continent. The nearest approach, and the briefest.

The Stresa front would probably have crumbled anyway in time under the ideological strains of the partnership and the inexorable rise of Germany to military supremacy in Europe. Yet it was Mussolini who, in October 1935, precipitated its end by launching his Abyssinian adventure. The Duce's attempt to carve out a new Roman Empire in Africa not only transformed the amity of the three Stresa powers into the rancour of their long League of Nations 'sanctions' dispute. It also diverted Italy's eyes, and her strength, from the middle Danube to the upper Nile. By the time that Empire had been won, Hitler had outstripped Mussolini on the continent. From 1936 onwards, Italy's famous 'Watch on the Brenner' became a watch with binoculars only.

This then was the position as the year 1938 drew near : Hitler growing in confidence, strength, fanaticism and appetite ; Mussolini, once his teacher and Vienna's protector, now fast becoming the cynical 'has-been' of European politics ; the Western democracies slowly arming for war with Germany but still thinking only of peace ; the Stresa front with Italy buried under the sands of Abyssinia ; America isolated from, and disinterested in, the problems of the Old World ; and, in the very centre of that world, an Austria as divided at home as she was isolated abroad. The Führer, who was very partial to Destiny, might almost be forgiven for thinking that his cue had come.

CHAPTER ONE

The Turn of the Year

A STRONG whiff of Nazi gunpowder hung over Europe at the turn of the year 1937–38. When and how the explosion would come was still uncertain ; there seemed less doubt where. Throughout the continent, wherever the threatening trails were uncovered, they all led down the Danube to the same place : Vienna.

From London, the young Foreign Secretary, Anthony Eden, sent a private message to Guido Schmidt, the even younger Foreign Minister of Schuschnigg's Cabinet, warning him that, according to Western intelligence reports, German aggression of some sort against Austria seemed imminent.[1] The Austrian Government had already built up the same disturbing picture from the telegrams of its own Military Attachés abroad and, just before Christmas, the Chief of the Austrian General Staff, Field-Marshal Lieutenant Alfred Jansa, had ordered new defence works to be built along the German border.[2] In Warsaw, the Polish Foreign Minister Joseph Beck declared gloomily that 'he saw black for Austria and feared that the die would be cast for her during 1938'.[3] And in Berlin the Nazi leaders themselves had begun to talk and act like High Priests preparing for some appointed sacrifice on the Teuton altar. One member of the Austrian Legation summed up the atmosphere there at the time : 'I often had the feeling that we were being treated as living corpses'.[4]

Against this background, the funny stories then current in Central Europe that the Führer was spending hours poring over maps and pictures of Vienna, designing stern 'Thousand-Year Reich' buildings to replace its Baroque and Victorian Gothic, lost most of their humour.

Of all the Nazi leaders, including Hitler, it was Hermann Göring who had been sharpening his Austrian knife the longest and the loudest. As early as November 1936 (only four months after the signing of the July Pact 'truce') Göring had literally banged his fists on the table in rage when discussing with foreign diplomats the Austrian problem and Italy's patronage of Vienna. The Austrian Minister in Berlin, Dr. Tauschitz, describes in a telegram to his Foreign Office [5] how Göring had shouted in one of these 'temperamental' talks : 'It's simply inadmissible that Italy should push herself in between the two German states, playing the policeman and preventing their union. I just will not accept this much longer and I mean to go down to Rome very soon and make this perfectly clear to Mussolini. Italy's interest in maintaining Austrian independence is laughable and is purely a petty prestige question. The *Anschluss* will come one day, in one way or another.'

This last point Göring did indeed put quite bluntly to Mussolini in precisely those words when, in January 1937, he visited Rome to play Foreign Secretary and collect another decoration. According to an eye-witness of the scene, the startled Duce asked to have the remark translated into French to make certain he had understood it properly. He then 'shook his head vehemently', but said nothing.[6] The passive gesture of disapproval was symbolic. By this time, the whole military and diplomatic deadweight of the Abyssinian adventure was tied to Mussolini's heels, preventing him from acting with his old freedom and energy in the Danube Basin.

Göring left Rome more than ever convinced of the 'inevitability' of the *Anschluss*, and more than ever inclined to give destiny an early helping hand — in the shape of a firm push in the back. The International Sporting Exhibition, held in

Berlin from November 2 to November 21 of that year, provided the next opportunity. As Hitler's Chief Game Warden (there is no better translation for the title, though the English words sound rather thin beside the resounding original of *Reichsjägermeister*), Göring played host for three whole weeks to the sportsmen — and politicians — of Europe. Guido Schmidt had been invited, in both capacities, together with a large and carefully chosen party of official guests from Vienna. This sporting occasion was, indeed, to mark a significant stage in the harassing and stalking of the Austrian quarry.

Game Warden Göring must have been as happy during those three weeks as at any time in his life. His idea of shooting was not only a pretext for diplomacy ; it was a sort of sanctified parallel to it. The organized slaughter, the medieval code of ethics, the emphasis on speed and skill sharpened by an illusion of danger, the master-servant atmosphere of the chase, the supra-national appeal, and above all, the living links with the pleasures and habits of Germany's legendary warrior heroes of old : all this made Göring's sporting functions an ideal setting against which the Nazi *Herrenvolk* could display their gracious might.

Even after a generation has passed, when reading over the elaborate invitations sent around the world to his guests, one can almost hear the plump Marshal purring with delighted anticipation over a function that was to be supremely *his*. Hitler with a shotgun in his hands was somehow unthinkable ; Himmler preferred poison gas.

And, all the time, between the gala performance of *Der Freischütz* in the Berlin Opera and the ball in the Zoological Gardens ; between the dog trials and falconry at Mühlenbeck and the pheasant shoot for fourteen lucky selected guns at Braunschweig (where the guests were taken 'in my special train') ; between the prize-giving for the trophies of all countries and the stag hunt in the Chief Warden's own preserve at the Schorfheide, Göring pursued his Austrian game.

On the 17th of November, for example, one of the Austrian visitors, Count Peter Revertera, who held the key position of Director of Security in the border province of Upper Austria, was summoned, despite his evasive tactics, to a *tête-à-tête* with Göring at the Air Ministry.[7] After a few harmless opening rounds about the Exhibition, Göring turned his sights abruptly on to politics. He complained of Austria's defensive preparations and asked : 'Do you really think that, if the Führer wanted to force the *Anschluss*, Austria would be able to defend herself ? I may as well tell you that this union will be carried out no matter what happens, for the Führer is determined at all costs to settle the question, and nobody could protest.'

Having pointed out that the German 7th Army Corps 'would be enough by itself to sweep the table clean in a few days', Göring stressed that he personally was 'energetically opposed' to any policy involving bloodshed. This, he claimed, would be an 'inestimable tragedy' for the German people, as well as 'completely futile' for the Austrians themselves.

The Chief Game Warden, now wearing his less convivial uniform of Air Marshal, then developed this theme of Austrian helplessness with regard to the international scene. England, he said, would stand aside in any Austrian crisis because her Dominions were 'opposed under any circumstances' to supporting such an 'intervention in Europe'. France might want to act but was 'completely powerless and absorbed with her own problems'. With Rome, Germany was now 'on such a different and better footing compared with 1934 that today Italy would not put up a single soldier to help Austria'. Russia just 'didn't enter into the question', which left only Czechoslovakia and, concluded the Marshal contemptuously, 'we would clean *her* up on the way'.

As we shall see when the crux of the *Anschluss* crisis actually came in Berlin four months later, Göring was to some extent whistling in the dark. Right down to the fifty-ninth minute of the eleventh hour of Austria's murder, nobody in Germany felt quite confident that Mussolini would not be stung once again into protective action, while nervousness about Anglo-French retaliation, especially in Hitler's mind, remained really acute. But, in November 1937, across the great desk of his Air Ministry office at the Prinz-Albrecht-Strasse 5, Göring exuded confidence. Revertera was so impressed that he forsook the delights of the Sporting Exhibition, took the next train back to Vienna and immediately wrote down for Schuschnigg a long and detailed account of the conversation.

This report, a copy of which has survived the war, shows that Göring could use the rapier as well as the battle-axe. For, having disposed of the Austrian body politic with his military and diplomatic *tour d'horizon*, he then proceeded to flatter the Austrian soul. This part of Revertera's memorandum to his Chancellor deserves translating almost in full, for it is the reverse side of that same Teutonic medal which so many Austrians, the loyal as well as the wavering, wore next to their troubled hearts. Count Revertera writes :

'Goring then went on to explain to me that history would pass severe judgement on all those who felt compelled to oppose the fusion of the two German peoples, and that such endeavours were not only pointless but repugnant, since the whole trend of developments was leading to the unification of races. Thus the Italian, the South Slav and the Polish peoples had united against the old Austrian concept and the Czechs had made themselves independent. There remained in Europe only the German people, and they would do the same . . . whether one welcomed it or not. . . . However, the Austrian must realise quite clearly that, in this case, the German Government would not treat Austria like, for example, Bavaria, Württemberg, Baden and so on, and that the leaders of the Reich were well aware that the age-old history and

tradition of Austria would need to be thoroughly respected
by Germany and that this section of the German people
would have to be given the broadest possible measure of
autonomy within the framework of the Reich.' Austria
could, moreover, provide 'an enormous reservoir of leader-
figures for the German people as a whole, since there was in-
comparably more to be found in the Austrian racial branch
than in all other Germanic off-shoots'. Göring ended by
presenting the bouquet that smelt the sweetest of all to the
nostrils of Vienna's pan-Germans : 'Austria', he declared
solemnly, 'would be the cultural and artistic centre of the
whole Reich, though the political leadership would obviously
remain in Berlin'.

The bribe of countless top jobs for the Austrians in a
Greater Germany was crude enough and, as events proved,
spurious enough. Yet Göring was probably quite sincere in
the rest of what he said. As the Führer's very own people
(however much he detested them in many ways), and as the
'purest', most compact and most illustrious German-speaking
group along the borders of the Reich, the Austrians qualified
in theory for very pampered treatment. It was precisely
because of this racial barb that Göring's words could find
their mark in the heart of even so unqualified an Austrian
patriot as Kurt von Schuschnigg himself. As will be seen
very clearly when the story develops, he had laid bare the
central dilemma that few of the $6\frac{1}{2}$ million Austrians of the
First Republic ever solved for themselves : how much should
be rendered to the ancient and powerful godhead of the
German race and how much to the new and feeble Caesar
of the Austrian state ?

One last point should be noted before we leave the Berlin
International Sporting Exhibition of November 1937. Twice
at least during the 'informal' political conversations with
which the festivities were peppered, the actual time at which
the *Anschluss* in fact took place was foreshadowed. Once

The Austro–German dilemma: *Rivals?* (Austrian and Prussian cavalry in action against each other at Königgrätz, 1866)

Or Partners? Emperor Wilhelm of Germany visits Emperor Franz Josef of Austria in Vienna a few months before their armies took the field together in 1914

'Chief Game Warden' Göring, who also led the hunt for Austria

Dr. Tavs, the extremist Austrian Nazi leader, being released from prison in Vienna after his arrest in January 1938 for planning an armed revolt

was in the Göring-Revertera talk, when the Air Marshal declared that the Führer 'was contemplating the spring of 1938' for the 'liquidation' of the Austrian question. The second and startlingly accurate forecast was made by Dr. Wichart, a top Nazi official of the German Food Office, to the Lower Austrian peasant leader Leopold Figl,[8] who was one day to succeed Schuschnigg as Chancellor when, in 1945, Austria re-emerged from Hitler's clutches. 'My friend,' Wichart declared with great earnestness, 'the middle of March is the time for Austria. It's a question of make or break. Unless the *Anschluss* is brought about voluntarily then, it will be carried through by force.'

Figl also took his alarming news straight back to Vienna. Some in the Austrian capital thought he was 'seeing Nazi phantoms'. Others feared he was describing the inevitable writing on the wall. It came to the same thing.

At all events, in Göring's sumptuous shooting-lodge at Karinhall, the *Anschluss* had already taken place before his Exhibition guests arrived. A fresco outline of Europe in the medieval cartographers' style had been painted earlier that year on one of the walls with the boundary between Germany and Austria removed. Göring cheerfully admitted during his Nuremberg trial [9] that he had deliberately ordered the map to be drawn this way in order to find a pretext for introducing the delicate subject of Austro-German relations with Mussolini, who paid an official visit to Berlin a few weeks before the Sporting Exhibition opened. No opportunity was lost to rub Austrian noses as well on the offending fresco. Among those to whom Göring showed it was Guido Schmidt, who visited him more than once in Berlin and who corresponded with him regularly. According to von Papen,[10] Göring looked at the astonished Foreign Minister of Austria with a grin and explained : 'Good hunters know no frontiers apart from game boundaries'.

We must now turn from these significant social sidelights

of Berlin and glance briefly at how Hitler's thinking was shaping at the time — inasmuch as it concerned Austria and is revealed to us today. Here, of course, the key document is the record which a certain Colonel Gerhard Hossbach of the German Army wrote down from memory, five days after the event, of a harangue delivered by the Führer to his service chiefs in the Berlin Chancellory on November 10, 1937.[11]

The gathering was a select one. Apart from Hitler, there were present only the War Minister (von Blomberg) ; the Commanders-in-Chief of the Army, Navy and Air Force (von Fritsch, Raeder and Göring) ; the Foreign Minister (von Neurath), and the one General Staff officer who was to achieve such unexpected post-war fame when, in 1945, his memorized notes were discovered among the Nazi archives and dubbed by the historians 'The Hossbach Memorandum'.

The six men entered Hitler's study at 4.15 in the afternoon and did not escape from the Führer's eloquence until half-past eight in the evening. What they heard during that four and a quarter hours was solemnly described by Hitler as his 'political testament, to be treated as such in the case of my death'. Like many ordinary wills, it was a complicated and rather confused declaration of intention ; so much so that its validity as a firm 'blueprint for the future' has been rightly called into question.[12] But whatever its true significance for Hitler's long-range strategy, it has some bearing on the more immediate question of the *Anschluss*, particularly when read against the broader contemporary background we have been setting out.

After a rambling introduction on economics, the Führer began his central thesis by declaring quite bluntly : 'The path of force is the only way to solve the German problem and this path can never be without risk'. Assuming, therefore, that this decision to use violence, with its attendant dangers, was accepted as the basis of all he was about to say, the only questions which remained to be solved were those of 'When' and 'How'.

Then followed a journey into the future. Hitler laid down the period 1943-45 as the 'latest possible period for solving the German territorial problem'. After that, he claimed, factors of recruitment, food supply and armaments quality would tip the scales of advantage ever more against the Reich. However, Germany would have to strike even before that ultimate date if one of two special opportunities presented themselves. The first was a civil war in France, or similar 'social tensions' there which would tie down the French Army; the second, armed conflict between France and another state (presumably meaning Italy) which would also prevent her 'proceeding against Germany'. Hitler said he saw this second eventuality as being possible 'fairly close' due to current tensions in the Mediterranean, and declared he was determined to exploit it 'even as early as 1938' if it occurred.

In either special case, the exploitation was to be the same : the invasion and subjection of Czechoslovakia and Austria which, the Führer told his generals, was the 'first aim' of German policy. The absorption of these two states, he pointed out, would bring 'considerable political and military relief'. Germany's strategic frontiers would be shorter and easier to defend ; manpower for twelve fresh divisions would become available ; and the German forces as a whole would be 'freed for other objectives'.

The diplomatic risks of all these military fireworks were also reviewed by Hitler and pronounced to be acceptable. He thought it was 'highly likely' that England had quietly written off Czechoslovakia and 'probable' that France had followed suit. In any case, the British Empire's 'disinclination to be involved in a drawn-out European war' would keep England out of the conflict, and this attitude would 'certainly not be without its effect on France'. As regards

Italy, there was 'nothing to fear over Czechoslovakia' but Hitler was notably cautious from that direction about Austria. 'How, on the other hand, the Italian attitude to the Austrian question is to be assessed cannot be judged at the moment', he admitted, and added that this would 'to a large extent depend on whether the Duce was still alive'.

Now it is clear that anyone who had tried on that 5th of November 1937 to read this as Hitler's time-table for aggression would have got sadly lost in the months that followed. To begin with, both Austria and Czechoslovakia were swallowed up within the next year and a half without either of the Führer's pre-1943 test-cases arising. France remained internally weak and demoralized, but neither went to war with herself nor with anyone else. The Duce, on the other hand, was very much alive when, to Hitler's unspeakable joy and relief, he delivered his little godchild Austria up to the Nazis without as much as a murmur only four months later. And when the 'drawn-out European war' did finally break out, Britain and her Dominions leapt into it as one man, to defend not just a country which Hitler had attacked, but a cause which he lived and died without ever glimpsing.

It is also worth noting for our special purposes that, though the *Anschluss* was, in fact, lying just round the corner of the year, Czechoslovakia is mentioned *before* Austria throughout in Hossbach's notes : indeed, for the French civil war eventuality, only an attack on the Czechs is foreshadowed. It seems obvious from the brief discussion which followed Hitler's monologue that this emphasis was no lapse of memory on Hossbach's part. Both Blomberg and Fritsch devoted their recorded remarks afterwards entirely to the Czech problem. Blomberg stressed the strength of Czechoslovakia's border defences which had 'assumed the character of a Maginot Line' and had 'made our attack extremely difficult'. Fritsch added that, as Commander-in-Chief of the Army, he had already ordered a special staff study to be undertaken that winter

with the object of mastering the Czech fortifications and even
asked whether, in view of what the Führer had said, he should
postpone the leave he was due to start in only five days' time.
Hitler graciously indicated that the matter was not quite so
urgent as that. The seven men then turned to concrete
armament questions without, apparently, Austria being mentioned by so much as one word.

What then was the bearing of this solemn conclave on
Hitler's current and future plans ? One plausible explanation
was given by Göring at his Nuremberg trial. He maintained
that shortly before the conference started, Hitler had confided
to him that the whole object of the exercise was to apply the
strongest possible psychological pressure on the generals, and
particularly on von Fritsch, to speed up the German armament
tempo, with which Hitler was 'thoroughly dissatisfied'. It
was for this reason, Hitler allegedly told Göring beforehand,
that he intended to sketch the European political situation in
alarming colours, and von Neurath had accordingly been
called in as Foreign Minister to lend weight to all this.[13]
Admiral Raeder supported this version of events in his evidence at Nuremberg, claiming that, just before the meeting
opened, Göring had passed on to him the news of Hitler's
real intentions.[14] Göring's story also gets indirect support
from the Hossbach Memorandum itself which concludes :
'The second part of the conference was concerned with
concrete questions of armament'.

Yet, despite all this, it would be wrong to dismiss this
famous conclave as being purely and simply a tactical move
to squeeze more arms out of Schacht and the generals. Hitler
was incapable of talking for hours on end with one such
simple aim always in view. The harangue which those six
men heard on November 5, 1937, came from the heart as
well as the head, and reflected the Führer's dreams for the
future as well as his calculations for the present. Even if it
was not a time-table for aggression, it was a ticket for the

journey : and the first stops, Prague and Vienna, were clearly marked.

The real significance of Hitler's language on this occasion was, in any case, its tone rather than its content. The phase of preparation for Germany's territorial break-out was over ; the phase of execution was beginning. Its major stages (the reoccupation of the Rhineland the year before had been but a nervous trial run) were to be launched first, in Central Europe and second, assuming the West continued to give no trouble, in the East. Each of these steps would involve the clear danger of war, and it was this risk which, from now on, Hitler firmly entered down on all his political accounts — on the credit rather than the debit side. What Colonel Gerhard Hossbach recorded for posterity was not just the Führer's impatience over German rearmament but the driving force behind this impatience — the mounting torrent of Hitler's own megalomania and of his supreme confidence in himself as a 20th-century Wotan whom the puny mortals of Europe's Chancelleries could never resist. That November meeting thus both reflected the mood of the time and, by reflecting, deepened it. Psychologically, the turn of the year 1937–38 was the beginning of hostilities.

It need not surprise us that those Nazi plans which were already being hatched at various levels for the overthrow of Austria were not mentioned at this meeting. In the first place, Hitler was painting a broad canvas without regard to the details. In the second place, he was talking to a group of generals at least two of whom (Blomberg and Fritsch) he distrusted intensely as being too 'soft', and both of whom were to be sacked only eight weeks later in a general purge of the Conservative 'moderates'.

Finally, all the underground plotting that had been going on sporadically for the past four and a half years between Berlin, Munich and Vienna was Nazi party skulduggery, of which the German General Staff and the German Foreign

Office were only patchily informed. This dichotomy of the SS as a 'state within a state' had come out very clearly as regards Austria in the abortive Nazi *putsch* of July 1934, when neither the bewildered German Minister in Vienna nor his Military Attaché were told until the last moment of the action carefully mounted by Hitler's plenipotentiary in Munich since the spring. And despite the 1934 fiasco, and despite all the protests of von Papen, who had been sent to Vienna to ride the fiasco down, these secret terrorist links were never broken off. Indeed, they had increased steadily again throughout 1937, as Hitler grew more and more restive at the dawdling pace of Papen's 'evolutionary' policy. It was in these various murky party channels, which often operated against one another and in ignorance of one another, that the threat of the *Anschluss* took on its clearest shape as the year wore on.

Early in May 1937 the first written evidence fell into Austrian hands that Germany was breaking her 'non-interference' pledge of the previous summer. A police raid on the Austrian illegal Nazi headquarters in the Helfersdorferstrasse in Vienna yielded accounts of secret talks which Austrian party leaders had held with Hitler and other members of the régime, as well as correspondence between Austrian and German SS officers, cover addresses for a courier service, and proof that both German money and propaganda material were being pumped in large quantities into the Austrian Nazi underground. Papen, who was in Berlin at the time, drew up a special report for the Führer, admitting that 'very incriminating papers' had been found.[15] The disclosures cannot have been entirely new to Hitler, but Papen makes it clear by his injured and anxious tone that they were quite new to him.

On returning to his post, he counter-attacked by forbidding the leader of the Austrian Nazi 'Radicals', Captain Leopold, or any of his staff, to set foot in the German legation in Vienna. In July 1937, probably at Papen's insistence, a circular was sent round from the Brown House in Munich to all party offices in Germany, calling attention to the fact that 'the maintenance of political connections with Austria is forbidden'.[16] Though another spurt of 'evolutionary' tactics was, in fact, tried out in Vienna that summer, the Brown House circular remained a dead letter, and may even have been written as one.

At all events, the indefatigable Captain Leopold, on his visits to Germany that autumn, seems to have had no difficulty in finding encouragement for his violent schemes in some Nazi quarter or other, despite the fact that he was personally reprimanded by Göring in October for having overplayed his hand. In January 1938 it became clear, not only that Austro-German Nazi intrigue was as thick as ever but that, this time, Leopold and his contact men in the Reich were playing for maximum stakes.

The first news of this turn for the worse reached the West through a garrulous lieutenant of Oswald Mosley's British Fascist movement called Spranklin. This worthy had been on a tour of German and Austrian Nazi party offices, during the course of which he had had a long talk with Captain Leopold in Vienna. Leopold confided to his spiritual brother from Britain that an armed *coup* against Austria would be staged by his group in the spring 'with support from Germany' and that it was hoped to bring out some sections of the Austrian Army in the revolt against Schuschnigg's government. Spranklin could not wait to get back to England with his exciting news and, on January 20, told the story to the British Consul-General in Munich, Mr. St. Clair Gainer, on his way home. The British diplomat immediately informed his own Embassy in Berlin as well as his Austrian colleague in the Munich Consular Corps, Herr Jordan.

It must have been an alarming day for the Austrian. That same evening he was told by another 'absolutely reliable source' of a threat recently made in private conversation by

Hitler himself, also to the effect that a 'thrust against Austria' was coming in the spring.

If Schuschnigg did not come to his senses, the Führer had allegedly declared, then he would 'share the fate of the late Chancellor Dollfuss'. The Austrian Consul-General promptly sent both these reports in a secret telegram to Vienna,[17] where they fell like two more weighty pebbles on the growing pile of gloom.

The air of Europe was, of course, buzzing with rumours at the time. Had they not already received other indications which pointed the same way, Vienna might have smiled at Herr Jordan's 'absolutely reliable sources', and London might have written off Spranklin's story as a fantasy. As it was, the Munich reports fitted an existing pattern and, only four days later, there came the proof that Captain Leopold was neither lying nor boasting.

For months past the Austrian State Police had entertained the gravest suspicions about the activities of the so-called 'Committee of Seven'. This was a panel of prominent Austrian Nazis and pan-Germans which Schuschnigg had allowed to form in the spring of 1937 with the declared purpose of building a bridge for political co-operation between his 'Fatherland Front' and certain 'moderate elements' of the Nazi movements. It was soon clear that the Seven were more interested in dynamiting bridges than in building them. Their offices in the Teinfaltstrasse duly became the 'Brown House of Vienna', the acknowledged headquarters of all Austrian Nazi radicals for whom the 'evolutionary' policy, represented by Papen and apparently tolerated by Hitler, was anathema.

In mid-January 1938, the Austrian security authorities had stumbled on the cypher code in which all the Committee's documents and communications with Germany were drawn up. Armed with this and prodded, no doubt, by Herr Jordan's telegrams from Munich, the Austrian police swooped on the Teinfaltstrasse building on the evening of January 25, and also arrested at his home a certain Dr. Tavs, one of the most virulent of the 'Seven' and the Gauleiter-designate for Vienna.

The papers found at party headquarters and at Tavs's home, when deciphered with the aid of the captured code, surpassed the worst fears of the Austrian Government. The most important of them described a so-called 'Plan of Action for 1938'. This was to begin the following April with nation-wide acts of provocation and sabotage by the Austrian Nazis, leading up swiftly to street clashes which would be too violent for the police, who were anyway Nazi-infested, to control. The moment Schuschnigg was forced to order his army into action, the German Government was to leap to the defence of its 'persecuted brethren in Austria' by demanding, on the threat of a German Army invasion, the formation of a new Austrian Government in which the Nazis were to share equal power with the Fatherland Front.[18]

One detail of the plot even called for the murder of the German envoy, von Papen, in his Legation by Nazi thugs dressed as Austrian Monarchists of the 'Iron Legion' move-ment. This was not as fantastic as it sounded. For the past four years, Hitler, Göring and von Neurath had been warning the generals and statesmen of Europe that a Legitimist *coup* in Austria was the one 'provocation' that would automatically lead to German military intervention. Indeed, as we shall see, the only vague General Staff plan that existed on the Berlin files for the invasion of Austria was for this contin-gency ; it had been called 'Operation Otto', after the name of the exiled Habsburg Pretender.

An anti-Restoration pretext for action was in fact about the best Hitler could hope for, and there were many Nazis on both sides of the Austro-German border to whom the sacrifice of von Papen seemed a very cheap price to pay for it. For the extremist 'Committee of Seven' in Vienna, his death would remove the supreme champion of 'evolution' from the scene ; for the radicals in Germany, it would destroy the very symbol of 'Conservatism' against which a decisive blow was being prepared during those same January weeks, with Papen himself on the purge lists. Rumours that the German Legation in Vienna had 'leaked' some of the incriminating material about Tavs to the Austrian police began to make sense against this background of intrigue and *sauve-qui-peut*.

At all events, whether over Papen's dead body or not, the 'Action Plan for 1938' was designed to crush Schuschnigg by force in the spring. Other captured papers contained detailed 'mobilization orders' for the Austrian SA and SS in support of the German march-in, for which the 8th German Army Corps garrisoned in Württemberg was 'earmarked'. There was even appended a survey of the probable diplomatic repercussions throughout Europe, which sounded like a cracked but very faithful echo of the analysis Hitler had given his generals the previous November. Italy was to be informed beforehand of the action ; Britain could be relied upon to act as a brake on an anyway reluctant France ; and, if need be, a plebiscite could eventually be arranged in Austria to persuade the Western Powers that the 'will of the people' had, in fact, been done.

The Austrian Nazi radicals who were standing by to carry out this scheme were, of course, consistently ahead of 'moderate' party opinion in Germany as well as Austria — if only because their own political future depended on revolution rather than evolution. And their leader at the time, Captain Leopold himself, was probably ahead of anybody on either side of the border. (He, too, was arrested in the wake of the Tavs disclosures, but released after 36 hours for lack of evidence.) Yet, whatever vested interests they had in violence, nobody in the Teinfaltstrasse would have dared to draw up a *putsch* programme as detailed and far-reaching as this without someone high in the German hierarchy knowing and approving of it, at least as a 'contingency plan'.

Exactly to whom the threads of this conspiracy led in Germany itself is still, however, unclear. Some of the sheets of the so-called 'Tavs Plan' had the initials 'R. H.' scribbled on the corners. The Vienna Police President, Dr. Skubl, was convinced at the time that those initials stood for Rudolf Hess and that no less a person than Hitler's deputy was in fact pulling, from Berlin, the wires of the seven Nazi marionettes in Vienna. But all the mountains of German party documents captured after the war revealed no conclusive evidence of this, and even Schuschnigg, looking back on the incident, has stated that he has 'no authentic explanation to offer' for the mystery of the initials.[19]

It is possible that Hitler himself did not know how far this particular 'Action Plan for 1938' had been carried. Then, as always, the Führer was alternating between prodding Destiny and waiting for it, between making plans and breaking them. This was not so much vacillation as opportunism, for a policy of 'keeping the options open' offered the maximum play for his instincts and the maximum dividend for those swift and sudden strikes so beloved of all dictators. This ambivalent approach applied with particular force to Austria, the home-land which had ridiculed and rejected him, and above all to Vienna, from whose gentle face he had picked only the sores of anti-Semitism.

The aim, of course, was not in doubt : there was nothing so sacred or so inevitable in Hitler's political calendar as the *Anschluss*. Apart from these personal complexes which drew him like a magnet to his native country, the absorption of Austria into the Reich had, for him, a blend of historical and racial compulsion behind it. By bringing Vienna safely under the German heel and driving on south-eastwards down the Danube, Hitler would solve the riddle that even Bismarck had left severely alone — how to combine the mastery of

Central Europe and of the Balkans in one strong hand. This feat would truly establish him as 'the greatest of all the Germans'; and, as he muses in *Mein Kampf*, he had always regarded the position of his birthplace — at Braunau-am-Inn on the very frontier between Austria and Bavaria — as a sort of certificate from Providence that such was indeed his appointed task in life. 'This little town', Hitler wrote as early as 1924, 'is situated at the very border of those two states whose reunion must be regarded . . . as the supreme task of our lives, and one to be achieved by any means possible. German-Austria must be returned to the great German motherland. . . . Even if such a union should prove detrimental from the economic point of view, it must take place. Peoples of one blood should belong to one Reich.'

Above all, the doctrine of race demanded the *Anschluss*, and this doctrine was at the very centre of Hitler's political philosophy — or, rather, was a substitute for it. What *la patrie* was to the French and *Haza* to the Magyars, what the city-state was to the Athenians and the class-struggle to the Communists, all this and more was racial purity and unity to the Führer : a mystic crucible into which the nation's memories and hopes, its traditions and its culture were thrown, there to be purified of dross and reduced to one communal essence beside which the individual was of no account.

The 6½ million Austrians belonged first and foremost in this crucible, though how to get them there — whether to lure them in or push them in — seems always to have been an open question in Hitler's mind. He never forgot the chilling fiasco of the 1934 Vienna *putsch*, and clung in his saner moments to the 'evolutionary' policy which von Papen had insisted on erecting over its ruins. But violence was as inseparable from Hitler's mind as a crucifix is from a cathedral. It was an ever-present alternative, and to meet it, schemes like the Tavs plan were drawn up, scrapped and revived again by the Führer's lieutenants.

The Anschluss

The problem for Hitler was when to stress which approach, and how far to go with either stick or carrot. It was even more of a headache for the unfortunate Schuschnigg, to whom we must now return on that alarming January 25 in Vienna.

NOTES

1. See Martin Fuchs, *Un Pacte avec Hitler* (Plon, Paris, 1938), p. 197.

2. *Der Hochverratsprozess gegen Dr. Guido Schmidt*, Öst. Staatsdruckerei, Wien, 1947, p. 219. (Hereafter referred to as Schmidt Trial Protocols.)

3. In a talk with the visiting French Foreign Minister Delbos which was reported to Vienna.

4. Prince Johannes Schwarzenberg, Secretary of Legation in Berlin in 1938, now Austrian Ambassador to London. (Schmidt Trial Protocols, *op. cit.* p. 202.)

5. No. Z 255/Pol., sent from Berlin on November 24, 1936.

6. Paul Schmidt describes the scene in *Hitler's Interpreter* (Heinemann, London, 1951), p. 64. (See also Documents on German Foreign Policy (H.M.S.O.), Series D, Vol. I, No. 207, for Göring's own account.)

7. The account which follows is based on Reverter's deposition in 1947 (Schmidt Trial Protocols, *op. cit.* pp. 292-297).

8. Quoted in Schmidt Trial Protocols, *op. cit.* pp. 83-84.

9. Deposition at Nuremberg (I.M.T., Vol. 9, p. 300).

10. Franz von Papen, *Memoirs*, p. 401.

11. German original text in the Nuremberg Documents, Vol. 25, pp. 402-413. (See also Documents on German Foreign Policy (H.M.S.O.), Series D, Vol. I, No. 19.)

12. Notably by A. J. P. Taylor in his *Origins of the Second World War* (Hamish Hamilton, London, 1961).

13. Göring's deposition at Nuremberg, I.M.T., Vol. 9, pp. 344-345.

14. Raeder's deposition at Nuremberg, I.M.T., Vol. 14, pp. 44-46.

15. See Documents on German Foreign Policy, *op. cit.* Series D, Vol. I, No. 223.

16. As above, No. 243.

17. The telegram is reproduced in full in the Schmidt Trial Protocols, *op. cit.* p. 507.

18. See Schmidt Trial Protocols, *op. cit.*, depositions of Schuschnigg, Police President Dr. Skubl and others.

19. In a letter to the author, 10.2.1962.

CHAPTER TWO

The Road to Berchtesgaden

THE Austrian Cabinet was summoned to an emergency session on the night of the Teinfaltstrasse raid, and the agitated Ministers did not leave the Chancellory for their beds until 3 A.M. the following morning. They agreed over the immediate security measures to be taken : arrest of the leading conspirators and their deportation to Germany, if Hitler would take them in. Opinions were divided over the best diplomatic action.

One group, headed by Zernatto, the Secretary-General of the 'Fatherland Front', urged full publication of the conspiracy in the world's press, coupled with an appeal for the sympathy and support of the Western Powers, especially England.[1] But Schuschnigg overruled both propaganda in the West and protests in Berlin. He was prompted in this by two deep-seated impulses which were to weaken his own and Austria's position in the crisis that loomed ahead — his personal dread of publicity and his general policy of 'doing nothing to provoke Hitler'. However, at this juncture, the tactics of saying nothing for the moment about the Tavs plot were probably sound. Taken by itself, without any dramatic Austrian counter-move, the affair was not weighty enough to arraign Germany in public and stir the heavy consciences of the Entente Powers. On the other hand, it was an invaluable card to hold in reserve for any private show-down with Hitler. This prospect was anyway now edging towards Schuschnigg with the chilling inevitability of a glacier.

Papen, in a telegram to his Führer two days after the raid,[2] suggested that the Tavs incident had served to 'make the Federal Chancellor conscious of the impossibility of letting the present state of affairs continue' and that, as a result, he was now 'most eager for the personal meeting contemplated'. Put in such a bald fashion, this was just another of Papen's hopeful exaggerations to serve his own ends. Schuschnigg did not need the police raids of January 25 for evidence that Hitler was breaking his July 1936 pledge of 'non-interference'. Fourteen solid tons of proof had piled up that same month on the platforms of Salzburg railway station — subversive propaganda material printed in Germany for the Austrian Nazis and smuggled across the border as 'official post of the German railways'.

In any case, it was the depressing outlook on the diplomatic horizon as much as the mounting security threat at home that was driving Schuschnigg to the distasteful idea of a direct encounter with Hitler. The new year had brought fresh signs that Italy had become more the mouthpiece of Berlin than the champion of Vienna. In Budapest early in January, at the last meeting ever to be held of the Rome Protocol signatories (Italy, Austria and Hungary), the Italians had simply echoed Hitler's demands by insisting that Austria should walk out of the League of Nations and join the anti-Comintern pact, to prove the sincerity of her foreign policy 'as the second German state'. Austria's alternative diplomatic umbrella — the so-called 'Stresa front' of 1935, by which England, France and Italy were at least pledged to 'consultations' if Austrian independence were threatened — was also splintered right down to the handle by the Abyssinian quarrel. The long hoped-for *rapprochement* between Italy and her Stresa partners, on which Schuschnigg pinned nearly all his hopes, still seemed a distant and dubious event. Britain's rearmament which, as seen from Vienna, was the only other prospect of stiffening the West and restraining Germany, also needed another year or two to gather momentum.

All this was a sombre background against which the latest emergency had to be placed. Only five days before the Tavs plot was unearthed in Vienna, Hitler's Foreign Minister, von Neurath, had warned the Austrian envoy in Berlin that the Austrian situation was 'like an overheated boiler which would explode unless a valve could be found to let off the steam'.[3] Schuschnigg can be forgiven for believing, after the 25th of January, that, as neither Mussolini nor the Western Powers were ready to grope for the valve and ease this pressure, it was high time he tried to do it for them.

The idea of a personal meeting between 'the two German Chancellors' had already been revived during all the commotion of that critical turn of the year described above. It was probably raised for the first time by Papen in a long talk with Schuschnigg just before Christmas 1937. At this discussion, held at the Chancellor's request, Papen used all his guile to try and mobilize Austria more wholeheartedly behind Hitler's political campaigns. 'The Führer', he told Schuschnigg, 'is trying to restore the world position of the Reich. In this process, Germany has to demand more than the mere passive assistance from Austria. She must insist that, wherever possible in existing circumstances, Austria should support with all her heart and soul this struggle of the German world for its existence.'[4]

Schuschnigg remained non-committal, and there matters rested until early in the New Year, when Papen returned from a visit to Berlin with Hitler's express authority to suggest an encounter. A preliminary invitation 'for a personal meeting in Berchtesgaden' was handed over to the Austrians on the 7th of January 1938 and 'accepted in principle' by Schuschnigg the following day.[5] For weeks, the project then hung fire. Hitler seemed at a loss to know how best to exploit the opening and once, during this period of indecision, asked von Neurath somewhat helplessly what he would do 'if the meeting produced no results'.

Schuschnigg, for his part, dreaded the thought like a visit to a jungle dentist, and was only prepared to go, with heavy heart and feet, for the same reasons of dire necessity. He later described his acceptance of Hitler's invitation as 'one of the most painful and difficult decisions of my whole life'. The risks of a fiasco were obvious to both the Chancellor and his closest advisers ; the latter were particularly worried that their shy gentleman from the Tyrol, whose real ambition in life had been to become a respected provincial lawyer, would prove no match for the greatest political clown of the century.

In some ways, their fears proved prophetic enough ; yet they had to be balanced, before the great encounter, against the dangers of a refusal. Quite apart from the eternal nightmare of 'provoking Hitler', these included the disadvantage of appearing intransigent before that very world opinion on which Austria's hopes of survival ultimately rested. So when — doubtless after more prodding in Berlin by the tireless Papen — the formal telegram of invitation arrived in Vienna on January 26, Schuschnigg again accepted.

Feverish preparations for the meeting now began. It was in these, rather than in the acceptance as such, that the Austrians committed the first of a whole series of questionable tactical manœuvres. The Tavs affair had been such a gross breach of Hitler's 1936 pledge of 'non-interference' that Schuschnigg, despite all the obvious inequalities of the Austro-German equation, could go to Berchtesgaden with a clear bargaining advantage. Papen's jumpy enquiries about the matter in Vienna, and the even jumpier precautionary counter-measures reported from Goebbels' propaganda machine in Berlin, had revealed German fears of publicity clearly enough. Armed with this weapon, Schuschnigg's best approach was to defend by attacking. Above all, his clear course as the injured party was, on no account, to yield another inch of ground.

This, indeed, was the brave way he seemed to start out at

a distance of three weeks from the meeting. Papen was told in advance on the 26th of January (perhaps a mistake) that the Austrians would be complaining or enquiring about a number of disturbing incidents, ranging from the Teinfalt-strasse plot to the indiscretions of the British Fascist, Mr. Spranklin. Schuschnigg was moreover quite emphatic that he was only coming to Berchtesgaden to get the July Agreement underlined and, if anything, strengthened from Austria's point of view, by another affirmation of Austrian sovereignty.

Yet, at the very moment this cavalry charge was being trumpeted in the enemy's face at the front, the Austrians began, behind the lines, to prepare for a further retreat. On the Austrian side, this was of course envisaged merely as an exchange of mutual concessions. To Hitler, who grabbed a mile of rope the moment he was offered an inch, it was all the same thing. Like Neville Chamberlain in London during these same months of slow surrender, Schuschnigg in Vienna made the fatal error of assuming the Führer to be one of them — a statesman with enough normal responses to make normal negotiation possible. His mistake was even more tragic than Chamberlain's, both for himself and for his country. It was also more understandable. As an Austrian, Schuschnigg understood better than most the historical processes that had formed Nazism, and he had enough loyalty left to the German race to hope against hope that it had not produced a new Attila.

This was one factor in the strange domestic prelude to Berchtesgaden which now opened in Austria. Another was that congenital fear of any clear-cut action which the Austrians have always possessed, that legendary 'curse of half-and-halfness' for which their national poet Grillparzer had once upbraided the Habsburgs. This again was rooted in their history, in those centuries of embattled existence at the racial and political cross-roads of Europe which made them lean to compromise as a people like the willow leans to the wind.

There was also one down-to-earth and immediate political calculation behind the steps Schuschnigg now took. The split in the Austrian Nazis' ranks between the 'radicals' and the 'moderates' always looked real enough so long as both were on the run (though it disappeared as if by magic when they smelt victory), and one of the Chancellor's first thoughts on weighing up the Tavs affair had been to use it to widen this split and absorb some of the horrified moderates into his own camp.

For all these motives, conscious and subconscious, Schuschnigg ordered his advisers to speed up the discussion of fresh compromises with the Austrian Nazis almost on the very day he had told Hitler's envoy that no further yielding was possible. He later [6] explained his tactics in these words : 'When the invitation (to Berchtesgaden) became imminent, I pressed for the conclusion of these domestic political talks, in order to get a basis for negotiation at Berchtesgaden, or rather, in order to be able to show Hitler that we had already of our own accord made the maximum internal concessions possible and were therefore not able to pay any higher price'. This approach presupposed for its success that Hitler would not receive in advance the full details of Austria's 'maximum internal concessions' (which he promptly did) and would not then follow his usual tactics of demanding twice what he had been offered (which he also promptly did).

Apart from the Chancellor himself, the key figures in these domestic truce talks were Guido Zernatto, of the 'Fatherland Front', and Artur von Seyss-Inquart, the leader of the 'moderate' or 'evolutionary' pan-German camp. It was a paradox quite typical of the Austrian situation that Schuschnigg stood almost as close to Seyss-Inquart, the man who was inevitably to become his greatest political enemy, as to Zernatto, who remained his staunchest supporter. This was partly personal. Like Schuschnigg, Seyss-Inquart was a devout Austrian Catholic ; like him, an intellectual who had followed the same legal career before being sucked up into politics ; like him, a former officer of the Imperial Army who had fought on the same Isonzo front ; and like him, a shy cultivated person who found refuge from the world in music (it was a long discussion about the Austrian composer Anton Bruckner which first brought the two men together).

Yet there was more to the paradox than these personal links. For Schuschnigg had almost as much respect for those theories of his political rival which helped to drag Austria down as for the devotion of his own lieutenants, struggling to the last to keep the country afloat. This was because Seyss-Inquart was not, in fact, a conscious traitor ; treachery grew out of his actions but did not inspire them. By his own strange lights, he was even an Austrian patriot, seeking to lead his countrymen, peacefully and voluntarily, into the *Zusammenschluss,* or fusion with Germany, which would pay full regard to Austria's own character and traditions. In this, he was the *reductio ad absurdum* of the Austrian dilemma, not so much a turn-coat as a man who always wore his national costume inside out. It was the racial lining that showed, while the red-white-red, though close to his heart, was hidden.

These muddled and cultivated Catholic gentlemen (Glaise-Horstenau of the 1936 pact was another) were not even careerists at heart, though they may have developed the taste for office as time went on. They were the earnest grave-diggers of the Austrian Republic, praying that the corpse would sprout wings in some Germanic heaven, and happily humming Wagner with every swing of the shovel. We have seen Göring going straight for their hearts by offering Vienna cultural supremacy in a common Reich ruled from Berlin. And had it not been for the fact that the Germany of 1938 was Nazi, Schuschnigg himself would not have found the idea too repugnant. This may be one psychological explanation for all the Chancellor's ill-fated manœuvres, both before Berchtesgaden and after. Though it was Hitler he had to deal with, his olive branches were subconsciously offered to that other 'eternal' Germany with which Austria was so closely bound and which he hoped and believed would outlive the swastika.

Seyss‑Inquart's attempts to incorporate 'acceptable' Austrian Nazis into the 'Fatherland Front' and to settle a number of Hitler's lesser grievances had been going on in a desultory way for many months. In the autumn of 1937 he had summed up these demands in his so-called 'Little Programme' which, despite its modest-sounding name, was quite big enough to open the trap-door under Schuschnigg's feet. The Chancellor, through Zernatto, had resisted these concessions so adamantly before Christmas that, early in the New Year, Seyss-Inquart told Berlin he was about to throw in his hand and abandon the whole task of building a bridge between the Austrian pan-Germans and the Government. The machinations of the extremist Austrian Nazis under Captain Leopold, who were doing their best to dynamite the bridge before it was built, were another factor in Seyss-Inquart's decision. But his mood of resignation was not allowed to last for long.

As he admitted at his Nuremberg trial,[7] Seyss-Inquart changed his mind after receiving fresh written instructions from Göring on the 7th of January ; at the same time he also agreed to take no further steps whatsoever without getting the Field-Marshal's approval in advance. Two months before the *Anschluss*, therefore, Göring emerges as its chief wire-puller, and it was already clear in Berlin (though not to the still trusting Schuschnigg in Vienna) that Seyss-Inquart was a mere puppet in the game. He was now jerked into action again.

In the week that followed the acceptance of the formal invitation to Berchtesgaden on January 25, these 'domestic truce talks' were resumed with new impetus from the Chancellor's side and by February 2, Seyss-Inquart could report to Hitler that most of his 'Little Programme' had now suddenly been agreed to by Schuschnigg. The Nazi demands conceded were listed under eight headings.[8] Some were mainly prestige issues, such as the release from jail of the last conspirators still held for their part in the abortive Vienna *putsch* of July 1934. Others, though harmless sounding, were significant enough in a Nazi context, like the 'thorough settlement of press problems' promised by Schuschnigg. At least one point, the inclusion of officials from the so-called 'National Opposition' in organizations like student and athletic clubs, enabled the pan-Germans to strengthen the already firm grip they had on the windpipe of Austria's youth.

But the most damaging concessions were those which opened the doors of constitutional power itself to Austrian Nazis. Schuschnigg agreed, for example, to 'the development of political, military and economic relations with the Reich through the inclusion of persons from the ranks of the National Opposition'. In a crucial talk with Seyss-Inquart in Vienna on February 1, the Chancellor went even further. According to the reports promptly sent back to Berlin, he hinted that he was prepared to carry out a sweeping Cabinet reshuffle which would establish 'equality' for Seyss-Inquart's group of 'moderate' Nazis and pan-Germans, and suggested that his good friend might himself become a Minister in the process. There was nothing outrageous in these suggestions to Schuschnigg's eyes. He still liked and respected Seyss-Inquart, and held him to be as loyal an Austrian as any devoted pan-German could be. The mistake was not to see how little loyalty that condition had, in fact, left his friend to play with. An even graver error, of course, was to offer Hitler such concessions so far in advance. These juicy morsels, which were meant to appease the Führer's appetite, only served to sharpen it.

For the moment, however, Hitler had other prey to devour at home. At this point, the negotiations with Schuschnigg become briefly suspended and then galvanized into life again by one of the most extraordinary episodes of pre-war diplomatic history. To the men in Vienna, the odd beginning of this interlude and its even odder end were marked by two urgent calls that von Papen paid on the Chancellory within 48 hours of each other. On February 5, 1938, Hitler's envoy, who had always been the personification of sprightly self-assurance, called on Schuschnigg 'looking like a man who had become old and grey overnight'.[9] The note he handed over was not, as had been expected, another document in the Austro-German negotiations, but his own recall from Vienna which had been abruptly telephoned to him from Berlin, without explanation, at 9 P.M. the night before. The interpretation Papen himself put on it[10] was that Hitler had tired of his slow 'evolutionary' policy in Austria. It looked, indeed, as though the Führer had resolved on more drastic methods to drag the Austrians to their senses and to their destiny.

This was suggested by the general context of Papen's recall. Hitler had been engaged for the past three weeks in one of the most critical fights of his career — the elimination of all the 'respectable' conservatives left in his régime who might not only have formed a brake on his ambitions, but also a rival centre of power. The War Minister, Blomberg, had conveniently put his head on the block by his scandalous marriage to a prostitute, thus showing more daring in his private life than Hitler credited him with as a soldier. With him was sacked the C.-in-C. of the Army, Fritsch (the second 'anxious man' of the Hossbach Memorandum) and no fewer than 16 other senior generals.

On the 27th of January Hitler took over himself the Supreme Command of the Armed Forces and turned his attention to the German Foreign Office. As with the army purge, all those in high places who might be suspected of 'dragging their feet' were removed. Von Neurath was replaced as Foreign Minister by Ribbentrop ; Dirksen and

Hassell, the ambassadors in the key allied capitals of Tokyo and Rome, were both recalled ; and, last of all it seems, Hitler gave the order to withdraw Papen from Vienna. The name of a radical Nazi functionary was mentioned as his successor.

Things never got that far. Papen left Vienna by the midday train on February 5, a mixture of fury and panic, having smuggled copies of his Embassy files into Switzerland, doubtless to have something with which to blackmail Hitler in an emergency. Not many people who saw him off at the station would have staked a week's salary on his life, let alone on his political prospects. Yet to everyone's astonishment, he returned to Vienna, reinstated as German Minister, only two mornings later ; and that same afternoon, more affable and persuasive than ever, called on Schuschnigg with Hitler's written invitation to Berchtesgaden. Papen's own version of this Jack-in-the-box performance (which is unfortunately the only one we have to go on) is that, at his interview with Hitler on the 6th, a distraught and absent-minded Führer suddenly came to life when Papen put forward his 'last wish on retirement' — the realization of the long-planned Schuschnigg visit. The ex-envoy was restored on the spot to his office, without regard for either appearances or protocol, and sent back to Vienna by the next train to arrange the meeting as rapidly as possible.

Even allowing for Papen's embellishments, the incident was a dramatic one. This is perhaps why its importance has often been exaggerated. As we have seen, Hitler knew all about the projected meeting ; indeed, only two weeks before, in the middle of his domestic purges, he had found time to authorize a fairly precise telegram of invitation to Schuschnigg, naming both Berchtesgaden as the place and 'the middle of February' as the time.[11] True, Hitler had not then finally made up his own mind on the subject. Yet, with or without Papen's farewell call, the issue would anyway have arisen within the next few days, and Hitler's decision would, in all probability, have been the same. A diplomatic success abroad was the dictator's obvious diversion from a domestic battle at home. Austria was the equally obvious choice. Twice in January her Chancellor had agreed to pay him a visit and the reports from Vienna had suggested that he would be coming in a very pliant mood. It was not entirely a coincidence that in 1938, as in 1934, a blow at Austria should have come hard on an internal German crisis. The July *putsch* in Vienna had followed the liquidation of Roehm and his SA. Four years later, the purge of the generals was to lead into the *Anschluss* itself.

Even if the Berchtesgaden meeting would almost certainly have taken place without Papen's chance reminder, he undoubtedly helped to set the stage for this dreadful event. He knew that his immediate personal future was now at stake in making the visit a resounding success from Hitler's point of view and, within a few hours of returning to Vienna, Papen set to work on Schuschnigg accordingly. Whether the earnest promises he made to the Austrian Chancellor on February 7 exceeded his authority or not, they had the same impressive effect. Papen pledged his Führer's word that 'no additional political demands' would be made at the conference and that Hitler would reaffirm all his obligations under the 1936 Pact.[12] Indeed, the envoy went on, he was empowered to state that Austria's political situation after the meeting 'would on no account be worse than at the moment'.

A moment's reflection should have caused the Austrians to doubt this rather odd assurance. Blomberg and Fritsch, now removed from the scene, had both been regarded in Vienna as the two principal military opponents in Berlin of any violent solution to the Austrian problem. On the diplomatic front, von Neurath, for all his failings, was to be preferred a dozen times over to the restless and ruthless Ribbentrop. But Papen, oozing Germanic good fellowship, even managed to turn these spectres into peace doves. He suggested that the recent upheavals in the Nazi régime, so far from complicating the proposed conference, would enable it to be held in a 'uniquely favourable atmosphere', since the Führer now needed 'tranquillity in his foreign relations' to master his domestic troubles.[13]   As a more tangible bait, Papen promised the publication of an agreed joint declaration after the meeting in which the basic principles of the July 1936 Pact would again be reaffirmed.

Schuschnigg probably did not believe all of these promises ; yet neither did he need them.   Not only had he made up his mind already, without Papen's persuasion, to go to Berchtesgaden ; he now began, entirely on his own initiative, to work out during the four days that remained a fresh series of 'maximum concessions', going beyond the 'Little Programme', to take there with him.   To prepare for a further gratuitous withdrawal of this sort, even on paper, when the watchword of the day was 'No change on 1936' was demoralizing enough for his supporters.   Far worse ; it destroyed the only bargaining position he ever had when, not surprisingly, the news of this secretly prepared retreat reached Hitler in Berchtesgaden a few hours before Schuschnigg's own arrival.

To keep a fair balance, one must be careful not to judge the Austrian Chancellor with too much historical hindsight. At this moment, neither Schuschnigg nor any other European statesman yet had the proof *ad oculos* that Hitler was an obsessed fanatic with whom reasoned argument was impossible ; the Berghof meeting was, indeed, Hitler's diplomatic début in this rôle.   Nor, for all the ugly reports received in Vienna, could Schuschnigg bring himself to believe that the *Anschluss* was inevitable, much less that it would come in a bare five weeks' time.   Having said that, however, his tactics in these last days before Berchtesgaden still remain questionable in logic and calamitous in outcome.

Once again, it was the industrious Zernatto, Secretary-General of the 'Fatherland Front', who was given the task of working out these new Austrian fall-back positions. The result was a list of ten points, the so-called '*Punktationen*', which were put before Seyss-Inquart in Vienna on February 11, the very eve of the visit to Hitler.[14] On all fronts, they marked a further voluntary Austrian withdrawal from the positions which Schuschnigg had conceded less than a fortnight before by accepting Seyss-Inquart's 'Little Programme'.

The attainment of a 'real press truce' mentioned in that programme had now blossomed into a promise 'to appoint a person to the Federal Press Office who would have the task of helping to solve all questions connected with the German and Austrian pan-German press'. The 'development of military relations' between the two countries, envisaged in the 'Little Programme', now read : 'Training and equipment are to be fused to the maximum extent after the pre-conditions for the closest possible military collaboration (*Zusammenleben*) have been created'. The increased political recognition for 'acceptable' Austrian Nazis and pan-Germans, promised in principle at the beginning of the month, now took on concrete form : three men from this camp were nominated for the Austrian Council of State ; another for the Economic Council ; another (Göring's brother-in-law, of all people) for the Directorate of Sports ; and yet another for the Civil Servants Chamber. As regards the 'Fatherland Front' itself, the appointment of selected Austrian Nazis to official positions at all levels of the organization was now promised, the process 'to be substantially completed in about three months'.

The Ten Points even gave ground on that ideological front which was so vital in the Austrian's own struggle of race versus state. Point Seven, for example, opened with the words : 'There are certainly some important basic concepts of a non-party-bound National Socialism which can be organically incorporated into the political ideology of the new Austria'. It would have been difficult to think, in February 1938, of a more egregious and dangerous piece of nonsense. After five years of Hitler, it was crystal-clear that there was not, and never could be, any such thing as a National Socialism that was not 'party-bound'. And, after four years of his unbroken meddling in Austria, it should have been equally clear that the only party the Austrian Nazis were bound to was the NSDAP in Germany.

It was this strange illusion — that Austrian Nazism could somehow be treated as a force apart from Hitler in all these negotiations — that doomed Zernatto's '*Punktationen*' from the start. For, in them, Schuschnigg had worked on the basic assumption that Seyss-Inquart and the Nazi 'moderates' were independent as well as on his side ; indeed, from the Chancellor's point of view, the whole object of Zernatto's labours was to establish Seyss more securely than ever before as the leader of these 'moderates' and the principal liaison channel with Germany.

Theoretically, of course, the attempt to split the Nazi camp into two, absorb the digestible part into the 'Fatherland Front' and isolate the fanatics made sense — though in terms of practical politics, it was as illusory as the tactics adopted by the Austro-Fascists and Austro-Marxists five years before of trying to conquer their rivals by dividing them. Yet there were at least two aspects of Zernatto's Ten Points which were hazardous even in theory. The first were the specific concessions offered in the propaganda and military fields, which simply opened these central floodgates to direct pressure from Germany. The second was the mere fact that any or all of these points should have been laid before someone like Seyss-Inquart less than 24 hours before the Berchtesgaden meeting. There was little need to discuss them with him if they were to be raised with his master in Germany the next day. On the other hand, the journey to Berchtesgaden itself would be pointless if, through these last-minute Vienna talks, the Führer learned in advance of the retreat which his guests were busily planning. The Ten Points, even kept as a secret between

Schuschnigg and Zernatto, were demoralizing enough. Conveyed to the Führer, they were like ten bullets fired into the Austrian delegation.

Duly conveyed they were, and in typically Viennese fashion. The Ten Points had been drawn up in draft form by Zernatto on the morning of February 11, and were laid before Seyss-Inquart that afternoon at the headquarters of the 'Fatherland Front'. These discussions — in which only the Chancellor, Seyss and Zernatto took part — dragged on with interruptions until 9 o'clock that night and, during one of these pauses, Seyss-Inquart summoned one of his colleagues, a certain Dr. Kajetan Mühlmann, to the building. Mühlmann was an art critic by profession, a 'moderate' Nazi by persuasion and a political busybody by passion. He was one of those human corks who bob up and down in the surge of all great events, yearning to turn the tide of history but content if they can just ride on the foam. This particular cork was to have a very exciting time. He was to be the first outsider to learn of the new concessions Schuschnigg was making, and the first to inform Hitler of them.

According to his own rather oily version of events,[15] he was received by Seyss-Inquart at about 5 o'clock in the afternoon, given an outline of the Ten Points which were still being debated elsewhere in the building, and told to leave immediately for Berchtesgaden with the news. The gloss Mühlmann put on his mission after the war was that he should contact Papen (who had gone ahead to prepare the visit) and Keppler (who was the Führer's Commissioner for Austrian Affairs) with the object of preventing any last-minute sabotage of the promising negotiations by Captain Leopold and his Austrian Nazi fanatics.

This might have been one motive of Seyss-Inquart's for, on the 8th and 9th of February, the dreadful Captain had launched some more of his terrorist actions. However, an appeal to the German side to be on their guard against Leopold's sniping had nothing secret about it and could have gone far more quickly by telephone ; what could not be safely sent by any means except special courier was the startling news that, before the meeting of the two Chancellors had even begun, Schuschnigg was prepared to reduce his maximum demands still further in the earnest search for peace. It seems as plain as a pikestaff that Seyss' main motive in packing Mühlmann off to Germany in the first train after their talk was to rush the news to Hitler of this well-meaning Austrian compliance. The situation was well worth a special messenger. The gestures of legality which Schuschnigg was asking of Hitler in the Ten Points were meaningless ; the Führer was pre-pared to sing the praises of virginity at the very moment of rape. And, for that matter, the expansion of Nazi power and influence which the Austrian concessions offered on all fronts were like a direct enticement to rape.

Mühlmann acquitted himself efficiently enough in his rôle of Nazi Mercury. He arrived at Berchtesgaden at 7 A.M. the next morning and poured out his story over breakfast to Papen and Keppler. These two evidently thought his news of sufficient importance to be brought immediately to Ribben-trop. According to Mühlmann (though here his account is in dispute), they whisked him off to Ribbentrop's hotel where he repeated his tale to the new Foreign Minister. The four men spent an hour together discussing the significance of the message, and the meeting was only broken off because it was high time for Papen to leave for the Salzburg border post to welcome Schuschnigg there in the Führer's name. Ribben-trop declared himself so impressed by Mühlmann's news that, before getting into his car, he informed the breathless art critic that he might be summoned before Hitler himself later that day.

Mühlmann was to enjoy this brief but glorious triumph, which was also to be climax of his nosey-parker's career. (For him, as for so many other Austrian Nazi intriguers, the

Anschluss itself brought disappointment. Seyss-Inquart re-
warded his services by appointing him 'State Secretary for
Cultural Affairs' in the last short-lived Austrian 'Cabinet'
formed as the German troops marched in. But by the time
the appointment was gazetted on March 15, Austria had disappeared even as a quasi-independent protectorate, and Seyss-
Inquart's two-day Cabinet with it. This did not stop the art
critic, in true Austrian style, from using the resounding title
of 'Herr Staatssekretär' socially — until Hitler's Gauleiter for
Vienna, Josef Bürckel, warned him that the police would be
after him unless he dropped it.)

Before following Papen down to the Austro-German
border on the morning of February 12, we must look briefly
at Schuschnigg's final preparations for the journey in Vienna
on the previous night. The discussion over the Ten Points,
to which Seyss-Inquart returned after he had despatched his
messenger, lasted another four hours. The three participants,
at least in retrospect, all emerged with different ideas about the
outcome. Schuschnigg gave the impression to some of his
colleagues that he had agreed to the Ten Points as they stood,
at least as a basis for negotiation with Hitler.[16] Zernatto, on
the other hand, declared later that same evening that he was
still 'not finished with the talks'. Seyss-Inquart maintained at
his Nuremberg trial [17] that he had tried to squeeze still more
out of Schuschnigg by holding out for an even greater freedom
of movement for the Nazis within the 'Fatherland Front'. But
he admitted that his eve-of-Berchtesgaden meeting on February
11 had given him two-thirds of his demands ; and the important thing, for him as for Hitler, was that the Austrian Chancellor was prepared to go that far.

One more incident is worth recording about these last-
minute Vienna discussions because it lights up again that
strange, ambiguous relationship between Seyss-Inquart and
Schuschnigg. The Chancellor had gone on the assumption
that Seyss and his circle knew nothing of the imminent meeting

The scene in the Chancellory in Berlin as Göring conveyed birthday wishes
to the Führer

Hitler's home in Berchtesgaden

Hitler and his generals

Schuschnigg and his generals

with Hitler, and had intended to let him into the secret during these final talks. As even the Austrian Federal President, Dr. Miklas, had only been informed himself a few hours before, this was fairly privileged treatment — treatment which showed that Schuschnigg still regarded Seyss as being basically a trustworthy Austrian. In fact, Seyss-Inquart had been told all about the Berchtesgaden meeting the day before by the ubiquitous Mühlmann, and now gently indicated to a somewhat astonished Chancellor that he was already 'in the know'. (Quite how Dr. Mühlmann discovered the great secret is uncertain ; though as two of Göring's sisters were married to Austrians and as our art expert often took tea with both ladies in Vienna, his opportunities were obviously considerable.)

During these tense days, Vienna's Carnival season reached its climax, and one of the last engagements Schuschnigg had to fulfil before leaving for Germany was the Ball of his own 'Fatherland Front'. It was a glittering occasion, attended by the whole Government and, according to one eye-witness, the entire Diplomatic Corps except the German and the Russian Ministers. For the first time at such a social function, Schuschnigg wore the dress uniform of the *Sturmkorps* leader of his Front. It was also to be the last time. This ball, held under the shadow of Berchtesgaden, was in fact almost the last festive assembly of Schuschnigg's followers, the last parade of that 'Christian, authoritarian and corporate state' which Dollfuss had created four years before.

There is something very fitting about the fact that Austria should have waltzed away the last hours of her real independence. It was especially appropriate that the 'Fatherland Front' should have blossomed out for the last time on a dance floor. More than anything else, the Vienna Carnival season, with its 'compulsory' balls for every institute, society, trade and profession in the capital showed that, socially at least, the Austrians were very close at heart to the 'corporate citizens' Dollfuss and Schuschnigg tried to make out of them.

Shortly before midnight on February 11, the Chancellor had to do another quick-change act — this time into the sporting garb of a Viennese leaving the capital for a week-end's skiing in the Tyrol. This was the alibi the Austrian security authorities had chosen to explain Schuschnigg's departure ; he was to leave on the ordinary overnight train to Innsbruck, but his special carriage would travel only as far as Salzburg before being uncoupled to await the dawn. So the skis and other holiday paraphernalia were noisily loaded aboard and then, before the whistle blew, the Chancellor paced up and down the platform with his colleagues, trying to look like a man who has nothing more alarming on his mind than the prospect of poor snow.

In fact, during these last minutes in Vienna, Schuschnigg seems to have been seized with uneasy premonitions. A mood of anticlimax seized him after all the hard bargaining and the even harder make-believe of the day. He had a heavy feeling that nothing good would come out of the journey he was about to begin : the ultra-Austrians would surely criticize him for any concession made to Hitler, and the Nazis would, just as surely, call any concession too small.

This was all prophetic enough in its way. Even more so was a vision Schuschnigg suddenly had during these moments of the Führer himself. He turned to his Foreign Minister, Guido Schmidt, just as they were boarding the train and said, only half in jest : 'You know, it would really be better for Wagner-Jauregg to undertake this trip instead of me'. Professor Wagner-Jauregg had nothing to do with politics. He was the most distinguished Austrian psychiatrist of the day.

NOTES

1. See Schmidt Trial Protocols, *op. cit.* p. 92.
2. Documents on German Foreign Policy, Series D, Vol. I, No. 279.
3. Schmidt Trial Protocols, p. 135.

4. Documents on German Foreign Policy, *op. cit.* Series D, Vol. I, No. 273.

5. The texts are reproduced in Schmidt Trial Protocols, pp. 556-557.

6. In written testimony at the Schmidt Trial, see Protocols, pp. 584-585.

7. I.M.T., Vol. 16, p. 100.

8. For Seyss-Inquart's report, see Documents on German Foreign Policy, *op. cit.* No. 282.

9. The description of the Austrian Foreign Minister, Dr. Guido Schmidt, who was present. See Schmidt Trial Protocols, p. 53.

10. See Papen *Memoirs*, *op. cit.* p. 407.

11. See Schmidt Trial Protocols, *op. cit.* p. 557.

12. See Schmidt Trial Protocols, *op. cit.* p. 579.

13. Papen, *Memoirs*, pp. 408-409, and Schmidt Protocols, *op. cit.* p. 584.

14. For their full text, see Schmidt Trial Protocols, pp. 557-559.

15. See Schmidt Trial Protocols, *op. cit.* pp. 249-250.

16. See, for example, Guido Schmidt's own testimony at his trial, Schmidt Trial Protocols, *op. cit.* p. 448.

17. I.M.T., Vol. 15, p. 674.

CHAPTER THREE

Face to Face

THE place, they said, had been called after Berchta, a
wicked fairy who dwelt in the crags of the Hoher Göll
mountain above, nursing her eternal spite against mankind in
a blanket of thunderstorms. On that February 12, 1938,
Berchta seemed to have come right down to the village to
deal with the visiting Austrian Chancellor, quite undismayed
by his Jesuit upbringing.

The first premonition of danger reached Schuschnigg the
moment his car crossed the German frontier post three miles
out of Salzburg. Very suitably, the immaculate messenger
of ill-tidings was Herr von Papen, who was waiting at the
barrier to greet the Führer's guests. Papen was bubbling over
with good spirits, and assured the Chancellor that Hitler too
was 'in an excellent mood'. By the way, added Papen in-
nocently, would there be any objection to the fact that several
generals had turned up, 'quite accidentally', for the meeting ?
In reply to Schuschnigg's question, the envoy named these as
Keitel, the newly appointed Chief of the *Wehrmacht* High
Command ; von Reichenau, the Commander-in-Chief of the
4th German Army Group at Leipzig, and the Air Force
general Sperrle, who had previously commanded the Nazi
'Condor' Legion in the Spanish Civil War.[1]

In its small way, this was a crucial moment. The sum-
moning by one side of Commanders-in-Chief to what had
been arranged as a private political discussion between the two
Chancellors was a clear breach of faith, and a menacing one.
Either it meant that matters of top-level military importance
were to be introduced into the talks by Hitler, which was

contrary to all previous understanding ; or else, as proved the case, that the meeting itself was to be held against a background of blackmail and threats. Had Schuschnigg been a little less afraid of provoking Hitler, had he possessed a little more of Dollfuss's political vanity, or a grain of his murdered predecessor's intuitive peasant instinct, he would have fought the first round of Berchtesgaden there and then at the frontier post by requesting either the withdrawal of the German generals or permission to fetch some 'military advisers' of his own from nearby Salzburg. The garrison commander would have sufficed, provided he turned up in full regalia.

But Schuschnigg was not Dollfuss. He hated fuss and scenes. He failed to see how much of politics, especially Nazi politics, was made up of bluff, bluster and appearances. As for his own modest person, there was almost no insult he was not prepared to endure on that journey if it would win his country a few more precious months of life. So he neither protested nor enquired further about the generals and, on that chilling note, the drive to Berchtesgaden began. For all Papen's chatter, the short trip to the village can have done little to soothe Schuschnigg's nerves : Hitler had obligingly transformed this beautiful little wedge of border territory into an armed camp for the occasion, with motorized convoys on the roads and planes droning overhead.

Soon after reaching the village, all the passengers in the convoy left their cars and mounted half-tracked vehicles which were waiting to take them up the steep icy road to the Berghof, Hitler's mountain retreat. The first iron gate barrier to appear was opened without challenge by a smartly turned-out sentry. It so happened that, four months later, this very same soldier was assigned to guard duty outside the room of the Hotel Metropole in Vienna where the ex-Chancellor Schuschnigg began his long spell as Hitler's prisoner. Berchta had thought of everything on that cold and cloudy February morning.

On this occasion, however, Hitler was still the host and not the gaoler. He greeted the Austrian party in polite and even friendly terms on the broad entrance steps to the Berghof, wearing his brown SA jacket with the swastika armband and a pair of black trousers. The three generals, already in evidence at his elbow, had little to say (they confessed later that they had not the slightest idea why they had been summoned). After a formal introduction of the two delegations, Hitler led Schuschnigg upstairs alone to his first-floor study with the famous panorama windows that looked across at Salzburg and his homeland Austria. Soon after 11 A.M. the door closed behind them, and this first and last parley between 'the two German Chancellors' began.

As no interpreter was needed, and as Hitler left no record of the meeting, the only authoritative account of what followed is that jotted down from memory soon afterwards by Schuschnigg.[2] According to this very full summary, Hitler dismissed his guest's polite opening gambit about the splendid scenery with the words : 'Yes, but we have not met to talk about the lovely view or the weather' ; and on that uncompromising note, the Führer launched straight into an attack against Austria for failing to pursue a 'German foreign policy'.

The following exchange then took place, with Hitler's rage steadily mounting and Schuschnigg's resistance steadily melting :

Hitler : 'Austria has anyway never done anything which was of help to the German Reich. Her whole history is one uninterrupted act of treason to the race. That was just as true in the past as it is today. But this historical contradiction must now be brought to its long overdue conclusion. And I can tell you this, Herr Schuschnigg, I am resolutely determined to make an end to all this business. The German Reich is a Great Power ; nobody can and nobody will interfere if it restores order on its frontiers.'

Schuschnigg : 'I am aware of your attitude towards the Austrian question and towards Austrian history, Herr Reichskanzler, but you will understand that my own views on this subject are basically different. As we Austrians see it, the whole of our history is a very essential and valuable part of German history which just cannot be wished away from the overall German picture. And Austria's contribution is a considerable one.'

Hitler : 'It's absolutely zero — that I can assure you ! Every national impulse has always been trampled underfoot by Austria : that was the chief preoccupation of the Habsburgs and the Catholic Church.'

Schuschnigg : 'Despite that, Herr Reichskanzler, there are many Austrian achievements which cannot be separated from the general German cultural scene. I'm thinking among others of Beethoven, for example. . . .'

Hitler : 'Indeed ? I regard Beethoven as a Lower Rhinelander.'

Schuschnigg : 'He was an Austrian by choice, like many others. It would never occur to anybody, for example, to describe Metternich as a Rhinelander.'

The Führer evidently found this intermezzo — which meant so much to his sincere and cultivated guest — both irrelevant and irritating. Without even conceding the point, he mounted his favourite hobby horse of Destiny and, as always when on that particular mount, went away at a gallop.

Hitler : 'I can only tell you yet again that things cannot go on as they are. I have an historical mission before me, and this mission I will fulfil because Providence has selected me to do so. . . . My task in life was marked out for me. I have travelled the hardest road that any German ever had to tread and I have achieved more in

German history than it was given for any other German to bring about. And, mark you, not by force. I am borne forward by the love of my people . . . wherever I go, I need the police only to control the masses and protect them from being crushed by their own tumultuous enthusiasm, not to protect me.'

Schuschnigg : 'I gladly believe you, Herr Reichskanzler.'

Hitler : 'I could call myself an Austrian with just the same right — indeed with even more right — than you, Herr Schuschnigg. Why don't you once try a plebiscite in Austria in which you and I run against each other ? Then you would see !'

Schuschnigg : 'Well, yes, if that were possible. But you know yourself, Herr Reichskanzler, that it just isn't possible. . . . We simply have to go on living alongside one another, the little state next to the big one. We have no other choice. And that is why I ask you to tell me what your concrete complaints are. We will do all in our power to sort things out and establish a friendly relationship, as far as is possible for us. . . .'

Hitler : 'That's what *you* say, Herr Schuschnigg. And *I* am telling you that I intend to clear up the whole of this so-called Austrian question — one way or the other. Do you think I don't know that you are fortifying Austria's border with the Reich. . . ?'

Schuschnigg : 'There can be no suggestion at all of that. . . .'

Hitler : 'Ridiculous explosive chambers are being built under bridges and roads. . . .'

Schuschnigg : 'If that were so, I must have heard of it. . . .'

Hitler : 'You don't honestly believe, do you, that you can lift a single stone without my hearing about it the next day ?'

Schuschnigg, of course, knew all about the measures taken to strengthen the Austro-German border, since he had himself ordered them. No defensive precautions could have been more legitimate ; their initial purpose was to repel any large-scale incursion by the 'Austrian Legion', those bands of desperate Austrian Nazi refugees whom Hitler had been training for the past four years as a para-military striking force poised right against the Austrian frontier. Yet, instead of making this perfectly reasonable point, Schuschnigg, according to his own account, only offered semi-excuses : he tried to explain away the North-Western defence works as being 'at the most those elementary precautions, taken on all Austria's borders, partly as a reprisal against Czechoslovak road-blocks'. If this was meant to soothe the Führer, it only succeeded in throwing him into an even greater fury. The dialogue continued :

Hitler : 'I only have to give one command and all this comic stuff on the border will be blown to pieces overnight. You don't seriously think that you could hold me up, even for half an hour, do you ? Who knows — perhaps you will find me one morning in Vienna, like a spring storm. Then you will go through something ! I'd like to spare the Austrians from that . . . the SA and the Legion would come in after the troops and nobody — not even I — could stop them from wreaking vengeance. Do you want to turn Austria into a second Spain ? I would like to avoid all that — if it is possible.'

Schuschnigg : 'I will make enquiries and have any defence work which might be in progress along the German border stopped. Of course I realize that you can march into Austria, but Herr Reichskanzler, whether we like it or not, that would bring bloodshed. We are not alone in the world and that would, in all probability, mean war.'

This remark touched off Hitler's standard lecture on the European diplomatic situation, the same lecture that had been recorded by Colonal Hossbach three months before, and echoed in the Tavs plot documents discovered only three weeks before. England 'would not lift a finger for Austria'. For France it was 'too late'. Her moment had come and gone in 1936 when Hitler had marched into the Rhineland 'with a handful of battalions', and she had remained passive. As for Italy : 'with Mussolini I now see eye to eye'. Despite the fact that the Führer himself was not half as confident as he appeared, it all sounded very convincing. He wound up with the following masterly mixture of threats and 'generosity' :

> 'Now I am going to give you one last chance, Herr Schuschnigg. Either we reach a solution, or events must take their course. Next Sunday I go before the German nation and, when I address the Reichstag, the German people must know where it stands. Think it well over, Herr Schuschnigg, I can only wait until this afternoon. And when I tell you that, you would do well to take my words literally. I do not bluff. The whole of my past record is proof enough of that. I have achieved everything I set out to do and have thus become perhaps the greatest German of all time. . . . And I am giving you, Herr Schuschnigg, the unique opportunity of having your name recorded as well in the roll of great Germans. That would be an honourable deed and everything could be settled. I am well aware that due regard must be paid to certain Austrian peculiarities, but that need present no difficulties.'

This old pan-German carrot, presented so skilfully right after the Nazi stick, left the Austrian Chancellor at a loss. For answer he merely asked the Führer what his concrete complaints were. By now, however, Hitler had achieved all he wanted at this first two-hour session. He had set the pace and the tone. He had taken the measure of his adversary, found no serious resistance and prepared him for the worst.

The instinct of the political impresario told him that the prologue should be ended there and then and that the main action should be reserved for later. So with a brusque : 'The details we can discuss this afternoon', he ended the talk. He rang a bell on the table, the heavy doors of his study swung open, and he led his dazed guest past 'a large and impressive bust of Bismarck' down to the dining-room for lunch.

If the first preliminary skirmish had been lost at the border, the main trial of wills between the two Chancellors had been almost irretrievably lost by Schuschnigg now. Hitler had been allowed to take the initiative at the start and never once had he been checked. The long catalogue of Nazi acts of violence and treason in Austria had not been used properly against him ; the Tavs conspiracy of the previous month, for which all the incriminating evidence existed, was not even mentioned, let alone produced in documentary form. Schuschnigg had not disputed Hitler's broad picture of the unified destiny of the two peoples. He had not so much as hinted that the Austrians might, in desperation, fight to defend their own country. Perhaps worse, he had not challenged Hitler's assumption that nobody else in Europe would, though, at the time, he still had his hopes of the Entente Powers.[3] Thus, though he had come to the poker table with a basically inferior hand, he had made it worse by throwing away his only good card and then disdaining to call even a legitimate fraction of his opponent's bluff.

Indeed, on the one issue where he was most vulnerable — conspiracy and meddling — Hitler seems to have got away with a piece of double bluff. Looking back on the meeting many years later, Schuschnigg recalled [4] that, at one point, Hitler accused him 'in all seriousness' of encouraging plans allegedly being hatched in Vienna by that indomitable anti-Nazi Jesuit priest, Father Muckermann, to assassinate the Führer. The archives of the German Foreign Office show that, on that same day, the 12th of February 1938, a secret telegram revealing this supposed plot had been received in Berlin from the German Legation in Vienna.[5] A 'reliable source' had passed the Legation an account of a tea-party given for Father Muckermann by Count Coudenhove-Kalergi, the leader of the pan-Europe movement. When Hitler's approaching visit to Rome was mentioned, the guest of honour was said to have declared in a hoarse whisper over the cream buns : 'While he is inspecting the Capitol, they can get close to him. I am convinced that the great Austrian plan will succeed.'

To his credit, Papen had only passed on this unsubstantiated tea-table rumour 'with reservations'. But Hitler knew how to exploit even tittle-tattle of this flimsiness. He was probably saving up the Father Muckermann anecdote to counter the detailed charges of German conspiracy he expected from Schuschnigg and, when these charges were not produced, he carried the attack into the Austrian camp instead. Thus, so far from pinning the Führer down for some explanation of the well-proven Tavs affair, Schuschnigg found himself disowning a 'Vienna Jesuit plot' against his host's life.

When the full text of Schuschnigg's own account is studied (and it is as scrupulously honest as it is unflattering), one thing stands out. Whenever the Austrian made a meek withdrawal — as on the question of the border defences — Hitler, instead of being pacified, was driven into an even more berserk attack like the reflex of Pavlov's dog. And on the one single occasion when Schuschnigg reproached him outright, the Führer himself drew back. This was when the Austrian Chancellor, in an oblique reference to the murder of his predecessor, remarked : 'If it had not been for the 24th of July *putsch*, things would have been settled between us long ago'.

For an instant, Hitler became sober, even contrite. He assured his guest he had had nothing to do personally with the assassination, but declared : 'You are right, Herr Bundeskanzler. I admit it. Dollfuss stands between us.' (This, incidentally, seems to have been the only occasion on which

Hitler was moved to address his guest by his correct official title. During the rest of the conversation, though Schuschnigg never failed to use the formal style of 'Herr Reichskanzler', the Führer employed in return the somewhat contemptuous form of 'Herr Schuschnigg'.) If ever there was a moment for a counter-attack, it was here ; and if ever there was a time when the tiny five-foot spirit of Dollfuss might have been called to the aid of his country, it was now. The chance slipped by, and, the next second, Hitler had resumed his tirade.

Though this is a fair analysis of the position on Schuschnigg's own evidence, it should not be read as an indictment of his courage. Of all the leading Austrian personalities of the day only one or two — President Miklas, for example, or Bürgermeister Schmitz of Vienna — might have found voice to hit the monster back in his own lair, because both their pride and their emotions ran higher. Schuschnigg seems to have been less offended than troubled, and less outraged than dazed. He can be forgiven for both feelings. Alone of all the statesmen of Europe, he really knew, by lunch-time on that 12th of February, what was in store for the continent. And, by then, his own battle was as good as lost.

During lunch, which lasted until nearly 2 o'clock, Hitler changed masks again, and became once more the correct host who had greeted them on the terrace of the Berghof that morning. The Führer's table talk, a monologue as ever, was a string of amiable reminiscences : how horse transport had failed in the last war and why he was going over to motorization in the *Wehrmacht* ; how he had just been offered yet another house by a 'grateful' German community but had been obliged to refuse the gift 'because his income simply did not permit the upkeep of so many establishments'. The nearest he seems to have got to politics was when describing his plans to rebuild Hamburg. The largest bridge in the world and the tallest office buildings in the world would be constructed there, so that American visitors to Europe could see that the new Germany could beat them at their own game. With the harsh buzz of Hitler's threats still ringing in his ears, Schuschnigg must have sat there opposite him in a polite trance, as the courses of the simple meal were changed by a line of muscular SS men wearing white waiters' jackets.

Over coffee, which was served in an adjoining glass-walled winter garden, Hitler suddenly excused himself and withdrew, leaving the Austrians alone with the German generals. Here they were left to wait for nearly two hours while the Führer and his advisers drew up their ultimatum in another room. The suspense was made a little more bearable for Schuschnigg, a chain-smoker, by the fact that now, for the first time, he was permitted both cigarettes and a stiff drink. Both were normally banished from this house of abstinence and evil.

Hitler was meanwhile busy upstairs with Ribbentrop, Papen and Keppler, his SS 'adviser' for Austria, mixing an even stronger political brew for his guests. This was only to be expected for, by now, he had all the ingredients he needed. He had had, since dawn, Seyss-Inquart's betrayal of the 'Ten Points'; and during the morning, further indications of an Austrian retreat had landed at Berchtesgaden in an urgent situation report telegraphed via Berlin from Rainer, another prominent Austrian Nazi. This worthy had even claimed that, in the final Vienna talks, Schuschnigg promised Seyss-Inquart 'the Ministry of Interior, combined with Security, and the Ministry of Finance'.[6] Though this seems exaggerated, there certainly had been some talk, and even more speculation, all that month in Vienna about new ministerial posts for Austrian Nazis (Glaise-Horstenau, for example, had been tipped as a future Minister of Defence). Coming on top of his highly satisfactory 'softening-up' session with Schuschnigg himself, these latest reports from Vienna must have removed the Führer's last doubts about the duty he owed to Providence on that day.

At 4 o'clock in the afternoon, the blow was delivered.

The Austrian Chancellor and Dr. Schmidt were summoned into a small room near the winter garden where they found Ribbentrop and Papen facing them across a table. Of Hitler there was no sign. Ribbentrop was too new to his post to be versed in the complicated back history of Austro-German relations, so he began by pouring out more of the familiar Nazi bromide on the subject. Both peoples, he said, were, after all, Germans and could not be 'kept apart for ever by artificial barriers' ; perhaps it was to be Schuschnigg's 'historic task' to facilitate their union. According to Ribbentrop's version,[7] Schuschnigg responded with such enthusiasm to these overtures that even the German Foreign Minister was secretly taken aback.

The two sheets of typewritten paper which Ribbentrop then handed over took away for good any fleeting enthusiasm Schuschnigg may have shown. They were the result of the prolonged drafting efforts which had been going on in the Führer's study since lunch : Nazi Germany's price for allowing the continuance of the Austrian state. And, as Ribbentrop re-marked when presenting them, they were 'the maximum that Hitler was prepared to concede'.

At his Nuremberg trial, Ribbentrop maintained that Hitler personally dictated the document, though it is likely that Keppler had prepared the draft. At all events, what Schusch-nigg now held in his hands [8] made a mockery of his presence at Berchtesgaden as the head of an independent government.

Hitler's terms were also set out in ten points — perhaps no coincidence. The first was a fairly harmless clause binding Austria 'to consult from time to time with the Government of the Reich on foreign policy issues of mutual interest'. Then came a far more dangerous ideological clause : 'The Austrian Government recognizes that National Socialism is compatible with . . . allegiance to the Fatherland Front, provided that National Socialists recognize and respect the Austrian Constitu-tion in carrying out their ideas. The Austrian Government will therefore take no steps which would have the effect of outlawing the National Socialist movement within the above context.'

Point 4 demanded 'a general amnesty for all persons punished . . . for their National Socialist activities'. Point 7 required the removal of Schuschnigg's two trusted propaganda chiefs, Minister Ludwig and Colonel Adam, as part of 'the smooth execution of a press truce'. The next clause, dealing with military matters, went a step further. It named the 'moderate' Austrian Nazi, Glaise-Horstenau, as the next Austrian Minister of Defence, and called for the exchange of 100 officers as part of 'a systematic cultivation of comradely relations' between the two countries. For similar purposes of 'assimilation' on the economic front, another Austrian Nazi, Dr. Fischböck, who was *persona gratissima* in Berlin, was nominated as the new Minister of Finance. And to cap everything, Hitler demanded the appointment of Seyss-Inquart as Austrian Minister of Interior 'with authority over security'. All these measures were to be carried out within the week, by February 18.

A quick glance back at what Hitler had learned since dawn that day shows where he had got his encouragement to make these monstrous demands, and even most of his concrete ideas. The first clause simply tightened the screws on Austria's pledge, made as far back as 1936, and just reaffirmed by Schuschnigg, to pursue a 'German foreign policy'. The ideological trap the Austrians had baited for themselves with Zernatto's dangerously vague admission in Vienna that some basic element of National Socialist philosophy 'could be organically incorporated into the new Austria'. The German formula of 'compatibility' now produced was a logical Nazi extension of this.

Hitler's demands on press and army merely took, yet again, Schuschnigg's own eve-of-Berchtesgaden discussions on these issues by the scruff of their necks and pushed them

further. One of Zernatto's points had offered the appointment
of a Nazi press officer to the existing apparatus in Vienna ;
Hitler ignored that and demanded instead the dismissal of the
two chief figures in the organization. Another Zernatto
clause had promised 'the closest possible fusion' in military
training and equipment between the two armies. Hitler
simply spelt this out in general staff terms and added a War
Minister of his choice for good measure. Even the appointment of Seyss-Inquart to the key post of Interior and Security
had, according to Hitler's information, been weighed by
Schuschnigg in the preliminary Vienna talks. This was the
only point on which Hitler was almost certainly misinformed ;
yet, from Schuschnigg's behaviour that morning, he could
hardly be blamed for believing even this to be possible.

All in all, it cannot be denied that the unfortunate Austrian
delegation had unwittingly helped to dig its own grave at
Berchtesgaden. Schuschnigg's problem now was how to
scramble out alive. What might be called negotiations, for
want of a better term, now commenced.

Schuschnigg began by protesting that Hitler's terms
flouted the pledge, given him only four days before by Papen
on the Führer's behalf, that no 'additional political demands'
would be made at Berchtesgaden. At this, Papen declared in
tones of outraged innocence that he, too, had been taken
'completely by surprise'. Somewhat oddly, the two Austrians,
instead of tackling the central issue of Hitler's impertinence in
choosing their next Cabinet for them, then started up a debate
on the ideological problem raised : where could the boundary
be drawn between Nazi ideology and the Nazi party, between
political convictions and political action ? Ribbentrop confessed that he didn't know, and what must have been a rather
rambling and pointless discussion between the four men was
fortunately interrupted by a summons from Hitler. The
Führer would now be glad to see Herr Schuschnigg again
upstairs.

Before leaving the room, the Chancellor told his Foreign Minister to go on doing what he could to reduce the German demands, and thus two separate sets of talks now developed in the Berghof. During his long and tough discussion with Ribbentrop, Dr. Schmidt did succeed in filing down several of the sharp edges of Hitler's ten points. Some of these gains can be seen by comparing Ribbentrop's original typewritten sheets handed over in the afternoon with the text of the joint protocol as it was actually signed six hours later.[9]

Thus the obligation on Austria to 'consult' with the Reich on foreign policy issues of mutual interest was toned down a shade into a promise 'to enter on a diplomatic exchange of views'. The problem of finding some safe elbow-room for the Austrian Nazis within the 'Fatherland Front' was eased for Schuschnigg by dropping all those confusing ideological elements which the Austrians had unwisely raised. In the final text this clause was bad enough for Austria, but it was at least reduced to its factual barebones : 'The Federal Chancellor states that Austrian National Socialism shall in principle be given the opportunity of legal activity within the framework of the 'Fatherland Front' and all other Austrian organizations. This activity shall take place on an equal footing with all other groups, and in accordance with the constitution.'

As for amnesty, the clause finally agreed was confined only to German Nazis imprisoned in Austria ; it thus excluded a free pardon for the thousands of *émigrés* in Hitler's 'Austrian Legion'. On press 'co-operation', the Austrians managed to scramble back to the last-ditch position adopted in the Vienna talks : a 'moderate' Nazi, Dr. Wolf, was appointed by name to serve in the Austrian Press Bureau, but the demand for the removal of Schuschnigg's two existing propaganda chiefs was dropped.

The military price was also fixed lower than Hitler had at first demanded, though it was higher than the 'maximum' Schuschnigg had been prepared to discuss on the eve of

Berchtesgaden. The exchange of officers '*up to* one hundred' and the other 'comradely' provisions remained. The insistence on a pro-Nazi Austrian War Minister was, however, modified to a change in the Austrian Chief of Staff : General Jansa, whom Hitler knew would have cheerfully led the Austrian Army on to the field against the German invaders, was to be replaced by a certain General Böhme, who evidently worried Berlin less. Finally, on the economic front, the Nazis' nominee, Dr. Fischböck, was to be appointed 'to a leading post' instead of to the Ministry of Finance itself.

These compromises, which seem mainly to have been wrung by Dr. Schmidt out of a Ribbentrop who was very unsure of his facts, were by no means negligible. Had Austria come to Berchtesgaden to treat for surrender terms after some military disaster in the field, they would have indicated a diplomatic triumph for the vanquished and magnanimity on the part of the victors. Considering that these were supposed to be discussions between two independent neighbours and ex-allies, all that can be said is that they reduced Hitler's attempted murder to manslaughter on a few counts.

That is also the most that can be said of the treatment which Schuschnigg was meanwhile getting at the Führer's hands upstairs. After being kept waiting again for some time outside the heavy doors, the Austrian Chancellor was re-admitted to the study to find Hitler pacing up and down the floor like a caged lion. The following exchange then took place : [10]

Hitler : 'Herr Schuschnigg, I have decided to make one last attempt. Here is the draft. I'm not prepared to discuss it and I will not alter one syllable. Either you sign or there is no point in us going on : we shall have reached deadlock and I shall then have to make my decisions accordingly during the night.'

Schuschnigg : 'I know its contents and, in the present

circumstances, I can do nothing but take note of it. I am willing to sign it with you, but you must realize, Herr Reichskanzler, that my signature by itself is of no value to you. According to our constitution it is the President . . . who appoints the Ministers of the Government and amnesty questions are also his prerogative. All my signature means therefore is that I am prepared to vouch for this and try and get it carried out.'

Hitler (thoughtfully) : 'Yes, there you are right. . . .'

Schuschnigg : 'And for this reason I can give no guarantee about the time limit laid down — three days.'

Hitler : 'That you *must* do !'

Schuschnigg : 'I simply cannot.'

Then followed the famous scene for which Hitler had been laying his preparations all day. With a rage that was probably half-genuine and half-simulated, he marched to the study doors, flung them open and bawled 'General Keitel' into the ante-room. The Führer's newly appointed *Wehrmacht* commander was just dodging a blunt question from Dr. Schmidt as to whether Germany was or was not contemplating military action against Austria.[11] (The Foreign Ministers had broken off their talks for a brief interval and a general *causerie* seems to have been taking place outside Hitler's room.) At Hitler's summons, and the clear tones of anger in his master's voice, Keitel abruptly broke off the polite discussion and, with what Schmidt described as a 'chilly and hostile glance', hastened to the Führer's side. As Keitel approached, Hitler turned to his guest and dismissed the Chancellor of Austria in words that might have been used to a manservant : 'I shall have you called later'.

Keitel's own testimony is the only historical record of what followed in the next few minutes, and the account he gave at Nuremberg [12] removed any doubts that Hitler's summons had been the purest bluff. The Führer, he said, had merely motioned him to take a seat, remarking that he had 'nothing particular to discuss', but that the Austrian Chancellor had wanted to leave the room for a brief conference with his advisers.

Schuschnigg and Schmidt would have given a great deal to have known this at the time. Instead, both men thought that the game was now really up, and Schmidt was heard to make the doleful remark that it would not surprise him if they were 'arrested the very next minute'. Even Papen, waiting outside Hitler's study doors with the horrified Austrians, seems to have been taken aback by this violent turn of events ; he offered to mediate and tried, without success, to gain immediate access to the Führer.

It must have been some time during this agonizing interval that the Austrians managed to get through, for the first time that day, to their own 'advance headquarters' just across the border at Salzburg. Here Schuschnigg had left behind a group of intimates, including his secretary, Baron Frölichstal, with orders to alarm the garrison if no word came from him by 6 o'clock that evening — a clear indication that the Austrians had crossed the frontier hoping for the best, but fearing the very worst.

Those instructions had been issued at breakfast time and, ever since, the Austrian party at Salzburg had waited in vain for some sign of life from their Chancellor. The garrison commander was said to be counting off the final minutes with a watch in his hand when the telephone rang at last with a laconic message from the Berghof. It told them nothing except that 'the talks are still continuing'. This did little to satisfy all the nervous curiosity in Salzburg. Perhaps regrettably, it did just enough to prevent even a token display of Austrian force on this wretched and demoralizing evening in the country's history.

In fact, over at Berchtesgaden, no talks of any substance seem to have gone on between Schuschnigg's second stormy encounter with Hitler and their third and final conversation. The Führer's main object in forcing the pause was to allow some forty-five minutes to tick away in an atmosphere as menacing and crisis-laden as he could make it. Outside his study, the Austrians continued to mull over the details of the German terms with Ribbentrop and Papen, though, as Schuschnigg had just told the Führer he was willing to put his own signature to them, this discussion had become rather academic.

On the other side of the great wooden doors, Hitler passed some of his time by talking to Dr. Mühlmann, our Nazi art critic and amateur Talleyrand from Vienna, who was summoned to the presence with a bursting heart just before 6 o'clock. Mühlmann's own account of the meeting,[13] in which he represents himself as having saved Austria single-handed from invasion that very night, reads like a typical fantasy of wish-fulfilment. Hitler's only purpose seems to have been to get an Austrian Nazi's opinion of the character of Schuschnigg and Seyss-Inquart. The Führer's own opinion of Mühlmann was summed up by the fact that, when the art critic pleaded to be allowed to sit in at the actual negotiations, he was dismissed with an impatient wave of the hand, and found himself 'outside the door almost in the same second'.[14]

Yet Mühlmann added his tiny grain of sand to the Austrian burden that day. When, in reply to Hitler's question, he declared that the Austrian Chancellor was a man of honour who would carry out what he had promised, the Führer got his own impressions confirmed : his blackmail victory would be safe in the keeping of Schuschnigg's Catholic Germanic conscience. This meant that, provided the Austrian leader pledged his word there and then with his signature, he could safely be allowed a day or two to win over his colleagues and his President.

Schuschnigg was accordingly called in again to find Hitler wearing yet another mask — the mask of magnanimity. He announced to his guest that 'for the first time in his life' he had decided to go back on a decision. The Austrian Chancellor, in signing the terms, would not be pledging their fulfilment that very instant but would be given three days to have the agreement put into effect.

It speaks volumes for the dazed state Schuschnigg was in that he should have even regarded this as a 'concession'. The original draft had given Austria only a week's grace. Less than an hour before, Schuschnigg had himself accepted a reduction to three days, merely pointing out that, owing to the constitutional position, the last word did not rest with him. The only thing Hitler had in fact dropped was that threatening cloak of military menaces which Keitel had been called in to display like some tailor's dummy. For Schuschnigg, who had already heard the German tanks rattling past Mozart's sacred birthplace, this was enough. Hitler's ten-point demands, as modified by the two Foreign Ministers, were promptly sent down to be retyped for signature. The Führer was moved to declare that this agreement had solved the Austrian problem for the next five years ; 'by then', he added, 'the world will anyway be a different place'.

This language was not exactly reassuring. Nor was Hitler's remark, a few moments later, that his new *Wehrmacht* was such a uniquely powerful instrument that it would be 'unjustifiable before history' not to make use of it. The Austrians got one final slap in the face over the press communiqué to be issued about the meeting. Schuschnigg had only come to Berchtesgaden on the promise, conveyed by Papen, that the talks would publicly reaffirm as their basis the compromise agreement of 1936. He now sought to have this point written into the joint statement.

Hitler would have none of it. He knew that he had won that day a diplomatic victory of the first magnitude, and he was determined that its propaganda exploitation should be his alone, and at the time of his choosing. So he insisted instead on two bald sentences which described the day's stormy events as 'an informal meeting, prompted by the mutual desire to talk over all questions pertaining to relations between Germany and Austria'. (Goebbels, that same evening, whetted world appetite for the truth by revealing over his German press network that 'very weighty and serious matters' had been discussed, the full nature of which would be revealed 'in due course'.)

And so, after putting their signatures to the retyped agreement, and declining Hitler's offer to stay for supper, Schuschnigg and Schmidt made their farewells, climbed onto the tracked vehicles again, and clattered away from the Berghof in the darkness down the steep hill to their waiting cars. On the drive back to the border, Papen once more preserved the decencies of protocol by accompanying the visitors, and even tried to cheer them up. 'Well,' he remarked, 'that's how the Führer can be, you've seen it now for yourselves. But the next time, you will get on much better. Believe me, the Führer can be absolutely charming.' The next time Hitler got in touch with the Austrian Chancellor was through his Gestapo.

Schuschnigg could not have dreamt that his own freedom, and that of Austria, would be snuffed out so completely a bare month hence. But he himself admits to driving away from Berchtesgaden feeling that there was now 'little room for any hope'. Well he might, for in accepting Seyss-Inquart as his new Minister of Interior, he had put one of the major keys to domestic power in Nazi hands. It was the retreat on this one issue which collapsed the centre of Austrian resistance, whatever ground had been won back on the flanks.

The real meaning of the disaster went even beyond putting that particular man in that particular job. The sacrifice of the principle had been worse, if possible, than the sacrifice of the post. Hitler had been allowed to tell the Austrian Chancellor whom he should put in his next Cabinet, and the most remarkable thing about the whole Berchtesgaden encounter is that the Austrians never once rejected the whole assumption behind this behaviour. They protested about Seyss-Inquart and they protested about the Ministry of Interior. But, even in their own accounts of the conversations, neither Schuschnigg nor Schmidt is on record as telling the Germans the blunt and irrefutable truth that it was absolutely no business of theirs which Austrian was given which portfolio. Never once was Hitler even reminded that he was talking to the Chancellor of a still sovereign state.

It is only fair to say again that this was not so much cowardice on Schuschnigg's part as a certain timidity induced by his own confusion and fatalism. The drugging propaganda of the 'common historic destiny', with its mixture of lies and truth, had numbed even his ability to distinguish any longer between interference and independence in Austro-German relations. He had set out for Berchtesgaden a free Head of Government in name, but not in spirit. He returned to Austria with considerably less of either liberty.

NOTES

1. Papen had learned of Hitler's decision to call in the generals from a secretary of Ribbentrop's soon after his arrival at Berchtesgaden in the early hours of the morning. Whether he had been ordered to break the news to Schuschnigg or did so on his own initiative is not clear.

2. The conversation extracts which follow have been translated and condensed from Schuschnigg's original German account in *Requiem in Rot-Weiss-Rot* (Amstütz, Herdeg & Co., Zürich). Where other details of the meeting are taken from other participants at the talks, these are indicated below.

3. In a letter to the author (10.2.1962) Schuschnigg maintains he had not believed Hitler when the Führer had tried to convince him that no help could be expected from Britain. This makes the Austrian Chancellor's tactics after Berchtesgaden even more difficult to explain.

4. Letter to the author, 10.2.1962.

5. See Documents on German Foreign Policy, *op. cit.* Series D, Vol. I, No. 292.

6. *Ibid.* No. 293 gives the original undated telegram from Vienna.

7. Evidence at his Nuremberg Trial, I.M.T., Vol. 10, pp. 276-278.

8. For text of Hitler's draft proposals, see Documents on German Foreign Policy, *op. cit.* No. 294.

9. *Ibid.* No. 295.

10. Here we return to Schuschnigg's account in the German original of *Requiem, op. cit.* (*Note* : All subsequent page references are to the better-known English version, Gollancz, London, 1947.)

11. See Schmidt Trial Protocols, *op. cit.* p. 61 and p. 458.

12. See I.M.T., Vol. 10, pp. 567-568.

13. Schmidt Trial Protocols, *op. cit.* pp. 250-251.

14. *Ibid.* p. 250.

CHAPTER FOUR

Suffering in Silence

IT must have been shortly before 11 P.M. on the night of Berchtesgaden that Schuschnigg got back to the familiar sanctuary of Salzburg — his ordeal, for the time being, at an end. The verdict that his waiting colleagues half expected to hear was written all over the Chancellor's face, but he seemed for the moment too exhausted even to pronounce it. The only one of the group to hear an outline of the story that night was the Provincial Governor, Dr. Rehrl, and he did nothing to dispel the general gloom by describing the news afterwards as 'appalling'.

The first man to be told the full truth about the Berghof meeting was Zernatto, who was on the platform when the Chancellor's special train pulled in to Vienna at 8 A.M. the next morning. The two friends breakfasted together on board and Zernatto's own account of their talk [1] shows that, though safely back in his own capital, Schuschnigg still had visions of Hitler dancing in front of his eyes. 'It was like meeting someone from another world,' he exclaimed, 'I might have been talking to an Indian instead of to the leader of the German people.' The disillusionment echoing in those words suggests what Schuschnigg had been hoping for, even from the head of the Nazi party, because he was also a German statesman.

There now followed three days of anguished argument inside the Government and the wildest rumour everywhere outside. Among the handful of people who were let into the secret, opinions were sharply divided. One group, which seems to have included Zernatto, argued that the best had been made out of a hopeless venture, and insisted that Hitler's terms would now have to be met as they stood, to keep the German Army on its own side of the border. As for Schuschnigg's performance, these men seemed to evaluate it rather like an encounter between a rabbit and a python : on getting back to his warren alive, the rabbit was to be congratulated on not having been swallowed up, rather than blamed for not subduing the monster.

Yet the critics were also not lacking, even among the Chancellor's closest friends. They included a number of ultra-Catholics, grouped around the influential Mayor of Vienna, Richard Schmitz, and their dismay was sharply echoed by every frustrated Monarchist or stifled democrat within the 'Fatherland Front' the moment he heard the dismal truth. This group questioned whether the acceptance of Seyss-Inquart, a crypto-Nazi appointed at Hitler's behest to the Ministry of Interior, was not too high a price to pay for a mere extension of the uneasy Austro-German truce on worse terms than ever before ; and they did not fail to point out that the laconic 'joint' communiqué dictated by Hitler had left out the one basic condition of Schuschnigg's journey — re-affirmation of the July 1936 Pact.

The Federal President, Wilhelm Miklas, himself stood at the head of this sceptical camp. As a 'parliamentarian' of the dissolved Christian-Social party, there was a great deal about the politics of the 'Fatherland Front' that displeased him anyhow. Moreover, a certain coolness, often bordering on animosity, marked his personal relations with the Chancellor. He had only been informed by Schuschnigg at the very last minute of the Berchtesgaden mission, and had given his approval, with marked reservations, over the telephone from the mountain pilgrimage resort of Mariazell.[2] On the Sunday after Berchtesgaden, when Schuschnigg appears to have given him a preliminary report, the President learned enough to raise prompt objections, though he afterwards claimed that the Chancellor 'had certainly not told him everything'.[3]

Indeed, Schuschnigg found the immediate week-end re-actions among his colleagues so divided that he approached von Papen on the Monday morning, and again that evening, for help in reducing Hitler's stiff terms : in vain, as a report sent back to Berlin late that night shows. This telegram,[4] marked 'Very Urgent, Very Secret. For the Führer and Chancellor', is Papen at his wily best. He writes :

'The Federal Chancellor, deeply impressed by his talk with the Führer, has been engaged in sharp conflict yesterday and today with the opponents of pacification, since he is deter-mined to carry out his Berchtesgaden pledge. The main obstacle is the placing of Security under Seyss-Inquart, which the President has so far refused to do. . . . I refused cate-gorically this morning to transmit to the Führer any proposal for weakening the Protocol that has been signed. The Federal Chancellor, who just received me, informed me that despite all opposition he hoped to put the agreement through to-morrow, provided both sides reaffirm the Pact of July 11 (1936) in the joint communiqué to be issued. . . . With these promises he hopes to overcome the resistance of the President supported by . . . the Schmitz group. I therefore ask for authorization to show a compliant attitude in this matter.'

The approval of Miklas was, of course, vital, as Schuschnigg had only secured those three paltry days' grace for Austria on the constitutional argument that the Cabinet appointments involved were the sole prerogative of the Head of State. On the afternoon of Tuesday, the 14th of February, with only 24 hours of the ultimatum left to run, a crucial conference was therefore summoned in the President's office. It was a small gathering. Apart from Miklas and Schuschnigg, there were present throughout the meeting only Dr. Schmitz ; Dr. Ender, a former Christian-Social Chancellor and Austria's leading constitutional expert ; and the President of the National Bank, Dr. Kienböck.

Schuschnigg gave another brief résumé of the Berghof talks and listed three possible courses of action : either he resign and a new Government be formed which would not be bound by the Berchtesgaden pledges ; or a new Chancellor be appointed to carry out the bargain ; or he remain in office and fulfil his own agreement with Hitler himself.[5] The debate which followed was both heated and rambling. It produced some very strange suggestions, of which the oddest was a proposal to pacify Hitler by ceding the Austrian frontier village of his birth, Braunau-am-Inn, to Germany. This was rather like trying to feed a toffee to a hungry tiger and, not surprisingly, the idea was dropped. It speaks volumes for the feverish frame of mind of those present that any idea so pathetically futile could even have been raised.

Schuschnigg argued throughout the meeting that, while he had no illusions about the gravity of Seyss-Inquart's appointment, he was convinced that Hitler would march if this, or any other key concession, were refused. In this belief, as we shall see later, Schuschnigg may have been as mistaken as he was certainly sincere. At any rate, we now know beyond doubt that the military 'preparations' Hitler was noisily organizing at that moment against Austria's borders were the purest bluff.

General Keitel's testimony at Nuremberg revealed that Schuschnigg had barely left the Berghof on the night of February 12 when Hitler began discussing with his generals how they could best simulate 'invasion manœuvres' on the Austrian frontier during the next 72 hours of his ultimatum.[6] That same night, while the exhausted Schuschnigg was on his way back to Vienna, a much fresher Keitel returned to Berlin to carry out the Führer's orders. On the following Sunday afternoon, while Schuschnigg was telling a few close friends in Vienna that Hitler was poised to march, Keitel held a conference in Berlin with Propaganda Minister Goebbels and the Chief of German Intelligence, Admiral Canaris, as to the best means of pretending that this was true. A deception plan was worked out by Canaris, based on token troop movements and rumour-spreading ; this was personally approved by Hitler, and launched from Munich next day by the formidable Admiral himself.

The contrast between these simultaneous activities in Vienna and Berlin is remarkable mainly for its irony. In fact, Schuschnigg did not need a new crop of rumours from Munich to persuade him that the Führer was preparing for war. He was convinced already, and it was this conviction of his that finally silenced the protesting Austrian President on the afternoon of February 14. With a troubled heart, Miklas gave in and agreed to his Chancellor's third solution : Schsuchnigg was to stay in office and the Berchtesgaden pact was to stay in force.

This was another moment, concealed but crucial, in the dying of Austria. For, once confirmed in power to carry out a pact with the devil which had horrified some of his closest advisers, the Chancellor found himself driven into the one thing most alien to his upright character : deception by half-truths and even untruths, both at home and abroad. The grave and debatable course which Austrian foreign policy soon took, and which is examined below, was all implicit in this domestic decision to retain Schuschnigg in office on the strength of his own arguments and on the basis of his own fears.

Papen was told the next day that the President had set his seal of approval on the Berghof agreement, but it was not until 9 o'clock that evening (strictly speaking, barely an hour before Hitler's three days of grace expired) that Schuschnigg's confirmatory message reached Berlin.[7] It merely informed the Germans that 'the measures promised by us will be carried out before February 18'. This was the dead-line Hitler had originally set for the complete execution of his desires, and he was quite content to return to it now that Vienna was committed without apparent possibility of withdrawal.

In exchange, Papen was able to produce the face-saving formula which Austria in general, and Schuschnigg in particular, needed so desperately. A joint communiqué published that same evening in Vienna and Berlin deceived the world even more than its laconic predecessor had done about the Berchtesgaden meeting. But this time, the deception was at least along agreed lines.

Without betraying by one syllable what had gone on at the Berghof, the statement described the talks there as 'an attempt between two Chancellors to clear up the difficulties which had arisen in implementing the July Pact'. Then followed a declaration that 'both Germany and Austria are determined to adhere to the basic principles of this Pact and to treat it as the starting-point for the development of satisfactory relations between the two states'. The communiqué ended : 'With this object, both sides agreed after the discussions of February 12, 1938, to put into immediate operation measures which will ensure that close and friendly ties between the two states are established, as befits their history and the general interests of the German people. Both statesmen are convinced that the steps they have agreed upon also constitute an effective contribution towards the peaceful development of the European situation.'

So Schuschnigg got his reaffirmation of the 1936 Pact, though with a most unpleasant twist which described this protective barrier as the 'starting-point' for future negotiations. And Papen got his diplomatic decencies publicly proclaimed, with even a dash of peace-making thrown in. He had proposed the last two sentences himself in a telegram to the Führer the night before.[8] To do him justice, they probably represented Papen's concept of what the Berchtesgaden meeting ought to have been, however wildly they misrepresented what had really gone on there.

Schuschnigg's last Cabinet, formed after Berchtesgaden
(Seyss-Inquart, *middle right*, half hidden)

Anthony Eden resigns over 'appeasement': leaving the Foreign Office on
February 22, 1938, ten days after Berchtesgaden

Two who saw eye to eye on Austro-German relations : Guido Schmidt, Austrian Foreign Minister and Herr von Papen, Hitler's envoy in Vienna

And two who did not : the Austrian Federal President Wilhelm Miklas (*left*) and Chancellor Schuschnigg

One final task faced Schuschnigg on that busy night of February 15 — the formation of his new Cabinet, with Seyss-Inquart holding the promised portfolio of Interior and Security. It was not until 2 o'clock in the morning that the list of Schuschnigg's ill-fated fourth and last Government could be announced. Seyss was there at his appointed place, though the Chancellor had done all he could to pad down this Nazi thorn planted by Hitler at the very heart of his adminis-tration. Dr. Skubl, the trusted President of the untrustworthy Vienna police, was reappointed State Secretary of Interior and given the additional office of Inspector-General of the Austrian gendarmerie ; through him, Schuschnigg hoped both to watch Seyss's every move and to limit his actual powers over the so-called 'Exekutive'.

Just as significant was the overall complexion of the new Cabinet, which represented, as far as was possible, a rallying of the 'Praetorian Guard' of the 'Fatherland Front' around their leader. Schuschnigg retained for himself the Ministry of Defence, with General Zehner, whom he had refused to shed at Berchtesgaden, as his State Secretary. Glaise-Horstenau, the pan-German Minister of Interior nominated as part of the 1936 Pact, had to be retained in the Government, though without a portfolio. To outbalance him and Seyss in the Cabinet, a number of Schuschnigg's closest political followers were now brought in for the first time, notably Zernatto, State Secretary Roth and Julius Raab.

Finally, Adolf Watzek, a prominent Vienna leader of the dissolved Social Democrat Party, was given the special post of State Secretary for Labour problems. This symbolized the attempts, which all but the incurable fanatics of Left and Right were now making, to grope towards each other across the graves of the 1934 Civil War and join hands in the face of a menace far greater than their party strife. In the last month of its five years of life, the 'Fatherland Front' thus took on its first faint tinge of a genuine national Coalition. It would be too much to say that, had this *rapprochement* come earlier, it could have held off the murder of Austria altogether. The burial would, however, have been a more decent one.

Once the essential defeat at Berchtesgaden had been as good as proclaimed in the new Cabinet list, Schuschnigg now had to decide how much of the whole disaster should be revealed, both to his countrymen at home and to his friends abroad. Considering what a national calamity the Berghof meeting was, Austrian public opinion had so far been misled with evasive tactics only partly justified by the earnest motives which prompted them. The initial propaganda line of the 'Fatherland Front's' press guidance had actually gone so far as to portray Berchtesgaden as an 'unqualified personal success' for Schuschnigg. This was even more naïve than deceitful, for it ignored both the bombshell effect which Seyss-Inquart's appointment would inevitably produce, and the impossibility of sealing Vienna off from all other sources of information. Sure enough, this guidance had barely appeared in the Government press when copies of Göring's *Essener Nationalzeitung* arrived in the capital with the ominous news that, at Berchtesgaden, 'a number of German generals had been presented to the Austrian Chancellor'. British, French and American papers available in Vienna filled in many of the gaps that Göring had left blank, and the Austrians were thus able to follow this first act of their tragedy at least from the outside, as though they were the spectators and not the victims of the action.

The result was a mood of panic and disillusionment that no 'Fatherland Front' propaganda could dispel. Papen, telephoning Berlin in the early hours of February 18, described Vienna as 'an ant-hill', with the banks under heavy pressure, the Stock Exchange uneasy and thousands of Jews packing their bags to emigrate.[9] Nor, despite the formation of his Cabinet, were Schuschnigg's difficulties in his own camp resolved ; the new Government immediately came under fire from no less a quarter than the Papal Nuntius in Vienna, and talk of the Chancellor's resignation cropped up again within 48 hours of his return to office. It was in an effort to save his own position, as well as to steady the nation underneath him, that he maintained his silence, refusing to take the country into his confidence even when the newly appointed Minister of Interior took off immediately for Berlin, issuing at least one order to his Ministry from the German capital.

Yet perhaps it was not silence that the Austrians needed to calm their nerves, so much as frank words of leadership. As we shall see, Schuschnigg was to be driven to this conclusion himself ten days later when, breaking out for one moment from his lifetime's shell of reserve, he electrified both Austria and the outside world with a rousing speech to Parliament. The magical if short-lived effect of that speech only went to show how much more could have been achieved had the Chancellor appealed to his people for support at the psychological moment — immediately after the return from Berchtesgaden.

As it was, Schuschnigg held his tongue throughout February about Hitler's menaces — inhibited by his own dread of histrionics, by a quixotic desire to keep faith with the leader of the 'other Germany', by uneasiness over his own rôle and by the fear that the facts might arouse even more panic than patriotism among his countrymen. For a statesman steering a dangerous course, this last argument was clearly a powerful one ; yet it ignored the maxim that the truth will out in the end, and usually causes less harm than rumour.

The parallel tactics which a desperate Vienna now adopted to the outside world are less easy to understand than these domestic subterfuges. Even after the policy of a public appeal to the Western conscience had been abandoned, there remained the possibility of a secret appeal to the Western governments. The call was duly sent, but it was a plea against action and not for it. Quite deliberately, and for the highest motives,

Schuschnigg now helped Hitler to steady the European boat that had been rocked so violently at Berchtesgaden. As things turned out, this did nothing to stop the wreck and lost him what slight chance he ever had of a Western lifebelt.

The first controversial step the Austrian Government took in this direction was to keep its own missions in all the key capitals of Europe in ignorance of the real truth for three whole days after Berchtesgaden. The second was to order those same missions to distort the few facts they were ultimately allowed to know. It was not until February 15, after Schuschnigg had won his battle with Miklas in Vienna, that he turned his attention to his envoys abroad. On that day, two circular telegrams were sent to Austria's Legations in the nine principal friendly or neutral capitals of Europe — Rome, Paris, London, Budapest, Prague, Warsaw, Belgrade, The Hague and Stockholm.[10]

Without going into detail, the first of these messages said that the Berchtesgaden talks had been 'accompanied by sharp disputes and rendered extremely difficult by the demands which the German side had made and by the pressure exerted to achieve those demands'. Only after many hours discussion, the telegram continued, had an agreement been reached by which the German Chancellor had repeated his promises of 'non-interference' and the Austrian Chancellor had pledged himself to carry out certain domestic measures which were 'inspired by a generous spirit of conciliation'. The heads of missions were told that, while they need not conceal the difficult nature of the Berghof talks, they should place their main emphasis on the reaffirmation of the 1936 Austro-German pact and on the unshaken position of the Austrian Government. This circular instruction, signed by Schmidt, was marked 'Approved by the Chancellor'.

A few hours later, a second telegram with much more precise guidance as well as a little more precise information was sent out to fourteen capitals, including the nine original ones. Though it contained no specific reference to Schusch-nigg's authorization, there is no reason to suppose that Schmidt despatched it behind his master's back, for it bore all the hall-marks of the policy that the Chancellor personally pursued in the following days.

This second message gave a summary of Austria's 'generous conciliatory measures' which was both sketchy and misleading. It was revealed, for example, that Seyss-Inquart would be taken into the new Government, but the essential fact that he was to be made Minister of Interior that same evening was not disclosed. There was, however, nothing sketchy about the fresh instructions now given, which went far beyond those already cabled. The Austrian envoys throughout Europe were told to treat the earlier references to the 'difficulties' of the Berchtesgaden talks as 'purely personal information' and to lay stress in all their conversations on 'the need for a general reduction of tension and Austria's confidence in the normal development of her relations with the Reich which had now been cleared up by the Berchtesgaden discussions'. And, as if to bolt a door that had just been locked, the telegram ended : 'All surmises which go beyond this do not correspond with the facts and must be energetically repudiated'.

Ever since the days of Kaunitz, Austrian missions abroad had complained of scanty treatment from Vienna. But, with these two telegrams, the Republic had outdone the Habsburgs. Throughout Europe, Austria's envoys were left more in the dark than many of their foreign colleagues about the supreme crisis of their country's history ; and all this at a time when the Foreign Offices of the continent were bombarding them anxiously for the truth and even proffering sympathies which, on instructions, had to be declined.

The only Austrian diplomats abroad who were spared making partial or complete fools of themselves in mid-February seem to have been the Ministers to Rome and the Vatican. Soon after receiving their cabled instructions, they were given the real story of Berchtesgaden by Dr. Funder, a confidant of the Chancellor's who happened to be visiting Italy at the time. The others were forced to rely for gradual enlightenment on private letters from Vienna or on cautious hints passed down the telephone. That these were inadequate is shown by the post-war testimony of a key diplomat of the period, Dr. Tauschitz, Austrian Minister in Berlin. Three nights after Berchtesgaden, this luckless envoy found himself at a diplomatic reception being congratulated by Hitler about an Austro-German agreement of which he had only the foggiest outline.[11]

At the root, these odd tactics probably sprang from that hallowed principle of Viennese bureaucracy : 'Why do anything simply if there's a complicated way ?' Other explanations were, of course, put forward, then and afterwards. These all rested on the great watchword of the hour which was to risk nothing, at home or abroad, which might provoke the Führer's wrath. To achieve this aim of maximum pacification, Schuschnigg and his advisers decided to enlighten the Western powers through their own envoys in Vienna who, they reasoned, could be more relied upon to avoid a fuss than Austria's nervous missions abroad.

Quite why the Chancellor was so determined to dissuade his friends from making this fuss on his behalf has never been satisfactorily explained. One argument, which he put forward himself after the war,[12] ran as follows : 'We had not yet abandoned our last hope, which was to keep Austria's nose above water by playing for time until a *rapprochement* between England, France and Italy would come into being and restrict Hitler's freedom of action. This was also Italy's view at the time. Parliamentary debates in Paris and London were only of use to us if they led to practical help. Otherwise, at this particular juncture, they only strengthened the case of our opponents.'

It is hard to link the second half of this reasoning with

the first. That Austria's salvation lay in anything which might restore the Anglo-French-Italian 'Stresa Front' of 1935 to life was clear enough, for this had at least pledged the three countries to 'joint consultations' in the face of any threat to Austrian independence. Yet precisely this threat now loomed up again at Berchtesgaden ; and in 1938, far more than in 1935, to stop Hitler's expansion into Central Europe was one of the very few truly common interests that still bound Rome, London and Paris together. Had Schuschnigg encouraged British and French Parliamentary debates in mid-February about Hitler's menaces and Austria's plight, this could only have revived and underlined those common interests, and made it far more awkward for Mussolini to abandon them when the Führer called Europe's weak bluff a month later. By actually damping down such debates, Schuschnigg only helped both his Roman 'protector' and the Western 'appeasers' to suppress their own consciences. Faint consciences they were, and faint would have been any hope built upon them. But it was the only hope ; and publicity, combined with defiance, was the only way of raising it.

In short, after Berchtesgaden, Schuschnigg and his advisers went on acting as diplomatists in a situation that was beyond· diplomacy. They were content to follow the West in anguish instead of leading the West in desperation. These were the actions of good but over-cautious men who feared the Devil too greatly and trusted their friends too much.

With this background in mind, we can now take a brief look at the actual impact of Berchtesgaden on the principal capitals concerned. It was to Rome that Schuschnigg turned first and foremost for advice ; in this, he simply acted as the captive of an alliance that had made military sense when Dollfuss launched it four years before but which was now fast becoming a hollow pretence that Austria was too afraid to abandon publicly, and Italy too ashamed.

Mussolini was the only foreign statesman who had been

informed in advance of the Berchtesgaden trip, and, immediately after the visit, Schuschnigg followed this up by passing him a text of the Berghof protocol before it had even received final approval from the Austrian President.[13] The Duce responded to this special treatment by helping Austria with great politeness into her coffin — once it was quite clear that nobody in Vienna, Paris or London was going to cry 'Murder !' too loudly.

Ciano's diary during this critical week is the most faithful mirror we have of the Italian dilemma. Pangs of conscience over abandoning the 'Watch on the Brenner' alternate with a cynical and fatalistic acceptance that the Rome-Berlin Axis would soon wipe out the Brenner frontier — and Austria with it — in any case. Thus on February 13, the day after Berchtesgaden, Ciano records in a resigned fashion that the *Anschluss* was now 'inevitable', the only remaining question being how to postpone it for as long as possible. Three days later, he describes a talk with the Austrian Minister in Rome, Berger-Waldenegg, during which this policy of despair was clothed in diplomatic language. The Austrian envoy was told that both Ciano and the Duce regarded Austria's attitude as 'absolutely correct' ; the decision to make major concessions to Hitler had been taken 'at a suitable moment'. The Italian Foreign Minister then actually went on to propose that Vienna should give 'further proof of Austrian independence' by joining Hitler's anti-Comintern Pact.[14] The next day, Ciano returns with relief to the frank secrecy of his diary and refers to 'The Austrian chicken that has fallen, or almost fallen, into the German soup-plate'.

This last entry is marked 'February 17, 1938'. Yet on the 19th, Ciano is found reproaching the same Austrian chicken for not having done more to stand up for itself. He records on that day a request being sent to Schuschnigg to defend Italy's attitude during the whole crisis coupled with a demand to deny 'the perpetual rumours about desperate and unanswered calls for help coming from Vienna'. In fact, Ciano writes, Rome had only learned about the Berchtesgaden developments 'when everything was already decided and Italy had no choice but to approve Austria's action'.

Within a week of his stormy meeting with Hitler, Schuschnigg thus had clear proof that Italy was concerned only with salvaging her own reputation out of the Austrian affair. Austrian independence was a wish but no longer an anchor of Italian policy. No tears or reproaches from Vienna would persuade the Duce to do more. Mussolini could only be goaded into action by some particularly gratuitous insult of Hitler's or else prodded into it by pressure from Italy's Stresa Front partners. This meant that, in fact, the only levers left for Austria to operate were in France and Britain, since it was only in those democracies that public opinion still existed as a real if dormant factor in politics, and a Parliamentary opposition was in being to challenge the actions of the Government.

The possibilities for an Austrian initiative come to life straight away when we move across to the Paris scene in the days after Berchtesgaden. In Rome, both the Duce and his tame politicians and press had opposed the Austrian cause with a sort of leaden shame-facedness, and there was simply no breach to be made in this wall of betrayal. In France, Parliament and the newspapers immediately came out in public agitation on Austria's behalf and the Government itself was lifted by the resulting tide of sympathy. The reaction in both Western democracies was not rigid but fluid and vigorous ; they thus offered the only small openings in Europe to a hard-pressed Austrian statesmanship.

The French were the first of the Western Powers whom Schuschnigg took into his confidence. The Chancellor was on good personal terms with M. Gabriel Puaux, the French Minister in Vienna, and knew him to be passionately devoted to the cause of Austrian independence. On the afternoon of Monday, February 14, two days after Berchtesgaden, M. Puaux was accordingly received by the Austrian Foreign Minister Dr. Schmidt and given a general summary of the disastrous meeting. This summary, though far better than nothing, still left him in the dark as to the full extent of Austria's retreat. 'We only accepted 20 per cent of Hitler's demands' he was assured by Dr. Schmidt.[15]

However, that same evening, at a dinner for the Vienna Diplomatic Corps given in the Hofburg Palace, Schuschnigg took the French envoy aside and gave both him and his British colleague a more frank picture of Austria's plight. The Chancellor was still smarting under the punishment he had received at the Führer's hands. 'Never', he told M. Puaux indignantly, 'had a head of government been treated by a foreign leader as I was treated by Hitler. Is this a madman who thinks he is a God?' On the subject of Hitler's intentions, Schuschnigg posed no such rhetorical questions. He told the French diplomat he was convinced that Hitler would not hesitate to use force, in the firm belief that Europe would not stir itself to stop him.[16]

On the 15th of February, the French Foreign Office received M. Puaux's disturbing reports on these conversations, and their gravity was confirmed only a few hours later when the new Austrian Cabinet list was published. Paris remembered again the warning that Aristide Briand had never ceased repeating until his death seven years before : 'L'Anschluss, c'est la guerre !'

Anger had to struggle against apathy, in France as everywhere. The German Embassy described the second of these moods in a jubilant situation report sent to Berlin on February 16.[17] 'In many places they are saying "Finis Austriae". The success achieved by German diplomacy (at Berchtesgaden) is characterized as a defeat for Mussolini, who had perhaps given up Austria in exchange for German support in the Mediterranean and North Africa. The Agreement is interpreted as an event of the greatest historical importance, representing the first step in the realization of a Greater German Empire of the Germanic Nation.'

Yet the underlying temper was not one of resignation, even if the immediate diplomatic action did not amount to much. As an initial step, the French Ambassador in Berlin, François-Poncet, was instructed to call on Ribbentrop and express his 'concern' at the Austrian situation. The envoy did not get very far; he was, in fact, stopped dead in his tracks by Hitler's new Foreign Minister, with a tirade of which the Master would have heartily approved.

In a memorandum of the talk circulated the next day to all German missions abroad (how much better informed they were than their wretched Austrian colleagues !) Ribbentrop records with relish : 'I expressed to the Ambassador my surprise at this communication. France and the world had to understand once and for all that, for a great power like Germany, it was in the long run impossible to view with complacency the incredible treatment that some of the Germans living on her borders had been receiving in the last few years. . . . As regards the future, I requested the Ambassador to take final note of the fact that the further development of the German-Austrian relationship was a German family affair, a matter that concerned Germany and Austria alone.' At this, François-Poncet beat a hasty retreat, and even agreed that the topic of Austria should not be mentioned as such in the communiqué of the conversation.[18]

Parallel with this *démarche* in Berlin went instructions to M. Puaux in Vienna to inform Schuschnigg that France 'regarded the independence of Austria as indispensable to the peace and stability of Europe'. The envoy delivered this modest crumb of comfort to the Chancellor on February 18, doubtless distressed that he could not offer more.[19]

In fact, something much more substantial was being debated at the time in Paris. Prodded by the press and a group of anxious Deputies, M. Delbos, the French Foreign

Minister, proposed to London that a strong Anglo-French note should be delivered jointly in Berlin, to reinforce the weak and separate enquiries the two powers were making there.[20] The French initiative came to nothing. Partly this was because public opinion in London had not been aroused so thoroughly as in Paris by the Austrian drama; partly because the British Government was even more reluctant than France to act without Italy in the matter; but mainly because the French proposal had barely arrived when, on February 20, Anthony Eden resigned as Foreign Minister in general protest against 'appeasement', and the Foreign Office was temporarily without leadership or guidance on such a delicate question.

It is, of course, quite possible to argue that nothing the Austrian Government could have done in these crucial days would have produced a different result. But one thing seems evident. Everything that the Austrian Government actually *did* do in that period only served to help along the actual and disastrous result. In Paris, for example, while the Government was trying to organize joint action with London on Austria's behalf, the Austrian diplomats were hard at work carrying out their instructions of February 15 from Vienna, calming down all their friends who were agitated for their future, and generally presenting Berchtesgaden as a cosy Teutonic tea-party. That these instructions appeared to some of the diplomats concerned to border on lunacy is clear from their own testimonies. Dr. Martin Fuchs, who, as Austrian Press Attaché in Paris, was asked to bear the main brunt of misleading the French press, actually defied his own Foreign Minister on the telephone and was threatened with dismissal from the service unless he complied.[21]

Even the Austrian envoy to Paris, Dr. Vollgruber himself, felt obliged to warn Vienna about the dangers of the 'hushing-up' policy. With the caution that befitted a senior official in a written report, he warned his Government on February 18 that the Austrian tactics of presenting Berchtesgaden in a rosy light might well have an unfavourable effect on the French initiative in London as well as dampening French popular enthusiasm for Austria at home.[22]   Indeed, there seems no question that Schuschnigg's resolute campaign to play down the February crisis had left many Frenchmen wondering whether they were not in danger of becoming more Austrian than the Austrians as the second and fatal crisis of March loomed up.

The Secretary-General of the Quai d'Orsay, M. Léger, in a sober review of the situation with Dr. Vollgruber on March 7, made no bones whatsoever about this concern over Austria's stand.   He declared that, though France was not disposed to go to war over Austria without Britain, there still remained the possibility that a fresh *coup* of Hitler's in Central Europe might force her to act alone, in the hope of 'dragging England behind her in the general commotion'.   But, he warned, one essential condition had to be fulfilled in Vienna before France 'drew her sword', either with Britain or before her.   This was, to quote Vollgruber's despatch : [23] 'That the case of assault be clearly established ; in other words, that the Austrian Government feels itself assaulted and reacts against this assault and that German propaganda is not allowed by then to persuade French public opinion that, in Austria, it is only the Government and a few diplomats who think as Austrians'.

No more searching criticism could have been made of Vienna's post-Berchtesgaden tactics.   It breathed the one urgent message that the Austrian Government had so far ignored : Austria in those weeks was not only the bad conscience of Western diplomacy, she was also the pace-maker, and if she settled down to a rather shambling trot, all hope was lost of spurring France and Britain into a gallop.

Perhaps it was a coincidence and perhaps not, that on the very day M. Léger's warning reached Vienna, Schuschnigg took the decision to scrap his entire policy of appeasement, come out from behind his wall of silence, and challenge Hitler before the world with his famous plebiscite. But, by then, Europe had witnessed three weeks of Austrian vacillation, so that his enemies could accuse him of perfidy and even his friends could doubt his resolution.

It was in London, even more than in Paris, that these doubts did most damage. Britain was the most powerful horse in the anti-Hitler stable. She was also the most reluctant starter. There was no guarantee she would respond under any goad ; on the other hand, it was quite certain she would never move by herself. To budge her should have been the prime aim of Austrian policy, for the 'anti-appeasers' in London were led by no less a man than the British Foreign Secretary, and, by 1938, they symbolized more defiance to Nazi Germany than all Mussolini's *Bersaglieri* put together. What, in fact, happened ? To begin with, we must look at the violent swings in the pendulum of British public opinion.

During the first 48 hours after Berchtesgaden, the response in Britain was completely moulded by the rosy accounts being put out by that odd propaganda partnership of Goebbels in Berlin and Schuschnigg in Vienna. On the day after the meeting (February 13), the *Observer* spoke of the meeting as 'a pleasant surprise', while the *Sunday Express* even referred to 'Austria's triumph'. Nearly all the national dailies of Monday, February 14, for lack of any facts or guidance to the contrary, continued in this approving strain. *The Times*, for example, commented with some justice at this particular juncture that 'there is no need to quarrel with an agreement with which the Führer, the Duce, and Herr von Schuschnigg are all apparently content'.

That same evening, the cat was let out of the Berchtesgaden bag as Seyss-Inquart was let into the Austrian Cabinet. Tongues began to loosen in Vienna ; intelligence reports began to come in from Germany, and the Austrian Government's campaign of deception was swept away overnight. For the next few days, a tone of puzzled but growing concern pervaded even the Right-Wing British press. The *Daily Express* spoke of the 'outright ultimatum' with which Austria had been presented, while the *Daily Mail* warned of the dangers facing Czechoslovakia if Hitler should succeed in his aim of 'amalgamating' Austria and Germany.

The Conservative *Daily Telegraph*, which at this time stood particularly close to the 'anti-appeasement' camp of Eden and Winston Churchill, came out with three strongly worded editorials on February 16, 17 and 18. The second article, entitled 'Austria succumbs', contained the passage : 'Whatever changes may have been introduced into German policy by the Nazi régime, it is now evident that the method of the mailed fist has been preserved without abatement. The ex-Kaiser at the height of his career was never more absolute, imperious and minatory than Herr Hitler showed himself at Berchtesgaden.' The last of the series, called 'The Awakening', sounded this warning note for the future : 'It should be evident that to talk about a settlement with Germany in the present mood is like the twittering of sparrows in a thunderstorm'.

The well-modulated tenor voice of *The Times* was missing from the angry chorus. Its own editorial comment, by contrast, reflected Chamberlain's policy of riding down the Austro-German crisis in the pursuit of a general accommodation with the Axis powers. In the longest and most influential of these articles, the paper wrote : 'Fundamentally, a close understanding between the two German states is the most natural thing possible. One of the least rational, most brittle and most provocative artificialities of the peace settlement was the ban on the incorporation of Austria in the Reich. . . . These crows are coming home to roost.

'Austria can never be anti-Germanic. Ultimately this is the real strength of the Reich *claims* [author's italics] upon it and the real difficulty of an Austrian Chancellor when he has to defend and define Austrian independence.'

There was, of course, much that was shrewd in this reasoning, and even the history was right in a telescoped sense. Unfortunately, it helped Goebbels' brand of history, based on the supremacy of race, the villainy of Versailles, and the doctrine that means are justified by ends.

This same division between acceptance and alarm which appeared in the British press cropped up also in the Cabinet and Parliament of Britain ; and here the direct influence of the Austrian Government was to play an even more decisively negative rôle.

The first discussion of the Austrian crisis in the House of Commons took place at question-time on the afternoon of February 16, the day after the formation of Schuschnigg's new Government and the publication of the deceptive joint communiqué. Mr. Eden was asked by a Socialist spokesman, Mr. Bellenger, 'whether, in view of the fact that the integrity and independence of Austria are declared objects of British policy, he has any official information concerning the week-end conversations between the Austrian and German Chancellors ; and, if not, will he ask to be informed of the purport of those conversations ?' [24]

The Foreign Office had already received, from its own secret sources in Germany, an outline of the disturbing truth about Berchtesgaden, and a sketchier version of the real facts had also been passed from Vienna by Mr. Palairet, the British Minister there. But, without the approval of the Austrian Government, Eden hesitated to go beyond the bald and misleading terms of the official Austro-German declaration. He therefore replied that he was 'not in a position to make any statement' until the text of the Berchtesgaden agreement was published, adding only : 'His Majesty's Government are meanwhile closely following developments'.

The Opposition were not content with this. Another of their influential spokesmen, Mr. Arthur Henderson, rose to ask : 'Will His Majesty's Government stand by the joint declaration of February 1934 to the effect that they reaffirmed the interest of this country in the integrity and independence of Austria ?'

Mr. Eden replied : 'I take it that the hon. Member is referring to the Stresa Declaration. That is quite true. Of course, that was a declaration by three Governments — Britain, France and Italy. Italy has not, as yet, consulted His Majesty's Government on the matter.'

Austria's plight was left for the moment on that indecisive note, but the Foreign Secretary knew that the debate would be resumed with greater intensity on the morrow. Indeed, during the rest of that critical week in British domestic politics, three factors began to interplay which might have turned the Führer's blackmail at Berchtesgaden, instead of the much vaguer issue of the Anglo-Italian talks, into the first full-scale public showdown between the 'appeasers' and the resolutely anti-Hitler camp in London.

The first was the fact that the Socialist Opposition now tried to make a major issue out of British policy towards Austria ; the leader of the party, Mr. Attlee, took personal charge, during the next 48 hours, of the campaign in the House of Commons to jog the Government into action. A second and more important circumstance was that this same concern over Mr. Chamberlain's 'passivity' also began to spread, during those same 48 hours, among the ranks of the Government's own supporters.

On the evening of Thursday, February 17, about one hundred Conservative M.P.s attended a special private meeting of the Foreign Affairs Committee in the House of Commons to discuss relations with the Axis powers in the light of the post-Berchtesgaden crisis. Mr. Harold Nicolson, who opened the discussion, appealed to the Committee to 'face the fact that adventurism is now in the ascendant in Nazi Germany and that the cautious people have been proved wrong'.[25] Winston Churchill, another 'anti-appeaser' in attendance, took an even stronger attitude, and declared it was time now to 'call a halt'.

By no means all of the M.P.s present were as resolute as this. But an agreed communiqué issued by them afterwards showed that a majority of the hundred — which represented an influential slice of Mr. Chamberlain's party — were prepared to take up the cudgels against Hitler then and there, if given the slightest encouragement. The statement made a blunt appeal, 'in the light of recent events', for 'a more positive attitude by this country in Europe'. The Foreign Affairs Committee, it added, was anxious that 'the Government should remain in no doubt of the future support of the party in such an eventuality'.

Mr. Chamberlain's Chief Whip in Parliament, Captain David Margesson, heard of these strong words being bandied about. He summoned the 'rebels' to his office and ordered them to issue a milder communiqué which would refer only to the need to 'maintain the authority of Great Britain in world affairs'. Too late : the original version had already been given to the press. This invitation to action was addressed to the Prime Minister of Britain by one of his principal Parliamentary Committees. It applied just as well to the Chancellor of Austria.

The third factor in the fluid situation was, of course, the personal dilemma of Mr. Eden himself during that week, and the link between the Austrian crisis and the timing of the Anglo-Italian *rapprochement*. It was on the latter issue that the British Foreign Secretary startled his colleagues and the whole world by resigning, at midnight on February 20, only eight days after Berchtesgaden. The specific motive for his step was disagreement with Mr. Chamberlain's view that Mussolini had given enough proof of good faith over the Spanish War and other issues to justify the immediate opening of 'peace talks' between London and Rome.

But, as Mr. Eden himself made perfectly plain in his

resignation speech to Parliament, this was but one facet of a general prospect which appalled him in Europe and of a general policy which disturbed him in Britain. That Hitler's unchallenged blackmail at Berchtesgaden had also influenced his decision comes out in the following passage of that short speech : 'Recent months, recent weeks, and recent *days* have seen the successive violation of international agreements and attempts to secure political decisions by forcible means. . . . It is quite impossible to judge these things in a vacuum. In the light . . . of the present international situation, this is a moment for this country to stand firm.' [26]

Indeed, we now know that, though far from optimistic about Austria's long-term prospects, Eden tried persistently, during his last three days in office, to include a discussion of that country's future on the agenda of the Anglo-Italian 'peace talks'. On February 18, for example, when he attended the council meeting between Mr. Chamberlain and the Italian Ambassador, Count Grandi, at 10 Downing Street, he twice intervened on Vienna's behalf. On the first occasion, he broke his silence to ask the Italian envoy 'what effect the opening of the conversations might have on the Italian attitude to Austria' ; on the second, he asked outright whether the Italian Government 'could now exchange views with the other Stresa signatories on the subject of Austria'.[27]

He got nowhere with either move, thanks to his own Prime Minister no less than to Count Grandi. But the fact remains that, during those same days after the Berghof meeting when Schuschnigg in Vienna was abandoning the search for potential helpers as too hopeless, His Majesty's Foreign Secretary in London was looking for any fresh evidence on which to base his great gesture of defiance to the Axis. This brief anticipation of events is needed to appreciate the irony of what actually passed between the two men in their last twilight of office.

On February 17, Mr. Eden had been pressed in Parliament

again, and much harder, for information on the Austrian situation. He repeated, for Mr. Attlee's benefit, his statement of the previous day that Britain stood by the Three-Power Stresa Declaration on Austria's independence, though he added, in reply to another question from Mr. Churchill, that 'we do not think it lies with us to take the initiative'.[28] Eden seems to have had Austria as well as Italy in mind when he said this. As if in elaboration, he twice stressed that no approach for advice or support had come to London from Vienna, either before the Berchtesgaden meeting, or after it.

This fact may well have puzzled the House of Commons ; it had certainly puzzled the Foreign Secretary. So much so that, when he received the Austrian Minister, Baron Franckenstein, that same day to discuss the crisis, Mr. Eden made a determined attempt to probe Schuschnigg's intentions and state of mind. As Franckenstein reported to Vienna in the evening,[29] he found the British statesman 'in a troubled mood'. The envoy began by trotting out the standard formula of deception that Vienna had circulated to its missions. Eden, aware of the truth, concealed his scepticism under polite expressions of sympathy for Schuschnigg's 'extremely difficult position'.

He then pointedly repeated in private what he had told Parliament in public, namely that Austria 'had not asked the British Government for help or counsel in any form'. In the language of diplomacy, this was a broad enough hint to the partner to declare his hand, and, to encourage the bid, Eden even provided Vienna with the right cards. Yet another demand for information on Austria had been tabled in Parliament under Mr. Attlee's name for the next day, February 18, and Mr. Eden now asked the Austrian Government outright for their wishes and guidance over his reply. He made no conditions or reservations whatsoever. As Baron Franckenstein told Vienna by telephone immediately afterwards, the British

Foreign Secretary had 'placed himself at our disposition'.[30] The envoy urgently asked his capital for instructions.

Considering that one of the most influential and respected figures of the democratic world had offered Austria his services, the reply that came back from Vienna a few hours later was curious in the extreme. Eden was requested to tell the House of Commons textually the following fairy tale : 'According to information in my possession, Austria has succeeded at Berchtesgaden in clarifying her relations with the German Reich in what we may hope is a favourable and durable fashion, through direct and detailed talks between the two heads of Government and *without the slightest disturbance*' [author's italics]. The proposed statement continued by saying it could be 'assumed' that the 1936 Austro-German Pact would now be 'observed in a friendly spirit' . This being the case, the Berchtesgaden meeting would thus have rendered a 'praiseworthy service to the cause of peace'. The formula suggested for a concluding declaration of British policy had been toned down to fit the rest of the text. It ran simply : 'The United Kingdom has a positive interest in the peaceful development of Austria, and of Central Europe in general'.[31]

It is worth noting that this was actually weaker and vaguer than the Stresa Declaration Eden had just reaffirmed. In the 1935 resolution, Britain, together with France and Italy, had specifically recognized 'the necessity of preserving the independence and integrity of Austria' and had pledged herself to joint consultations 'in the case of threats' to that independence. The odd situation thus arose on the evening of February 17 that Austria was officially requesting Britain to declare even less than the minimum support agreed on three years before at Stresa. Indeed, there was not so much as a formal demand from Vienna for those old obligations to be restated.

This was no slip of an oversubtle diplomat in the Ballhausplatz and no sabotage of a pro-Nazi official. The Austrian Foreign Office archives show that this draft for the House of

Commons declaration was, as befitted its importance, discussed between Schuschnigg and his Foreign Minister Dr. Schmidt. A few hours later Schmidt sent another telegram to London for Mr. Eden's personal guidance which pulled the carpet from under his feet completely. This second message flatly denied the existence of any 'Berchtesgaden agreement or bilateral treaty instrument of any kind', and requested the British Foreign Secretary to convey this point also in his parliamentary replies.[32]

By now, of course, the basic facts of the Berchtesgaden encounter were known in London, while many of the details had even been published in the responsible Western press. The declaration proposed by Vienna would thus have made Eden appear ridiculous before his own Parliament and public, as well as cutting across all his own personal instincts of defiance to the Axis. Accordingly, when he rose in the House of Commons the next morning to reply to Mr. Attlee's reiterated question on Austria (it was the first matter to be discussed) he ignored the whole of Schuschnigg's draft except the final sentence on Britain's attitude, which he echoed in a slightly more positive form than Vienna had proposed.[33] Five questioners from both parties stood up to press him for more information or signs of more positive British support. But, with the official gag of the Austrian Government rammed down his throat, there was nothing he could add.

Finally, Britain's one and only Communist member, Mr. Gallacher, got to his feet and asked : 'In view of the fact that Austrian independence has now been disposed of by Germany, is it not necessary that something very urgent should be done ?' To this last question Mr. Eden made no reply. He could not very well admit in public that it had been left to Mr. Gallacher to make the very point which both his own Prime Minister and the Chancellor of Austria seemed anxious to hide.

That same day, February 18, the British Ambassador in Berlin, Sir Nevile Henderson, followed his French colleague by calling on Ribbentrop to 'ask for information' on the situation. The envoy was ordered to use the same mild formula that Vienna had proposed to Mr. Eden 24 hours before : he merely voiced 'the interest that the British Government had always taken and would continue to take in the Austrian question'. Ribbentrop repaid like for like. He recorded afterwards that he had responded 'in a somewhat more conciliatory form' than he had shown in his treatment of the French Ambassador the previous day.[34]

And that was that ; or very nearly. Forty-eight hours later, when Eden and Lord Cranborne, his Under-Secretary of State, resigned in protest against their Prime Minister's 'soft' policy towards the Axis, the only effective rallying point inside the Cabinet for a more vigorous attitude over Austria — or anything else — had disappeared. Lord Halifax was immediately appointed in Eden's place, and all subsequent attempts made in Parliament to get Berchtesgaden discussed were simply brushed aside.

As we shall see, Hitler was hesitant enough when it came to taking the plunge over Austria a month later, and it was nagging uncertainty over the reaction of the three Stresa powers which still caused him to demur on the evening of March 11. Like all dictators who boast of flouting public opinion, it was, in fact, the one thing he was really frightened of. It is at least safe to say that this hesitation would have been more marked had the whole question of Austrian independence become a *cause célèbre* in the West by being linked publicly with Eden's resignation.

The paradox was that Schuschnigg was about the only figure involved in the drama who refused to establish such a link. The Führer himself surmised, in a talk with Göring on February 22, that the Austrian problem was really behind Britain's Cabinet crisis.[35] Papen in Vienna came to the same conclusion on February 24 after a 'somewhat dramatic conversation' with the British Minister there, who accused

Germany of having used 'the strongest pressure' at Berchtesgaden. 'I realise', Papen telegraphed to Hitler that night, 'that there is truth in the assertion that Eden's fall was due less to the Italian question than to his readiness to make a public declaration of solidarity with France on Austrian independence.' [36]

Mussolini, for his part, was the first to bend the Berchtesgaden crisis to his own purposes. Realizing that the affair could both weaken his position yet, at the same time, revive the fleeting spirit of the Stresa Front, he told Chamberlain three days after the Austrian surrender that, 'in this new situation', it was desirable to open talks for an Anglo-Italian settlement 'forthwith'.

Finally, we might quote Winston Churchill's speech to the House of Commons on February 22 during the debate on the appeasement issue. With typical breadth of vision, he put his finger on the one approach which could both help Vienna and get the controversial negotiations with Rome under way. Referring to these impending talks he said : 'If it were possible for Italy to discharge her duties in aiding Britain and France in defending the integrity and independence of Austria then, for the sake of that, I would go as far as any man in making concessions'.

With a little more encouragement from Vienna, Eden might have said just that himself when still Foreign Secretary. And perhaps, with a little more luck, skill and courage all round, those words could have been converted into an improvised Western policy. Whether such a policy could have saved Austria in the long run is highly questionable. But it might well have given Schuschnigg what was, after all, the declared aim of all his efforts — to gain a few more months of life in the hope that the European scales would tip in his favour.

As it was, the Berchtesgaden blackmail, which was a sort of diplomatic dress rehearsal for the *Anschluss*, was allowed to subside without a ripple. The appeasers in the West, and the Führer in Berlin, drew their own conclusions. This is the most powerful, if rather unfair, criticism of Schuschnigg's strategy : the results just could not have been worse.

NOTES

1. Guido Zernatto, *Die Wahrheit über Oesterreich*, pp. 210-215. Zernatto also states that Schuschnigg told him he had reproached Hitler with interference in Austrian affairs, but there is no record of this in Schuschnigg's own published version.

2. See Miklas's testimony in the Schmidt Trial Protocols, *op. cit.* p. 259.

3. *Ibid.*

4. Documents on German Foreign Policy, Series D, Vol. I, No. 297.

5. See Schmidt Trial Protocols, *op. cit.* p. 193, and Schuschnigg's account in *Requiem in Rot-Weiss-Rot*, *op. cit.*

6. See I.M.T., Vol. 10, p. 568, and Vol. 11, p. 28.

7. See Documents on German Foreign Policy, *op. cit.* Series D, Vol. I, No. 299.

8. *Ibid.* No. 298.

9. *Ibid.* No. 309.

10. For texts see Schmidt Trial Protocols, *op. cit.* pp. 561-562.

11. See Testimony of Dr. Tauschitz, *ibid.* p. 132.

12. Letter of M. Puaux to the author, 12.2.1962.

13. *Ciano Diaries*, *op. cit.* Entry for 15.2.1938.

14. See also Berger Waldenegg's telegram to Vienna of 16.2.1938. Printed in Schmidt Trial Protocols, *op. cit.* p. 565.

15. Letter of M. Puaux to the author, 6.5.1962.

16. *Ibid.*

17. See Documents on German Foreign Policy, Series D, Vol. I, No. 302.

18. *Ibid.* No. 308.

19. Letter of M. Puaux to the author, 12.2.1962.

20. See Schmidt Trial Protocols, *op. cit.* p. 530.

21. See Schmidt Trial Protocols, *op. cit.* p. 427.

22. *Ibid.* p. 567.

23. *Ibid.* p. 573.

24. For this and all the other Parliamentary entries for February 16, 1938, see Hansard, Vol. 331, pp. 1862-1863.

25. For this and all other material on this meeting, the author is indebted to Sir Harold Nicolson, who has given an account of the incident and made available his personal diary for March 1938.

26. Hansard, Vol. 332, p. 47.

27. See, on this, Anthony Eden, *Facing the Dictators* (Cassell, London, 1962), p. 581.

28. For this and all other Parliamentary entries for February 17, 1938, see Hansard, Vol. 331, pp. 2074-2075.

29. Telegram reproduced in Schmidt Trial Protocols, *op. cit.* p. 565.

30. *Ibid.* (Austrian Foreign Office Memorandum, 51,695).

31. Proposed Austrian Draft reproduced in Schmidt Trial Protocols, *op. cit.* p. 566.

32. *Ibid.*

33. For this and other Parliamentary material on Austria for February 18, 1938, see Hansard, Vol. 331, p. 2211.

34. See Documents on German Foreign Policy, *op. cit.* Series D, Vol. I, No. 310.

35. *Ibid.* No. 318.

36. *Ibid.* No. 324.

CHAPTER FIVE

The See-Saw

HITLER'S behaviour during the fortnight after Berchtesgaden typified his whole attitude to the Austrian problem : two-faced, opportunist and plain undecided. In most of his actions and utterances during the rest of February, the emphasis was on peace and the 'evolutionary solution'. Yet one is always being reminded that the pendulum of his mind, even while moving in this direction, was at the same time gathering force for the counter-swing towards violence.

The Führer began by carrying out some of his formal obligations under the Berchtesgaden pact. On February 16 his Deputy, Rudolf Hess, issued a circular instruction to Nazi party offices 'strictly forbidding Reich-Germans to meddle in the internal affairs of Austria, to carry on National-Socialist propaganda across the border, or to issue directions to Austrian National Socialists'.[1] This formality had been conducted at Ribbentrop's request, to enable the German Foreign Office to report to Vienna that Article 3 of the Protocol (non-interference) was thus 'duly implemented'.

Four days later, Hitler rose to make his much-publicised Reichstag speech, and another Berchtesgaden pledge fell due to be honoured. This was the Führer's parting promise to Schuschnigg after their Berghof talks that, on the following Sunday, he would 'mention the meeting with some favourable comment'.[2] Hitler discharged this obligation in the following passage :

'I express . . . before the German people my sincere thanks to the Austrian Chancellor for his great understanding and the warm-hearted willingness with which he accepted my invitation and worked with me, so that we might discover a way of serving the best interests of the two countries.' [3]

As a way of describing an occasion on which he had insulted, humiliated and threatened a guest who was also the head of an independent government, this was perfidious enough. The Führer then went on to destroy even the appearances of friendship by referring in the same three-hour speech to the 'ten million Germans' living on the borders of the Reich who were 'subjected to continuous suffering because of their sympathy and solidarity with the whole German race and its ideology'. The ten millions were the people of Austria added to the Sudeten minority of Czechoslovakia, and when Hitler announced in the same hoarse breath that he would not allow them to be deprived of the 'right of racial self-determination', everyone in Prague and Vienna knew what he meant.

This was the first frost to nip the tiny buds of Schuschnigg's hope after Berchtesgaden. A more severe one came when Hitler personally appointed a Carinthian Nazi, Major Franz Klausner, as the new chief of the illegal party in Austria. Schuschnigg's clear understanding at the Berghof talks had been that Captain Leopold and his fellow extremists would be withdrawn from Austria and that, in future, all Nazi affairs would be handled by the 'moderate' Minister of Interior, Seyss-Inquart. Hitler's understanding, it seemed, was that Leopold should merely be replaced by another of his stamp and the dichotomy of 'evolutionary' and 'revolutionary' Nazi leadership in Austria should continue.

This emerges in a memorandum found in the German archives of the conference which Hitler held on the afternoon of February 21 to carry out the hand-over.[4] Göring attended as well as Dr. Keppler, the Führer's Special Commissioner for Austria, and both Leopold and Klausner, who had been summoned from Vienna, were called in — first separately and then together — to have the position explained to them.

Hitler reproached Leopold for his 'insane behaviour' in allowing secret memoranda of their conversations and 'plans for conspiracies' to fall into the hands of the Austrian police (an obvious reference to the Tavs plot scandal of the previous month). Had the diplomatic situation been different, he added, such actions could have landed him 'in the most painful and mortifying predicaments' (an equally obvious reference to his relief that the secret now seemed safely locked away in Schuschnigg's 'German honour').

Hitler continued by saying that 'he had now put Austrian policy on a different basis'. The new Austrian leader, Klausner, was told that 'illegal activity must be transformed into legal activity', in support of the 'very hard task' that Dr. Seyss-Inquart had assumed. So far, the change of heart seemed genuine, if calculated.

But then Keppler, in view of all this talk of 'evolution', asked what should be done about the Austrian SA leader Reschny, who organized, from exile in Germany, the paramilitary invasion force of Austrian Nazi refugees which now masqueraded as the 'Hilfswerk Nordwest'. As the whole purpose of this movement was to finance and train Austrian extremists — at home and abroad — for the day of action, Hitler's reply to this question was highly significant. The memorandum records : 'The Führer does not want to hear of a dissolution yet, *since the need for intervention by force might still arise*' [author's italics]. Reschny was even ordered to expand his organization, provided he did not exceed the handsome budget of 700,000 Reichsmark a month allotted to him regularly from German party funds. In a letter sent on February 23 to SA-Obergruppenführer Reschny, informing him of Hitler's decision, Keppler added : 'The development of the Austrian question has now been taken hold of, and I believe that it will move faster than had previously been supposed'.

Naturally, when Hitler gave a formal audience in Berlin

three days later to all five 'disgraced' Austrian extremists,[5] he went to somewhat greater lengths to stress his newly declared policy of 'peaceful penetration', since this, after all, was the only explanation he could offer for their removal. Yet, even in his lecture to them, he left the final choice open. According to another of Keppler's revealing memoranda,[6] he told this crestfallen quintet of desperadoes, in the presence of Ribbentrop, that 'he did not *now* [author's italics] desire a solution by violent means, if it could at all be avoided, since the danger for us in the field of foreign policy grew less each year and our military power greater'.

In this connection, the Führer made the very significant remark that 'the Protocol signed by Schuschnigg was so far-reaching that, if completely carried out, the Austrian problem would be automatically solved'. It would be hard to think of a more searching, or more expert comment on Vienna's policy of trying to buy peace, or even time, with concessions to Berlin.

The only parts of this complicated double game which emerged clearly to Schuschnigg at the time were, of course, the threatening references to those 'ten million Germans along our borders' and the appointment of a new Nazi Gauleiter for Vienna. The fact that Klausner's reorganized illegal party network inside Austria seemed to be built on the SS (Kaltenbrunner, Rainer, Globocnig) rather than on the SA of Captain Leopold and his cronies did nothing to reassure the Chancellor. By 1938 the Reichsführer of the SS, Heinrich Himmler, and his henchmen like Heydrich, were already figures that caused a shiver in any anti-Nazi breast. It was Himmler who had received Seyss-Inquart when the latter flew to Berlin on February 16 'for consultations'. One wonders what the muddled Austrian Catholic and the ice-cold German heathen made of each other as they discussed police methods.

Partly because Hitler's actions had stung and disappointed him, and partly because some gesture of leadership was needed to restore his own shaken authority inside the 'Father-land Front', Schuschnigg now switched from silence into eloquence and from passivity into defiance. It was the first of a series of such sudden and rather puzzling oscillations which marked the doomed Chancellor's last weeks of power.

The occasion was a speech to the Austrian Parliament on February 24, 1938. The event had been well publicised in advance and, on the day, Vienna had been decked out with streams of red-white-red bunting which flapped along on the Ringstrasse next to the black crutched crosses, symbols of the 'Fatherland Front'. For once. Schuschnigg as an orator lived up to the stage setting.

He began by announcing with simple effect : 'The one and only point on the order of the day is : Austria'. He then called the roll of those who had fought for Austrian indepen-dence, from the great Empress Maria Theresa to his murdered predecessor, the little peasant Chancellor, Engelbert Dollfuss. This brought him to the conflict with Nazi Germany which he described, still more in sorrow than in anger, as 'this struggle of brother against brother . . . with its uncounted sacrifices, its destruction and alienation of men, and its blood-bespattered trails'.

But his tone sharpened when he came to the Berchtesgaden Pact : 'We knew exactly that we were able to go, and indeed we did go, up to that boundary line beyond which, clearly and unequivocally, appear the words — "Thus far and no further" '. At least the sentiment was right here, even if the facts were questionable, and this passage set the keynote for the remainder of the speech. Despite periodic reference to Austria's Germanic loyalties, what followed was one long and defiant indictment of Hitler. He attacked those countrymen of his who 'were wont to place National Socialism upon the altar of their thoughts' and reminded them that 'it is not Nationalism or Socialism which is the watchword in Austria, but Patriotism'. There were sarcastic references to unnamed 'foreign countries' who belittled Austria's economic progress, and an array of statistics to contradict the critics. He spoke at length of his country's 'immortality', of its determination to remain 'a free and independent state' and to preserve the borders that history had imposed on it. He ended with the almost frenzied shout : 'Until death : Red-White-Red ! Austria!'

It was a stirring performance for any man, and for Schuschnigg, a staggering one. For the first time in his political life, he had smashed through that wall of polished glass which always divided him from his hearers and had touched the heart of his audience. His first moment of passion had been his first moment of triumph.

The Federal Diet, which in those days passed for Austria's Parliament, responded to a man. The storms of cheering were taken up by the crowds outside and, as spontaneously as the Parisian would have chanted the 'Marseillaise', the middle-class Viennese broke out here and there into the old Imperial anthem of 'Gott Erhalte' and the 'Andreas Hofer' song of the Chancellor's native Tyrol. For many of them, as for Schuschnigg himself, the roots of any purely Austrian emotion were still planted in the ancient Empire that had preceded the Republic or in the even more ancient provinces on which that Republic rested.

It is a depressing fact that, barely three weeks later, that same Vienna Ringstrasse was resounding with far greater clamour to the strains of the Nazi 'Horst Wessel Lied', and that thousands of those same middle-class throats were joining in the chorus of welcome to Adolf Hitler. No one could look on the contrast with pride. Yet, to be fair, it showed less the fickleness of the Austrians than the emotional instability of all who stood anywhere between the fixed poles of Nazidom and ultra-patriotism, between the rival magnetisms of race and state. This central mass of psychological wobblers held the key to Austrian politics in 1938, and, in the long run, they

Seyss-Inquart (*left*), the Austrian crypto-Nazi appointed Minister of Interior in February 1938 in an attempt to placate Hitler, with Dr. Skubl, Schuschnigg's loyal Police President of Vienna

Austrian Nazi demonstrators in Graz (Styria) shortly before the *Anschluss*

Andreas Hofer — the Tyrolean peasant hero of the Napoleonic wars —
raising his levies above Innsbruck

Chancellor Schuschnigg, his would-be successor in the 20th century,
arriving at Innsbruck on March 9, 1938, for the speech that announced
his ill-fated plebiscite

could be won over only by dynamic leadership. Dollfuss, dead nearly four years, had been the last man to provide it from inside the country. Now, on February 24, in the last days of the Republic's life, it flickered up again in his successor. Like a man who tries to jump away from his own shadow, Schuschnigg strove in that hour to snap the ties of his background and temperament and to grow as great as the challenge.

During the next few days, the mood of the people swung over with unnatural violence to one of confidence and hope. Indeed, throughout Europe, the Chancellor's unexpected burst of energy and defiance had made its mark. The Germans were flabbergasted at the lion-like roars suddenly being uttered by the lamb of Berchtesgaden, and even Mussolini was moved to grudging admiration. In Paris, the entire foreign affairs debate in the Chamber of Deputies on February 25 was coloured by Schuschnigg's firmness the previous day. The Foreign Minister, M. Delbos, described Austria's independence as 'an indispensable element of the European balance', and one deputy was even moved to declare that 'France's fate would be decided on the banks of the Danube'.

This all showed what brave words from any quarter could achieve in a Europe divided between bombast and lethargy. Yet, at least as regards the impact abroad, Schuschnigg seemed almost to regret his boldness the moment he had displayed it. Two days after the speech, on February 26, von Papen paid a farewell call on the Chancellor (the india-rubber envoy was being recalled once again to Berlin, this time in honour). After some opening pleasantries, Papen launched into severe reproaches over Schuschnigg's behaviour. The speech, he complained, had been the immediate cause of the sharp French debate. The Austrian problem had thus 'again become the centre of discussion in Europe', and he went on to warn his listener that 'an Austrian independence supported by French or Czech crutches was unbearable for Germany'. Schuschnigg immediately retreated into his shell. He agreed that the effects of the French debate had been 'most disturbing' and even consented to publish a special article in the official *Wiener Zeitung*, 'which would draw a clear line between the problem of Austrian independence and French interests'.[7]

Papen concluded his account of what must have been, for him, a highly reassuring interview with these words : 'When taking leave of the Chancellor, I asked him not to delude himself into believing that Austria could ever maintain her position with the aid of non-German European alliances. The Austrian question would be decided only by the interests of the German people. He assured me that he was also convinced of this, and that he would let this conviction guide his actions.' This may have been a typical Papen telegram ; but it also sounds ominously like a typical Schuschnigg performance. Always, that massive ball-and-chain of Germanic loyalty was there, dragging at the feet even of his undoubted Austrian patriotism.

Schuschnigg later maintained [8] that his speech to Parliament had really been intended as a sort of 'last chance' offered to Hitler to declare his hand : if the Führer reacted strongly to this firm but reasonable language, no doubts could be left in anyone's mind that he intended violence. Considering how Hitler had behaved at Berchtesgaden and after, it is hard to see what further proof of his intentions was needed. Be that as it may, Schuschnigg was not kept waiting long for the answer. Indeed, in some parts of Austria, the local Nazis showed once again that they were one jump ahead of Berlin, for their reaction to the Chancellor's challenge was both immediate and ferocious.

The conflict raged fiercest of all in Graz. This Styrian capital, with its long border facing the Slav and Magyar East, was one of history's 'Germanic citadels', and, by 1938, most of the students and the pensioners who formed such a large part of its population had nailed the swastika onto these old Teutonic colours. Despite the efforts of the loyal Provincial

Governor, Dr. Stepan, and the local 'Fatherland Front' officials, the city often behaved more like an outpost of Hitler's 'Thousand Year Reich' than an ancient seat of the Habsburgs in the last weeks of Austria's freedom, and its betrayal had a strong influence on Schuschnigg's final manœuvres.

The Nazis of Graz (reinforced by 'flying squads' from outside) scored their first success on February 24, while the Chancellor was actually delivering his patriotic appeal in Vienna. They took control of a crowd nearly 20,000 strong which had gathered outside the Town Hall to hear the speech relayed, put the loudspeakers out of action, and even managed, with the Mayor's approval, to hoist the swastika alongside the Austrian colours from the roof of the building.[9] Elated with this triumph, they called a mass rally of 65,000 Nazis from all parts of the country for the week-end, in defiance of the Government's four-weeks' ban on political meetings. Only a bold show of strength by Schuschnigg — who ordered three battalions of the Vienna garrison, an armoured train and a squadron of light bombers down to Graz — caused them to think again and cancel the demonstration. This was both encouraging and depressing for the Government. Encouraging because it showed that Austria's Nazis would still scatter when charged ; depressing because it revealed that the Austrian police could no longer be relied upon to do the charging.

Indeed, Schuschnigg was now beginning to feel the full and sinister burden of carrying on his back Seyss-Inquart as Minister of Interior. The police force, always a political rag-bag, was now torn asunder completely by the dual control of a pro-Nazi Minister and a patriotic 'watchdog', Dr. Skubl, as his State Secretary. And, with every day that passed, Seyss-Inquart himself seemed to shed another shade of his faded Red-White-Red colouring and become a deeper brown. He persuaded the Chancellor to overrule Zernatto's plans for a wave of 3000 'Fatherland Front' meetings up and down the country on the grounds that it would 'provoke' Nazi reaction, and then promptly set out on a tour of provocation himself.

On March 1, he was in Graz, giving the Hitler salute to a jubilant torchlight procession headed by 5000 storm troopers in their forbidden Brown-Shirt uniforms. The following Sunday, March 5, he was in Linz — another Austrian provincial capital which was to carry a heavy load on its civic conscience for the year 1938. Here, from the balcony of the welcoming Town Hall, before a sea of banners in which the swastika mingled with the Black-Red-Gold of the old German Reich, this sworn Minister of the Republic told 50,000 listeners : 'Austria is German and only German. The National-German Reich is already a fact in the minds of men . . . and this National-German Reich of a common destiny it must be our aim to uphold.'

Seyss-Inquart's ambiguous decrees during that same week did as much damage as his speeches ; the slide into Germany's waiting arms was helped by a dozen of his officially pronounced compromises. The Nazi badge and the Hitler greeting, for example, though still banned in schools and offices, were now to be allowed 'in private'. The German anthem of 'Deutschland, Deutschland über alles' could be sung if a verse of the Austrian hymn were sung first. Both, of course, were set to the same theme from Haydn's famous Quartet. The same old music with two different modern texts — a perfect expression of the Austro-German dilemma that both the patriots and the Nazis were now trying to resolve by force, each in the opposite direction yet each with some logic on his side.

So, as the Ides of March approached, the Austrian tragedy began its final convulsions. Schuschnigg had one move left before Hitler brought the tale to its climax — a public appeal to the Austrian people and to the conscience of the world. He had rejected this step immediately after Berchtesgaden, when Austria's plight was in a sympathetic limelight abroad. He had hesitated to take it together with his rousing speech to

Parliament, when the domestic impact would certainly have been the greatest. It was the same decision and there were still the same arguments in his mind against it, notably the chronic fear of provoking Hitler. Yet, coming now, there were additional handicaps : an amenable Foreign Secretary was firmly established in London, while public opinion at home was enfeebled by the weeks of uncertainty and vacillation.

The plain truth was that, already at this stage, the Austrian Nazis were dictating the pace of events. Schuschnigg has freely admitted that his ill-fated plebiscite project was in reality a desperate defensive shot, fired on the retreat from the 'revolt' in Graz.[10] The Nazi strongholds of Styria were by now in a state of undeclared civil war. Characteristically, the Chancellor had first tried to buy off the violence and sabotage there with fresh sacrifices to the sacred 'German peace'. In pursuance of this hopeless policy, he had even removed his friend and staunch supporter, Dr. Stepan, from the post of Provincial Governor in the first days of March, replacing him by Dr. Trummer, a name more acceptable to the pan-Germans. But, to quote Schuschnigg's own words : 'Every concession on our part brought an avalanche of new and impossible demands'.

There seemed nothing left but the weapons of Austrian democracy, which had never been very sharp and which had anyway been locked up to rust for exactly five years. On March 6, after a week-end of deliberation, the Chancellor told Zernatto of his 'irrevocable decision' to appeal to the country, and fixed the plebiscite date for one week ahead, Sunday, March 13. Little did Schuschnigg dream, as the feverish secret preparations were launched that, by polling day, there would no longer be a free Austrian people to vote. He cannot be reproached for *naïveté* here. There was probably no one in Europe, including even Adolf Hitler, who would have guessed at this stage that Austria had less than a week to live.

In those first days of March, as the plebiscite project

ripened in his mind, Schuschnigg decided on three basic moves connected with it. Two were domestic and the third diplomatic. At home, he took the long-overdue step to open his régime up to the Left by starting serious negotiations with the workers; at the same time, he sealed his régime off politically to the Right, by formally rejecting any Monarchist solution to the crisis. His move abroad was to Mussolini, to consult that cynical and now rather battered Roman oracle about his plan.

The search for a truce with the Austrian Socialist leadership, driven underground or into exile after the brief though bloody Civil War of 1934, had been going on in a desultory fashion for more than a year. It was Hitler — who forced the Austrians to take so many decisions about themselves — who finally knocked some sense and urgency into the heads of the 'Austro-Fascists' and the 'Austro-Marxists'. Their own rivalries had paled into insignificance beside the common threat that arose at Berchtesgaden, for, instead of the wasteful political luxury of continuing to snap away at each other, there was now the danger that both camps would be swallowed up together.

Immediately after Berchtesgaden, therefore, businesslike contacts began.[11] The Catholic Mayor of Vienna, Dr. Schmitz, Schuschnigg's close friend but by no means his blind follower, approached the Socialist Trade Union leader Hillegeist; in a parallel move, Reither, the powerful Provincial Governor of Lower Austria, sought out one of the organizers of the illegal 'Revolutionary Socialists', Heinrich Widmayer. From these and other probings there finally materialized a three-hour meeting in the Chancellory on March 3 between Hillegeist, supported by twenty of his comrades, and Schuschnigg himself.

It cannot have been an easy personal encounter on either side. To the workers, Schuschnigg still wore the hangman's hood, for, as Minister of Justice, it was none other than he who had signed the death-warrants of the Socialist leaders executed as rebels after the Civil War four years before. And to the devout Jesuit-trained Chancellor, these spokesmen from the Austro-Marxist underground were still rather like the messengers of Anti-Christ, exhaling brimstone with every breath. Yet under the shadow of that even greater Lucifer across the border, the Left and the Right in Austria were now able to speak to one another without passion for the first time since 1934.

Hillegeist stressed in a dignified statement the workers' determination to join wholeheartedly in the struggle against Hitler, provided they could be made to feel that 'they were defending their own freedom as well as that of their country'. This very reasonable request was embodied in three basic demands submitted to the Chancellor : full ideological and political freedom for the Socialists ; the right to elect genuine workers representatives in the Government-controlled Trade Union movement ; and finally, a guarantee of better social conditions. Without committing himself over details, Schuschnigg pledged his word that the workers would certainly not be worse treated than any other section of the community and, as an earnest of his intentions, he nominated a Ministerial Committee of Three to continue the talks. The confrontation had been calm and businesslike. At last, there seemed to be an end to that dialogue between two deaf stutterers that had for so long passed for Austrian domestic politics.

Schuschnigg's decision, three days later, to hold his plebiscite only increased the urgency of a settlement from the Government's point of view. On their side, the workers held a mass meeting at Floridsdorf on March 7 — the first to be legally sanctioned for four years — at which the policy outlined by their spokesmen to the Chancellor was given formal support. Yet, despite this, the pact was never properly sealed, and when, at the end of that same week, the First Austrian Republic died, it took its inner wounds to the grave with it.

There were two main reasons why Schuschnigg hesitated
to the bitter end to give way in full to the workers' demands.
Each was a mixture of prejudice and commonsense. His first
and basic argument was that, whatever increased rights were
given to the Socialists within the Trade Unions, they could
not be allowed to re-emerge as an independent political movement outside the Unions. His régime stood or fell on the
all-embracing patriotic concept of the 'Fatherland Front', and
five years before, all the individual parties of Austria including
his own Christian-Socials, had been dissolved to make room
for this emergency constitutional experiment.

By 1938 the maintenance of the monolithic 'Fatherland
Front' was the only unanswerable legal argument he could
present to Hitler for continuing to ban the Nazis as a party
in Austria. He now feared that the Socialists, while only
demanding in theory those same civic privileges he was ex-
tending to the Nazis, were, in fact, aiming at political rights
which the Führer would promptly exploit for his own
protégés. Schuschnigg's second reason was the reverse of the
same medal : reluctance to move too far in public towards
the Austrian Left Wing in case Hitler should brand his régime
as having 'sold out to the Bolsheviks', and start 'protective
measures' accordingly. This fear was not fanciful. German
propaganda had already greeted the Floridsdorf workers'
meeting with allegations that a 'Popular Front' was forming
in Austria.

For their part, the Socialist leaders were, quite under-
standably, trying to combine resistance to Hitler with a political
comeback of their own. Thus, to some degree, each side
tried to balance the common peril against its individual
interests ; and each side, to a very marked degree, underestimated that common peril. As we shall see, it was not
until the morning of March 11 that agreement was finally
reached whereby a member of the 'Revolutionary Socialists',
Herr Sailer, was to appeal over the radio to the Austrian

workers that same evening to support the Chancellor's plebiscite. The truce came too late to have the slightest influence
on events, and the broadcast never took place. A few hours
later it was Schuschnigg who came to the microphone
instead himself, to announce the end of his plebiscite, and of
his régime.

It was certainly a tragic irony that the rival forces of
patriotism and democracy in Austria should have waited in
this way until the fifty-ninth minute of the eleventh hour
before touching fingers again. Yet to argue that Hitler would
have been held back had they met earlier is to ignore the
realities of power politics in the Europe of 1938. The Führer
struck the moment he saw that the mere threat of invasion
was enough to cow almost everyone in Vienna — 'Fatherland
Front', Monarchists and Socialists included — into submission;
and, even more important, when he judged that the risk of
outside aid to Austria had shrunk to acceptable proportions.
The only faint chance of checking him would have been
through a simultaneous stand on both fronts, the domestic and
the diplomatic. In March it still seemed too early for the one,
and almost too late for the other. The last-minute resurgence
of the Austrian Socialists behind Schuschnigg did them great
historic credit. At this stage, however, the country could
only have been saved by the will to fight, rather to
demonstrate, from inside ; and by the will to help, than to
talk, from outside.

There is a similar note of unreality about Schuschnigg's
dealings in these final weeks at the opposite pole of Austrian
politics, with the Legitimists. The Chancellor's own attitude
towards the Habsburg question was complex and wistful, like
so much in the man's nature. As befitted the son of one of
Franz Josef's most loyal generals, he was himself a passionate
Monarchist at heart. Yet, as equally befitted the leader of a
Republican state, he had the gravest doubts about Restoration
as a policy. His attitude to the crown was therefore like that

of a man towards an adored mistress whom he dared not make his wife. The usual pangs of conscience, with reproaches and misunderstandings all around, resulted.

This tug-of-war in the Chancellor's own soul was increased by two very practical factors, which also pulled in opposite directions. The first was the fear that, if he did beckon the Habsburgs back to Vienna, it would be Hitler, riding on a whirlwind, who would get there before them. Schuschnigg's anxiety never to provoke the Führer mounted in the final phase to a political neurosis, with imagination sometimes outpacing commonsense. But if ever this anxiety seemed justified, it was on the Restoration issue.

As Hitler's writings in *Mein Kampf* and in his so-called 'Secret Book' showed, the Habsburg dynasty was personally anathema to this frustrated ex-Austrian revolutionary. Its languid internationalism was an affront to his compact racial doctrines, and all his theories were infuriatingly upset by any such institution that could be so tenacious with so little virility. He also saw it as a potential political threat. A Restoration would not only keep the Austrians out of his clutches; it would revive old patterns and old affinities, as well as old rivalries, throughout the Danube Basin, and cross his wider ambitions in Central Europe. Domestic repercussions in Germany could also be feared, especially in the conservative Catholic provinces of Bavaria and Württemberg; the Habsburgs reinstated in Vienna might thus even weaken the Nazi régime at home.[12]

Whether Hitler's fears were real or imagined, personal or political, he fought the restoration concept with more consistency and vigour than any other aspect of the Austrian problem. In Vienna, and in every other capital of Europe, his emissaries never ceased to hammer home the warning that the return of the Habsburgs in any form might well set the German Army on the march. (As we have seen, the only plan that existed on the files of the German General Staff for an invasion of Austria bore the code-name 'Operation Otto' after the exiled Pretender.) It was Göring who, as usual, went around dotting the 'i's' and crossing the 't's' on the Führer's behalf. When he was visiting Rome in January 1937, for example, a member of the German Embassy asked him for instructions about handling the Monarchist question in conversations with the Austrian Minister there. A rather awed telegram[13] sent back to Berlin by the German diplomat concerned relates the advice he was given : 'General Göring then added that . . . if there was to be a restoration in Austria, it would force Germany into appropriate measures. In reply to a question I interposed, General Göring said we would then march in, and that would mean the end of Austria. When I remarked that surely I was not supposed to tell this to the (Austrian) Minister, General Göring replied that I might do so very definitely — the more plainly it was said, the better.'

Despite these warnings, and despite his disavowals then and later, there seems little doubt that Schuschnigg was toying with the possibilities of a Restoration in the winter of 1936/37, when the Monarchist movement in Austria was at its height. A revealing memorandum[14] written by the German Foreign Minister Baron von Neurath after his visit to Vienna in February 1937 shows that Schuschnigg had sounded him out very earnestly and exhaustively on the subject. According to this report, marked 'Strictly Confidential' in Neurath's hand, the Chancellor had told his visitor that 'there was great affection in Austria for the old ruling house and that the return to monarchy was considered the best means of quieting internal political conditions'. Von Neurath's blunt retort was that 'a Habsburg restoration would be the best way for Austria to commit suicide'.

Undeterred by this rebuff, Schuschnigg asked the German Foreign Minister to call on him again that afternoon (of February 23) 'to discuss the restoration question again in private'. At this second session, Neurath recorded, the

Chancellor began by saying that he was 'perfectly aware that a restoration of the Habsburgs could never be carried out against the wishes of Germany'. Schuschnigg added, however, that though he would of course consult Berlin before any such step, 'he could give no express assurance that he would in every case secure the advance approval of Germany'. After an interlude on Nazi problems in Austria, the Chancellor suddenly returned to the theme again like a dog to a favourite bone and asked whether German objections 'were directed merely against the House of Habsburg or against the introduction in Austria of a monarchy as such'. Neurath replied with some astonishment that Germany 'objected to the Habsburgs to begin with', and that the other question had not yet arisen.

When, in due course, Hitler persuaded Mussolini to add his support to the Anti-Restoration policy, Schuschnigg was left under no doubts as to the hazards of the scheme. Yet — and here the opposite pull of the tug-of-war was felt — he dared not drop the idea for the simple reason that he dared not drop its supporters. From the point of view of a besieged leader counting the reliable heads in his garrison, the Monarchists were the anti-Nazi fighters *par excellence*. They were, in fact, about the only section of the nation who, ever since 1918, had consistently and fervently pleaded the Austrian cause, as opposed to the pan-German cause of part of the Right Wing, or the Socialist International cause of most of the Left Wing.

The Austro-Fascist and the Austro-Marxist both looked abroad for inspiration and their roots in the soil of their own country were short and tangled. After the *Anschluss*, some elements of both camps tried brief flirtations with the Nazi conquerors because, in theory at least, there was something in either the Nationalism or the Socialism of Hitler's doctrines that looked acceptable. But, to the Monarchists, everything that Hitler stood for — politically, socially and ideologically — was abominable, partly because, ever since the battle of Königgrätz seventy-two years before, Berlin itself had been suspect. In short, the Legitimist was politically the only *natural* 100 per cent anti-Nazi, and, where he was Jewish as well, the percentage was doubled.

In this conflict of emotions and interests, Schuschnigg tried at first to compromise and get the best of both worlds. He started off by treating the Restoration as, ten years previously, his great clerical predecessor Chancellor Seipel had treated the *Anschluss* : something to be talked about but not done. Yet, because his own personal sympathies were so much with the Monarchist movement, the pace soon became too fast for comfort. By the end of 1936, 1456 Austrian municipalities had followed the example set by Axams in the Tyrol and had made the Archduke Otto their 'honorary citizen'. A New Year's message which the Pretender sent to them all alarmed von Papen with its 'urgent language'. The 'Emperor' had written to his 'subjects' : 'The times are past when we could content ourselves with wishes and expectations. What we neglect to do in these fleeting hours remains forever undone.'[15]

Schuschnigg had done nothing to discourage the young Archduke from using this sort of bold and direct approach. The Chancellor had paid personal pilgrimages to him in exile, while trusted intermediaries like Baron Karwinsky or the Legitimist leader Freiherr von Wiesner were constantly travelling between Vienna and Steenockerzeel Castle in Belgium where the Pretender lived. He was, in fact, treated between 1935 and 1938 as a sort of supernumerary member of the Austrian Cabinet and was kept better informed on some matters of state than the Federal President himself. His comments were welcomed and read with respect even where, as in the case of the July 1936 Pact, they expressed the strongest disapproval of the Chancellor's actions.

All this juggling with divine fire had to stop in a real crisis. The moment of decision came in February 1938, when the

Habsburg Pretender, like the Führer, put a pistol to Schuschnigg's head and told him to make up his mind. On February 19, exactly a week after Berchtesgaden, the faithful Wiesner arrived once again in Vienna from Belgium and put an urgent letter from his Emperor on the Chancellor's desk.

The first paragraphs showed that the young Archduke knew exactly how the cards lay.

'With the events of the last few days', he wrote, 'a new phase in the life of our people has begun. The enemies of Austria, by an act of violence that is without parallel, have succeeded in forcing your Government into a perilous position which dangerously impairs our further resistance.' The Pretender then declared that, because of his 'hereditary obligations', he must share the Chancellor's responsibilities in this hour of crisis, and outlined a three-point 'plan to save the Fatherland'. In foreign policy, he recommended a personal approach by Schuschnigg to the Western Powers; at home, he urged a further build-up of the Austrian Army and a political reconciliation with the workers. The formula was resolute and shrewd, considering that it was penned only three days after the real story of Berchtesgaden had emerged.

The real sting came in the tail. Referring to Schuschnigg's statements (as yet only in private) that he would resign rather than submit to further Nazi demands, the Archduke continued :

'However unexpected this may seem to you, if you consider that you can no longer withstand German or Ultra-National pressure, then I beg you, whatever the position may be, to hand over to me the office of Chancellor. . . . I could ask you to hand over only the Chancellorship to me so that, without altering the Constitution, the same advantages could be secured as through a formal act of restoration. . . .'

The signature — 'Otto, in a foreign land' — must have made Schuschnigg's Legitimist heart bleed. Yet the arguments failed to sway his political reason. To feel for the Pretender was one thing; to make room for him was another. Schuschnigg, though never corrupted by power, was none the less glued to office by four years of struggle. He genuinely believed that, under his guidance, Austria had a chance of surviving that struggle and that, meanwhile, the day of the double-headed eagle had not yet come. So, after nearly a fortnight spent in mulling over the problem, he sat down on March 2 and wrote his reply.

It was the same mixture of personal devotion and political rejection that Admiral Horthy had used to the Archduke's father seventeen years before, when the Emperor Charles, with the same easy assumption of sovereignty, landed in Hungary and asked the wily Regent for the keys of his Magyar kingdom. The time for the dynasty, Schuschnigg wrote, was in some happier tomorrow, when a new Europe, purged by war, would undergo a 'time of Resurrection'. But tomorrow, as Pretenders are always told, was a long way off. 'Our policy of today is tied to the present. The Austrian idea, including that of the House of Austria is, in my opinion, a concept which cannot be measured in terms of a generation. . . . Any attempt at a restoration, either in the next few years, or as far ahead as one can see, must assuredly, with one hundred per cent certainty, mean the death of Austria.'[16]

The Archduke and his followers might well have wondered why they had never received this blunt answer before. The Chancellor might well have replied that he had never been put a blunt question before. Wherever the fault lay, the whole Monarchist flirtation, which had been a typically Viennese affair of sweet words and faint resolves, was broken off with this farewell letter. Schuschnigg, who never held a political ace up his sleeve, had now discarded the one king in his hand.

With one way opened up to the extreme Socialist Left and another way barred to the extreme Monarchist Right, the Chancellor took his final preparatory step before appealing to the country by consulting with Mussolini. On March 7 he sent the Duce a full account of developments in Austria since Berchtesgaden and warned him of the likelihood of a plebiscite to save the situation. The intermediary entrusted with this message — Colonel Liebitzky, the Austrian Military Attaché in Rome — flew back to Vienna the next day with Mussolini's reply.

It was the familiar blend, as dispensed by the Duce over the past two years, of vague assurances for the future and no comfort for the present. The Italian dictator expressed long-term optimism, especially in view of the 'impending relaxation of relations between London and Rome'. As regards the immediate tension, he professed to regard Göring's 'word of honour', given to him the previous year, as sufficient guarantee that the Germans would not resort to force over Austria. Nevertheless, he counselled emphatically against the projected plebiscite, which he described as 'dangerous'. No good, he thought, could come of the idea, however the polling went. If the result were favourable for Austria, the Nazis would dismiss it as a fake ; if unfavourable, Austria would be doomed ; and if the vote were indecisive, it would be simply useless.[17] The plebiscite was thus 'a bomb which would burst in Schuschnigg's hands'.

This was the last personal message Schuschnigg ever received from his great protector. As regards Austrian domestic politics, Mussolini's reply showed either a refusal to face the facts or complete ignorance of them. For there was one point on which every actor in the Austrian drama and every foreign observer was agreed, whatever his allegiance : had the Chancellor gone through with his plebiscite as planned, the outcome at this juncture could only have been a substantial vote of confidence in himself and his anti-Nazi policy.

To some extent, this success was implicit in the very conditions of the poll. Schuschnigg cited for his general mandate Articles 65 and 93 of the 1934 Constitution. The first of these provided for plebiscites, though only in disputes over federal law ; so Schuschnigg took as his direct authorization the second article, which gave the Federal Chancellor power to lay down the overall lines of national policy, arguing that he could also submit to the people any major issue under this heading. At the same time, he retained the operating provisions of the earlier article, which fixed the minimum voting age at 24, and thus excluded all of the country's Nazi-infested youth.

Such juggling with the Constitution (which had itself been devised by jugglers for the benefit of tight-rope walkers) showed up the dismal truth that, by 1938, it was the rising generation from which Austria had most to fear. Yet it certainly increased what would have been only a plain majority on a wider vote into the prospect of an overwhelming majority on the restricted basis. According to one calculation, made by Schuschnigg's advisers, Austria had, at that time, about 4,400,000 electors — though after four years without elections, a certain margin for error was inevitable. Of these, 1,400,000 well-disciplined workers had just pledged their solid support ; Austria's 1,500,000 peasants would have backed Schuschnigg almost to a man without being asked, and so, on this issue, would the country's 400,000 Jews and half-Jews. Thus, even without the Monarchists and other 'Fatherland Front' stalwarts in Vienna and the towns, the Chancellor seemed sure of at least a 70 per cent victory, *provided* the emotional impetus could be sustained from the start and the plebiscite question was itself broadly enough phrased.

It looked as though both conditions would be amply fulfilled when, on the evening of Wednesday March 9, the Tyrolean Kurt von Schuschnigg rose at a mass meeting in Innsbruck to tell his native province and the world of his decision. True, the formula he asked his fellow-countrymen to endorse the following Sunday seemed so general as to be almost meaningless. It ran : 'Are you in favour of a free and German, an independent and social, a Christian and united Austria?' This was, at first sight, an extraordinary jumble, yet the order in which the various elements were introduced was not without significance.

First came liberty, and here, by implication, was the only anti-Hitler touch. Then, before either God or municipal housing, came the reaffirmation of loyalty to the German race. Unity finished up a bad sixth and the corporate state came nowhere. However, there was something here for nearly everybody — patriots, pan-Germans, workers and Catholics. And the only anti-Nazi minorities whose special interests were not catered for — the Monarchists, the Communists and the Jews — would give the Chancellor their desperate support in any case.

That evening, Schuschnigg found for a second time the right emotional touch, as well as a safe text. The proud old province and the uncertain young Republic were used to shore each other up. The Chancellor, himself wearing the loose grey jacket and green waistcoat of the Austrian Alps, ended his impassioned speech: 'Tyroleans and Austrians, say "Yes" to Tyrol. Say "Yes" to Austria.' And then, in Tyrolean dialect, he shouted out to them the same cry with which, one hundred and thirty years before, their peasant hero Andreas Hofer had emptied those same surrounding valleys for volunteers to fight Napoleon: 'Mannder, es isch Zeit!' ('Men, the time has come!') At that, twenty thousand throats roared themselves hoarse in the square, and the magic of the moment was caught by hundreds of thousands more listening on their wireless sets.

Alas for the legends of Austria, history did not repeat itself. Andreas Hofer, though facing even heavier odds against the tyrant of his day, actually drew his sword and fought on to the hopeless end. Schuschnigg appealed on Wednesday to the glorious past only to recoil on Friday before the terrible present. He was not hewn from the same human granite as the leader of that deathless billhook army. There was another vital difference : the tyrant he had to face was not a Frenchman.

NOTES

1. Documents on German Foreign Policy, *op. cit.* Series D, Vol. I, No. 304.

2. Schuschnigg, *Austrian Requiem*, p. 31.

3. Text in *Hitler's Speeches*, edited by N. H. Baynes, Vol. 2, pp. 1407-1408.

4. Documents on German Foreign Policy, *op. cit.* Series D, Vol. I, No. 318.

5. Tavs, Leopold, In der Maur, Schattenfroh and Rüdiger.

6. Documents on German Foreign Policy, *op. cit.* Series D, Vol. I, No. 328.

7. *Ibid.* No. 327.

8. *Austrian Requiem*, *op. cit.* p. 37, and conversation with the author at Salzburg, September 1960.

9. One of the best eye-witness accounts is in G. E. R. Gedye's *Fallen Bastions*, pp. 251 *et seq.* See also the accounts of Guido Zernatto, Oswald Dutch and Lennhof in their respective books.

10. Letter to the author, 10.2.1962 ; see also *Requiem*, *op. cit.* pp. 39-40.

11. For the best documentary account of these negotiations, see the testimony of the various Socialist leaders involved, given in the Schmidt Trial Protocols, *op. cit.* (for example, Friedrich Hillegeist, pp. 268-271; Karl Hans Sailer, pp. 264-268).

12. See Martin Fuchs, *Un Pacte avec Hitler*, pp. 300 *et seq.*, who has an interesting chapter on this.

13. Documents on German Foreign Policy, *op. cit.* Series D, Vol. I, No. 204.

14. *Ibid.* No. 213.

15. *Ibid.* No. 195.

16. The texts of both letters are reproduced, *inter alia*, in *Kurt von Schuschnigg*, by R. K. Sheridon, English Universities Press, London 1942, pp. 237-243.

17. See Schuschnigg's *Requiem*, *op. cit.* pp. 40-41. The author is also grateful to the late General Liebitzky (as he then was) for a personal account of the 1938 crisis given to him in Vienna in June 1960. See also Schmidt Trial Protocols, *op. cit.* p. 223.

CHAPTER SIX

March 10, 1938 : the False Dawn

ONCE again, the Chancellor returned to Vienna by the overnight train from the Alps after a decisive day in his struggle with Hitler. The capital he stepped out into on the early morning of March 10 was, however, a very different place from the frightened and bewildered city that had waited for him in silence after Berchtesgaden a month before. Vienna, always as quick to change as the surface of a mountain lake, had undergone another of her sudden transformations after the Innsbruck speech. For the last time, hope briefly supplanted doubt, and the natural fatalism of the people was swept aside by a new surge of purpose.

The Inner City rang that day like a tower of Babel with conflicting shouts. Though the defiant Nazi whip-crack of 'Sieg Heil !' still echoed through the streets, it was drowned for once under a variety of patriotic cries : 'Heil Schuschnigg !' 'Heil Front !' 'Heil Liberty !' (from the Socialists) and the lengthier 'Sunday is polling day ; we vote Yes !' These all added up to the simple slogan of 'Austria !' which somehow sounded less stilted now than at any time since it was launched as a rallying-cry five years back. Dollfuss, whose livid death-mask looked down on all the commotion from placards, could rest content at least with this part of his life's work.

The confident bustle extended to the political scene. One by one, as the day passed, spokesmen of the various anti-Nazi groups produced their pledges of full support for the plebiscite — Major Fey for the dissolved *Heimwehr* ; Karl Mittler for the underground Socialist 'activists' ; Dr. Friedmann for the Jewish Community ; Colonel Wolff for the Monarchists ; Cardinal Innitzer for the Catholics.

Only the local Nazi leaders themselves were, to begin with, uncertain, as they awaited their orders from Munich or Berlin. This uncertainty comes out most clearly in the last-minute discussions held on the evening of March 10 between the Chancellor and Seyss-Inquart, to try and determine how Austria's Nazis should behave on polling day. Hitler's fastidious henchman was now beginning to feel his Austrian heart flutter again in all this patriotic stir. His first act after hearing about the plebiscite project the previous day had been to consult with his cronies and then write long letters to both Schuschnigg in the Chancellory and Zernatto in the 'Father-land Front' headquarters to seek some sort of working compromise with them. In his message to Zernatto, for example, he declared that, as Minister of Interior, he would agree to the plebiscite, and even assure its smooth passage, provided certain technical 'irregularities' were removed and the voting formula was itself amended. Schuschnigg got a similar offer, coupled with a demand for increased Nazi participation in the Government, presumably as a price for such 'co-operation'.[1]

One of the Austrian Nazi underground leaders of whom we shall hear more later, Odilo Globocnig, was despatched to Hitler with a copy of this letter. Seyss's explanation at Nuremberg for this step was that, as the officially recognized middle-man between Schuschnigg and the Nazi movement as a whole, he was obliged 'to keep both sides informed'.

The Austrian Chancellor found time on that busy day to write a long reply to Seyss-Inquart which radiated confidence and a calm sense of superiority. He rejected insinuations that the plebiscite was in any way contrary to the Berchtesgaden agreement and bluntly told his rival that it was his own followers who, by their 'open revolt' in Styria, were trying to wreck the month-old truce. He continued : 'I am neither

capable nor desirous of playing a puppet's rôle. I carry the
political responsibility and I am the head of the Fatherland
Front. The grave situation in the country has been caused by
the fact that the Nazis will not keep the Berchtesgaden Pact
and are still trying to cause terror in the streets and in the
factories. I cannot be expected to look on while the country
is being wrecked by violence. I am in the fortunate position
of being able to call up the whole world as a witness of who is
right and who is seeking for peace. I am absolutely resolved
to do this at the time I think necessary.'[2] This was proud,
serene language, despite the fact that it came a month too late
and was to evaporate into thin air in exactly twenty-four hours
time.

Early that same night, these two earnest Catholic gentlemen, once military comrades-in-arms and now political
adversaries, followed up their courteous correspondence with
a long private talk. According to Seyss-Inquart's testimony,[3]
it was the Foreign Minister Dr. Schmidt who engineered the
meeting in the hope of at least neutralizing the Nazi faction
in Austria before Hitler broke his mysterious silence. In their
post-war accounts, both Schuschnigg and Seyss-Inquart seemed
to agree that the encounter was a success. Though rejecting
the idea of any formal 'Black-Brown' coalition as the reward
for Nazi support at the polls, the Chancellor hinted that more
of Seyss's nominees, like Jury and Reinthaller, might eventually
find themselves in leading federal or provincial posts. Schuschnigg made short work of his opponent's technical and moral
objections to the plebiscite, and finally extracted from Seyss-
Inquart the promise that he would appeal to his followers over
the radio to vote 'Yes' that coming Sunday. This was better
than the Chancellor had dared to hope for.[4] The only trouble
was that, by now, Seyss had practically no followers left.

He must have begun to suspect this for himself when he
hurried from his meeting with Schuschnigg to the nearby Hotel
'Regina' to attend a secret conference of Nazi 'Gauleiters'

summoned from all over Austria to discuss the plebiscite crisis. His report on the agreement just reached with the Chancellor was received by these worthies with a total lack of enthusiasm or even interest, and when they retired to another room to deliberate, Seyss found the door closed in his face. Small wonder : the 'revolutionaries' had just got their wind from Berlin of Hitler's reactions and were sharpening their knives for the morrow for anything from mass demonstrations to a new *putsch*.[5]

Of all this, the Chancellor was still blissfully ignorant. He went to bed that night confident not only that the Nazi threat to his poll had been removed but also that, on the other flank, the Socialists had finally been rounded up behind his programme. His tortuous negotiations with the Left Wing described above were, indeed, producing concrete results at last. The three-man Committee under Minister Roth, which had been appointed by the Chancellor a week before to hammer out a truce with the 'Revolutionary Socialist' leaders, found no choice in the end but to accept their irrefutable minimum claim for 'equal rights with the Nazis'. By March 10 it had been agreed that workers' organizations with genuinely elected officials should be given the same restricted freedom within the 'Fatherland Front' that Seyss-Inquart already enjoyed with his so-called 'Racial-Political' cells. A formal pact to this effect was, in fact, concluded the following morning between Roth and the Socialist spokesman, Karl Sailer, who was to launch the plebiscite appeal to the workers.

Even before this, practical co-operation between the Left Wing and the Right Wing in Austria had started up spontaneously, for the first time in the history of the First Republic, and during the last hours of its history. Small units of the *Schutzbund*, the old para-military striking force of the Socialists, emerged again from their years of underground existence and often brought their weapons out of the shadows with them. Most remarkable of all, Major Eifler, the 'military adviser' of the Revolutionary Socialists and ex-Chief of Staff of the *Schutzbund*, actually sat down with the ultra-Catholic Mayor of Vienna, Dr. Schmitz, to discuss joint armed resistance to the Nazis, should the situation deteriorate that far.[6] The irony of this particular contact can be seen from the fact that, in the Austrian Civil War only four years before, it was this same Major Eifler who had planned the *coup* against the 'Clerico-Fascists', Schmitz included, by a lightning armed action against the Inner City—mounted, if all else failed, on mobile municipal incinerators ![7] Eifler had as little luck in 1938 with his plans to fight the Germans as he had in 1934 with his plans to fight his own fellow-countrymen. The change of enemy was, none the less, significant : the common pull of the nation was at last replacing the rival tug-of-war of the parties.

An incident which took place in an outer suburb of Vienna on that same evening of March 10 showed that these tardy loyalties were also stirring in the breasts of Austria's Nazi-infected youth. 'Fatherland Front' officials working in the district on preparations for the plebiscite were approached by the leaders of several bands of local students who cheerfully admitted that, earlier in the week, they had taken part in Nazi demonstrations in the centre of the town for a fee of five Austrian schillings per day. This, they agreed, was excellent pay ; yet, in view of the coming poll, their consciences were beginning to trouble them. So, they asked, would the Front agree to pay them only four schillings per day to demonstrate in future for Schuschnigg and against the Nazis ?[8]

By any normal standards of patriotism, it was not very impressive for young Austrians to calculate the difference between Berlin and Vienna at exactly one schilling per day. But Austria in 1938 simply had no normal standards. The word 'Fatherland', which was already becoming rather old-fashioned in most other countries of Europe, was still new and strange on the lips of the First Republic. The Socialists distrusted it because it savoured too little of international brotherhood, and had anyway been coined as a political philosophy by the opposite camp of Dollfuss and Schuschnigg. As for the Nazis, they had a German fatherland of their own. It is to this 'other Germany' that we must now return, to see how Hitler was responding to Austria's final burst of defiance.

*   *   *

The German Legation in Vienna (temporarily without Papen, who was skiing in Kitzbühel) first heard that something drastic was in the wind on March 8. A memorandum signed that day by the Military Attaché, Lt.-General Muff, gives a detailed if roundabout report, whose ultimate source was Fritz Stockinger, the Austrian Minister of Commerce, to the effect that Schuschnigg had decided 'to hold elections in Austria as soon as possible'.⁹ It is not clear from the German archives whether this semi-accurate advance warning had reached Berlin by that same night. In any case, Hitler was not kept in the dark much longer. During the morning of Wednesday March 9, a few hours before Schuschnigg announced the news to the world, the Führer knew for certain that it was a plebiscite and not an election that was brewing in Austria and that the following Sunday was the date set.

This information did not come directly from Seyss-Inquart, whom Schuschnigg had informed and sworn to secrecy on his honour as a gentleman in Vienna the previous evening. In a sense, the nature of the betrayal was even more sinister and even more typical of the Austria of those times. The woman secretary of Guido Zernatto, that *fons et origo* of the Austrian patriotic movement, turned out to be a secret Nazi spy. While her chief was dictating to her his official instructions for the plebiscite in the late evening of March 8, she managed to smuggle out a note with the news to a prominent Austrian Nazi who had his office, very conveniently, in the same building. An emergency meeting of the illegal party leadership was held early the next morning, as Schuschnigg was on his way to Innsbruck, and one of its first decisions was to inform Hitler immediately of the impending crisis. This was done through a telephone call to Gruppenführer Keppler, the so-called Commissioner for Austrian Affairs in Berlin.

The Führer reacted with the astonished fury of a man stung by a bee that he had mistaken for a harmless bluebottle. Within an hour or two of getting the startling news, he had packed Keppler off to Vienna in a special plane to bring Schuschnigg to his senses. According to an urgent information telegram sent to Ribbentrop, who was then in London, Keppler's instructions were 'to prevent a plebiscite, or, if this is not possible, to have added to it a question on the *Anschluss*'.[10]

This initial response of Hitler's is typical of that see-saw between blackmail and outright violence which stamped all his feelings towards Austria. Keppler's task was, of course, only exploratory, and it seems clear that one of Hitler's main motives in despatching him to Vienna was quite simply to discover whether the news was true or not. (Keppler, indeed, testified at Nuremberg that the Führer had received his first message about the plebiscite with utter incredulity.)

None the less, Hitler had given his emissary fairly precise instructions on the assumption that the report was correct, and these instructions reflected a policy of preventing or altering the threatened poll by quasi-constitutional means. The proposal to amend the plebiscite formula with an additional question on the *Anschluss* revived those visions of a public trial of strength between the two German Chancellors that were always floating in the back of the Führer's mind. As early as July 1933, the month after the Nazi party had been banned in Austria, German planes had showered leaflets over Salzburg calling on Dollfuss to 'follow Adolf Hitler in the

Reich and legitimize his new policy by an appeal to the nation'. At Berchtesgaden only a month before, Hitler had returned to the theme, challenging Schuschnigg to a sort of grand joust of Teutonic knights, in which the weapons would be not lances but ballot boxes. And so again on the morning of March 9 : however swiftly his mood was to alter, the Führer's immediate reaction was not one of violence but of pained and incredulous shock.

This seems to have been the more or less spontaneous attitude struck by every leading German or Austrian Nazi as the plebiscite rumour was confirmed beyond all doubt by Schuschnigg's speech later that day. Göring in Berlin attacked the poll as a 'clear breach of the Berchtesgaden agreement' [11] and immediately set all his massive energy and influence at work to frustrate it. Papen, now back in Vienna from holiday, ostensibly just to pack up his personal belongings before returning to Germany, listened to the Innsbruck speech over the radio in his Legation. Keppler, straight off his plane, and one or two of the leading Austrian Nazis were sitting round the receiver with him. The general verdict, Papen claimed later, was that the plebiscite was 'a theatrical *coup*' and 'a mean trick of the Schuschnigg régime'.[12]

The new German Foreign Minister, von Ribbentrop, was, as we have seen, in London, where he had gone to complete his farewell calls as late Ambassador. In addition to the brief message received from his own Ministry, he had also listened there to the full broadcast of Schuschnigg's announcement on March 9 and had decided to tackle Lord Halifax, Eden's successor at the Foreign Office, on the subject the next morning. In his report of their conversation,[13] Halifax describes how Ribbentrop branded the proposed plebiscite as 'a fraud and a swindle' and appealed to Britain to use her influence in Vienna to get it cancelled. His Lordship reacted to this suggestion as though he had been asked by the former champagne salesman to cheat at cards. 'It seems a tall order', he replied icily, 'to say that a Head of Government cannot have a plebiscite if he wants to.'

Halifax went on to indulge in some very plain speaking. He told Ribbentrop that he 'attached the utmost importance' to the Austrian poll being carried out 'without interference or intimidation'. The situation in Vienna was 'highly charged with ugly possibilities' and he warned the German Minister against 'anything that might lead to or encourage violent action, for, if any explosion should occur at any time, it was quite impossible for any man to tell what might be the limit or the end'.[14]

By now, however, Hitler was rapidly steering towards the very 'explosion' Halifax was so concerned about. Until Schuschnigg had actually made his speech, the Führer stuck to the temporizing attitude he had adopted in the morning. During the early afternoon of March 9, for example, he ordered Seyss-Inquart in Vienna to take no formal steps 'but at the most to intensify the protest already made against the plebiscite'.[15] The Austrian Chancellor's broadcast, with its ringing tones of defiance, put an end to all that. Hitler no longer needed to await Keppler's return from Vienna to know that a supreme challenge to his prestige as 'the greatest of all the Germans' had been thrown down in the square at Innsbruck, and that the challenger was not likely to be bought off by mere words, much less defeated by them in an open vote.

The Führer's mood changed abruptly. He heard that Glaise-Horstenau, the pan-German Minister without Portfolio in Schuschnigg's latest Cabinet, was on holiday in Germany and ordered him, through the local Gauleiter, to come immediately to Berlin for consultations. (According to Glaise's testimony at Nuremberg, he had a $2\frac{1}{2}$-hour talk with Hitler in the Chancellory late that same night, without any decisive steps being agreed upon.[16])

Much more ominous were two other summonses that the

Führer sent out before dawn on March 10, after long telephone conversations with Göring. General Schobert, the Commander of the 7th German Army Corps, was ordered to report from his Headquarters at Munich, and General von Reichenau, the C.-in-C. of the Fourth Army Group at Leipzig, was also called back to Berlin immediately from Cairo, where he was attending a meeting of the Olympic Games Committee.[17] Both commanders would have a leading rôle in any military move mounted against Austria, while von Reichenau had been among the group of generals paraded for psychological effect before Schuschnigg at Berchtesgaden. This time, he and his colleagues were going to be something more than stage extras to support the Führer's monologues.

These decisions, taken by Hitler in person during the early hours of Wednesday March 10, were not propaganda gestures (indeed, they were never made public), but direct operational moves, either preliminary or precautionary in nature. They show that Hitler's Austrian pendulum was again swinging round from 'evolution' to 'revolution', and that the idea of a solution by force, or at least the threat of force, was already forming once more in his mind.

This became abundantly clear soon after daybreak, as the tension in Berlin grew and the tempo of the Führer's actions mounted with his anger. It also became equally clear that, whatever 'cloak-and-dagger' schemes Hitler had hatched or tolerated within the SS and SA organizations for a *coup* in Austria, the German Army as such had nothing better on its files in March 1938 than vague and totally unrehearsed invasion plans. The discrepancy was not surprising. Action against Austria had always been a closed affair of the party's, and the Army leadership itself had only been rendered politically 'reliable' in Hitler's eyes by the mass purges of the previous month. Indeed, the 'Old Guard' of Blomberg and Fritsch, which had fallen in February, had the reputation of being specifically opposed to any 'adventures' along Germany's southern borders — especially against the allies and blood-brothers of the First World War — and their removal from power had accordingly been received in Vienna with a sense of dismay.

Hitler's Chancellory was never a dull place. But on that morning of March 10 it must have resembled an angry bee-hive, an aspect it was not to lose for the next three days. Keppler, who had left Vienna by plane before dawn, presented himself in the building soon after 9 A.M. to find Hitler and a number of generals already at work. The Führer could only spare his special envoy a few minutes to hear a first-hand report on the Austrian situation, now made largely superfluous by Schuschnigg's speech. The military discussions were then resumed in earnest.

At about 10 o'clock, General Keitel, the Chief of the *Wehrmacht* Supreme Command, was himself called in. He was warned by Hitler that the Austrian problem had now become 'acute' [18] and that preparations were to be made accordingly. Left to himself, Keitel remembered the general staff paper 'Operation Otto' which had been drawn up the previous summer as part of a major study on war contingency planning for the German Armed Forces. This famous paper was invested after the war with an historical importance that it certainly did not possess at the time. True, it called for an immediate military invasion of Austria should a Habsburg restoration be attempted in Vienna. But this so-called 'special case' had not been taken very seriously by the German military strategists. Though the broad objectives of the operation were laid down, no proper mobilization plans had been drawn up and no detailed provision had been made for the Army's logistical or air support. Even the 7th Army Corps at Munich, which was to be the spearhead of the invasion, had received no special instructions from the Supreme Command before or after the February purge, and had conducted no separate invasion exercises of its own.

As late as the morning of March 10, 1938, therefore, when Keitel ordered 'Operation Otto' to be produced from the files, it was nothing more than a theoretical staff study which had been collecting dust ever since it was first drafted in June 1937. Keitel, whose anxiety to please the Führer was to become legendary, seems to have been somewhat apprehensive when Colonel Jodl handed him the inadequate paper. In the hope of finding something better, he summoned General Beck, the Chief of the Army General Staff, and told him to submit an immediate report on the preparations made for a 'possible invasion of Austria'. Keitel's nervousness can only have increased when he got the prompt reply that no such preparations existed to report on. At all events, it was Beck and not Keitel who was given the delicate task later that morning of going to Hitler and explaining the situation in person.

It was at this point, somewhere before noon on March 10, that the first concrete measures towards a military invasion were taken. On hearing Beck's negative report, Hitler ordered him to draw up immediate operational plans for crossing the Austrian border in force. The so-called 'Instruction No. 1', though not actually signed by Hitler until the following morning, almost certainly originated in the verbal directive which the Chief of Army Staff received from his Führer at this meeting.

This 'Instruction No. 1' blew all the dust off 'Operation Otto' at one puff.[19] Hitler reserved for himself personal control over the entire action. The 8th Army was designated to carry out the attack by land with the immediate objective of 'the occupation of Upper Austria, Salzburg, Lower Austria, Tyrol, as well as the rapid seizure of Vienna and the securing of the Austro-Czech frontier'.

The rôle of the German Air Force was 'to show and drop propaganda material, occupy Austrian airfields . . . support the ground forces if required and hold other bomber units ready for special tasks'. All units involved were told to be 'ready for invasion by midday on the 12th of March 1938 at the latest'.

The whole concept sounded as improvised as it was ruthless, a typically Hitlerian blend. The Führer's personal touch is also unmistakable in the political instructions given at the beginning and the end of the document. The invasion of Austria was to take place 'if other measures prove fruitless . . . and in order to establish constitutional conditions'. Though resistance was to be 'mercilessly crushed by force of arms', the invading troops were to try and create the impression by their behaviour 'that we do not wish to start a war against our Austrian brothers'. Hitler's mixture of stick and carrot towards the land of his birth thus persisted even in the moment of decision. It must be added that events were to prove his tactics perfectly right.

By the afternoon of March 10 it was clear to everyone in the Berlin Chancellory that Hitler had resolved to stop the plebiscite by fair means or foul. After lunch, he received Globocnig, the Austrian Nazi leader who had been kicking his heels ever since handing over the copy of Seyss-Inquart's letter the day before, and sent him back to Vienna to spread this message among the faithful, adding that detailed instructions would follow. Late that night, Glaise-Horstenau, the other Austrian temporarily at the Führer's court, was also called in again and told that Schuschnigg's poll would be stopped at all costs. He afterwards described Hitler as being 'in a furious and excited mood', and the whole atmosphere 'laden with danger'.

Those 'other measures' mentioned as a possible alternative to invasion in the Führer's 'Instruction No. 1' now began to emerge. At the end of the interview, Hitler tried to press into the Austrian Minister's hands two documents to take back with him to Vienna. The first was a draft letter of Seyss-Inquart's resignation from the Government ; the second was the proposed text of a broadcast by Schuschnigg on the

Austria's last fling — patriotic propaganda distributed in Vienna on March 10, 1938, for the anti-Hitler poll that Hitler stopped

The Chancellory in Berlin — outside the Führer's study where the first decision to crush Schuschnigg was taken, also on March 10, 1938

abandoned plebiscite.[20]   A moment or two later, Göring tackled Glaise-Horstenau on an even more sinister mission. The Field-Marshal, who was already emerging on the German side as the most uncompromising driving force in the crisis, pulled out of his pocket the draft of a telegram to be signed by Seyss-Inquart and sent to Berlin in which the despatch of German troops into Austria 'to restore order' was formally requested.

More of this notorious telegram, which Glaise was also asked to deliver, will be heard later. It is sufficient at this point to note that it makes its first appearance as early as the evening of March 10, barely 24 hours after Schuschnigg's public challenge. Though it was Göring who made the proposal, it is highly unlikely that he did so without Hitler's previous knowledge and approval.

And here, in trying to plot the chart of Austrian patriotism in those times, we come up against another frontier which ran submerged in all that tangled undergrowth of loyalties. Globocnig, the Austrian illegal Nazi 'Gauleiter' who had been sent back to Vienna early that day with a general message of defiance, would have taken anything back with him, including a Gestapo death warrant for Schuschnigg himself. He would have done so without even a pang of treachery, for he and his like thought of themselves as being already citizens of the 'Greater German Reich'. But Glaise-Horstenau, for all his pan-German sympathies, could still regard himself first and foremost as a Minister of the Austrian Republic. As such, he firmly refused both Hitler and Göring to act as their courier — no mean performance in view of angry pressure by the latter — and he flew back to Vienna the next morning with plenty on his mind but nothing in his hands.

For anything but his own conscience, it was a useless gesture. Hitler's message got there before him, and Glaise-Horstenau was forced to play the Führer's postman after all, back in his own capital.

NOTES

1. For details of these letters see Zernatto, *Die Wahrheit über Oesterreich*, pp. 286–289.

2. *Ibid.* pp. 290–292.

3. See Schmidt Trial Protocols, *op. cit.* p. 338.

4. See Schuschnigg, *Requiem*, *op. cit.* p. 43.

5. See Seyss-Inquart's testimony at Nuremberg, especially I.M.T., Vol. 16, p. 108.

6. See, *inter alia*, Schmidt Trial Protocols, *op. cit.* p. 266.

7. See Brook-Shepherd, *Dollfuss*, *op. cit.* p. 335.

8. This anecdote is recorded in Zernatto's *Die Wahrheit über Oesterreich*, *op. cit.* pp. 294–295.

9. Documents on German Foreign Policy, *op. cit.* Series D, Vol. I, No. 338.

10. *Ibid.* No. 339.

11. See Göring's testimony at Nuremberg, I.M.T., Vol. 9, pp. 332–333.

12. See Papen's Memorandum in the Schmidt Trial Protocols, *op. cit.* p. 380.

13. Documents on British Foreign Policy, Third Series, Vol. I, No. 9.

14. *Ibid.*

15. Documents on German Foreign Policy, *op. cit.* Series D, Vol. I, No. 342.

16. Nuremberg testimony of Glaise-Horstenau, I.M.T., Vol. 16, pp. 131–132.

17. Diary of Colonel Jodl, *op. cit.* Entry for 10.3.1938.

18. For this and the following sequence of events see the Nuremberg testimony of Keitel (I.M.T., Vol. 10, pp. 565 *et seq.*) and Jodl (I.M.T., Vol. 15, pp. 388 *et seq.*).

19. For its text, see Schmidt Trial Protocols, *op. cit.* pp. 576–577.

20. See Glaise-Horstenau's testimony at Nuremberg, I.M.T., Vol. 16, pp. 132 *et seq.*

CHAPTER SEVEN

March 11, 1938—Austria's Longest Day

IT began early enough and grimly enough, that blackest of Black Fridays in Vienna's history. At 5.30 A.M. the Chancellor was waked by his bedside telephone with an emergency call from the State Secretary for Security, Dr. Skubl. The Germans had closed the border at Salzburg an hour before and withdrawn all customs officials ; rail traffic had been stopped on their side of the frontier and massive troop movements had been noted throughout the night.[1] Schuschnigg hurried to his office in the half-light of breaking dawn, pausing on the route only to say a brief prayer in St. Stephen's Cathedral, where the priests were just reading first Mass at the side-altars. It seemed the sort of day when Austria would need all her patron saints.

At the Chancellory, he found his key officials at work and anxiously awaiting his arrival. Hornbostel, the Political Director of the Foreign Office, had already passed the news from Salzburg to the heads of the principal friendly missions in Vienna. Indeed, Mr. Palairet, the new British Minister, must have been aroused from his slumbers in the Metternichgasse Residence soon after Schuschnigg, for his urgent cable to Lord Halifax reporting the closure of the Austro-German frontier landed in London by 6.10 A.M.[2] Whether the British Foreign Secretary was waked up in turn we are not informed. It is unlikely.

Among the first telegrams that greeted the Chancellor was one sent during the night from Munich by the Austrian Consul-General there, Dr. Jordan. It bore the cryptic text : 'Leo is ready to travel'. No message in the code-books had a more ominous meaning : this was the pre-arranged signal to warn Vienna that preparations for an imminent German invasion of Austria appeared to have begun.[3] The telegraphed texts of that morning's German papers, rushed over by the Austrian Press Office, were just as disturbing. Goebbels, who had hitherto kept quiet about the plebiscite plan, had now trained all the guns of his propaganda machine onto it with one sudden blast. Among the more sinister inventive touches was one from the official Nazi news agency, D.N.B., alleging that hammer and sickle flags had been hoisted in Vienna and that combined shouts of 'Heil Moskau — Heil Schuschnigg' were resounding in the Austrian capital. It was not difficult to imagine how these stories could be exploited to justify the Führer in some 'anti-Bolshevik' crusade.

The Chancellor now tried to get in touch with the two men whom he was entitled to call upon for a formal explanation of these overnight moves : von Papen, the German envoy, and Seyss-Inquart, the Minister of Interior imposed on the Austrian Cabinet by Hitler at Berchtesgaden exactly a month before. In vain. If, in Munich, the lion was 'ready to travel', in Vienna, the fox had already bolted. Papen had flown out of the Austrian capital by special plane for Berlin at 6 that morning, before Schuschnigg had even left his own house.

Papen later testified [4] that he had been ordered by telephone to leave his post for Berlin 'immediately' on the previous evening, but had postponed his departure because he was 'no man for hasty decisions or unnecessary night-flights'. At first, he had assumed the summons meant simply that Hitler needed his advice ; later, he inclined to the view that the Führer wanted him removed from the scene of action, in case his 'evolutionary' tactics got in the way. Certainly, his last steps on free Austrian soil were placatory. According to a second telegram of the British Minister's sent to London at breakfast-time, Papen left word behind for the Austrian

Foreign Office 'not to attach too great importance to the closing of the frontier, which was probably due to a fear of disturbances'.[5]

More disquieting was the temporary disappearance of Seyss-Inquart, whom the pavements of Vienna seemed to have swallowed up. He was not to be found in his Ministry, his home, his private legal office nor at the underground Austrian Nazi Headquarters, transferred after the Tavs scandal to the Seitzergasse, though he was said to have called in there soon after daybreak. In fact, Seyss was also down at Aspern airfield, not to fly away but to meet his pan-German colleague Glaise-Horstenau, arriving on the early plane from Berlin. Glaise had flown in the interesting company of Dr. Hueber, Göring's Austrian brother-in-law, who was to take part in some pretty high-level family business before the day was over.

Another German plane had landed at Aspern shortly before them — the courier machine ordered to Vienna by Hitler the previous night to carry his written instructions to Seyss-Inquart. On hearing this, Seyss immediately had the Führer's letter collected from the German Legation, and he then read it through with Glaise-Horstenau on the drive to the Chancellory.[6] To their consternation, though hardly to their surprise, these two Austrian Ministers now found themselves being ordered by the head of a foreign power to deliver an ultimatum to their own Chancellor.

The nervous messengers of doom reached Schuschnigg's office at about 9.30 A.M., and spent the next two hours with him alone. After reproaching the Chancellor once more for his 'provocative' action, and painting a lurid picture of the mood in Berlin, they delivered the Führer's message : Sunday's plebiscite was to be postponed for at least two weeks to give time for a 'legal poll' to be organized in its stead on the lines of the 1937 Saar plebiscite. If the Chancellor refused, both of Hitler's spokesmen declared they would resign, and scarcely-veiled threats of Nazi violence in Austria and even of German military intervention were added. As the time-limit given for acceptance, 12 noon, was only thirty minutes away when their talk ended, Seyss-Inquart extended it in the Führer's name until 2 o'clock that afternoon and later confirmed this in writing. It was one of the last independent decisions he ever took.

At midday, Schuschnigg still seemed not only defiant, but confident in his defiance. Though prepared to discuss with the pan-German camp certain amendments to his plebiscite, he refused at this stage either to postpone it or cancel it altogether.[7] More than that; even before written confirmation of Seyss-Inquart's verbal demands reached his office, he called in the same Dr. Skubl who had aroused him before dawn and issued a series of emergency security orders which sounded for all the world as though he was preparing to call Hitler's bluff.

The 1915 class of Austrian reservists were called to the colours, ostensibly 'to keep complete order on the day of the plebiscite'; the police and the Vienna Front Militia were alerted; the security guards of the Federal Railways and of the capital's municipal plants were issued with arms, and the Socony Vacuum Oil Company in Austria was asked to supply extra fuel for motorized troop movements. The Nazi intelligence system in Vienna operated so swiftly and accurately that, half an hour later, a telegram reporting all these measures was on its way to Berlin from the German Legation.[1]

The Chancellor's mood of firmness remained uppermost when a group of his closest advisers gathered in his office to discuss the crisis shortly before 2 P.M. (Seyss had obligingly extended the ultimatum for an extra hour to allow this meeting to take place.) To the small group of his 'Inner Cabinet', which included Zernatto of the 'Fatherland Front', Perntner and Raab, the Ministers of Education and Trade, and Reither, the Provincial Governor of Lower Austria, he outlined the events of the morning.

According to Zernatto, whose eye-witness account is the fullest to survive,[9] Schuschnigg then advanced three alternate courses of action : first, total rejection of Hitler's ultimatum, coupled with a denunciation of the Berchtesgaden Pact and a public appeal to world opinion ; second, acceptance of the ultimatum, with the Chancellor resigning to make way for a new Government ; third, a compromise in which the technical changes proposed by Berlin for the plebiscite would be accepted, but nothing more. As at a similar critical meeting a month before, Schuschnigg had neatly drawn up, with a lawyer's clarity, two extremes and a middle course. Again, the middle course was adopted ; and, once again, it was promptly abandoned.

Seyss-Inquart and Glaise-Horstenau now turned up at the Chancellory for another and critical bargaining session. Schuschnigg's compromise solution was rejected out of hand, and he thus found himself driven into that very corner he had tried to avoid, where a flat choice between defiance and sur-render to Hitler had to be made. As always when faced with this stark alternative, Schuschnigg gave way. He put his dilemma before the Federal President Dr. Miklas, who had hurried in to the Ballhausplatz because of the mounting gravity of the crisis. It must have been around 2.30 P.M., during this conference with the Head of State, that the Chancellor decided to bow to the first German ultimatum of that day, and call off the plebiscite on which he had staked his own future and Austria's.

Compared with the resolution he had shown that morning, it seemed a surprising reversal ; indeed, most of his colleagues were taken aback when he returned to his own office to tell them of his decision. The only new negative factor to develop in the situation over lunch-time, which Schuschnigg learned shortly before going to the President, was that, despite repeated attempts to get through to Mussolini on the telephone for advice, the Duce was 'unavailable'. Though bitter enough, this was scarcely unexpected ; after all, the advice from Rome only the week before had been strongly against holding the plebiscite in the first place.

Nor can an explanation for Schuschnigg's abrupt withdrawal be sought in some sudden failure of nerve. His personal courage stayed with him to the end of that terrible day and, as he once pointed out, his much-publicized mental breakdown came, not then, but weeks later in a Nazi prison cell.[10]

It was not Austrian faint-heartedness which made him recoil before the prospect of violence so much as Germanic conscience. Had Italy been the aggressor in March 1938 instead of the 'protector', Austrian blood might well have flowed, whatever the odds. But against Germans — no matter what arm-bands they wore — Schuschnigg felt he simply could not draw the sword. In his own words : 'Already in 1934 — at the time of the attempted Nazi revolt — I was sure of one thing. Never again a war against Germany as in 1866, and never a civil war.'[11] That third alternative he was always drawing up on paper — resistance — never really existed in his heart. And, perhaps unfortunately, the art of bluffing was one he never attempted, let alone mastered.

Whatever the motives in the Chancellor's mind, and whatever the reactions among his colleagues, it looked as though his decision to abandon the poll had saved the freedom of Austria, if not her honour. Indeed, for the space of about thirty blissful minutes, everyone in the Chancellory, including Hitler's two spokesmen, believed the crisis was now over.[12] Their euphoria was to be shattered just after 3 o'clock when Göring leapt into action from Berlin and proceeded — for the first and probably the last time in history — to take over a whole country by telephone. This just gives us time to look at what was happening outside the Vienna Chancellory building during those eventful lunch hours.

In the Austrian capital itself, preparations for the plebiscite that had just been abandoned were, ironically, still in full swing. That particular Friday was a brilliant, warm spring day, with a touch of the relaxing Alpine 'Foehn' blowing in from the West. The pavements were already littered with leaflets for the Sunday poll, and Austrian military aircraft droned through the blue sky overhead unloading thousands more which fluttered stiffly down on the city like a stage snow-storm. A medley of waltzes and patriotic marches poured out over Vienna's radio station, and the streets were dominated by processions or lorry convoys of the 'Fatherland Front', be-decked with red-white-red ribbons, shouting slogans and scattering still more hand-bills as they moved along.

'Austro-Fascists' and 'Austro-Marxists' were at last united on this morning, though the police, unable to shake off over-night habits accumulated over four years, were sometimes severe with the cheering groups of workers — themselves more than a little unfamiliar with the idea of demonstrating for Schuschnigg's Austria. The legal arm of the legal Govern-ment seemed to have the capital firmly in its grasp. Steel-helmeted troops, reinforced by the Militia in their grey-green uniforms, bustled about everywhere. Even the arcades of the Opera House, where the sleepy horse 'fiakers' normally parked for hire, and where students or tourists queued up for tickets, were now filled with police cars, keeping order on the Kärntnerstrasse.

True, the very fact that the city was so dominated by this patriotic commotion did worry a few thoughtful people : where, they asked themselves, had all the Nazi 'activists' dis-appeared to ? They would have been far more perturbed could they have seen those same Nazis assembling at secret meeting-places in the outer districts and in the Vienna woods, with all the weapons they could muster and rations for a three-day 'operation'. Yet outwardly, the capital was calm. Gay music continued to come over the radio, and the Government had done nothing and said nothing to suggest what was going on behind the yellow Chancellory walls. So, until evening, the Viennese went on celebrating the new Austria that was dying at birth.

Abroad, the picture during the first half of that March 11 was a varied one. Italy, as we have seen, might have been on another planet that morning. Ciano's Diary for that day shows no diplomatic activity whatsoever on the Austrian crisis until the afternoon.[13] The Duce was allegedly at his country retreat of Rocca della Caminata and was not answering his telephone. It was the same instrument he had pointed out to Schuschnigg in a visit to the same house in 1936 with the words : 'Even here, I am always reachable for you in case of need'.

In Paris, by another ironic coincidence, the Chautemps Cabinet had fallen almost on the very day Schuschnigg announced his plebiscite. The Foreign Minister, Yvon Delbos, was therefore *in statu demissionis* on March 11, and was thus handicapped from the start when the second and more severe crisis broke over Vienna in the afternoon. It was in London where, for the moment, the centre of Western diplomatic activity lay, for the German Foreign Minister, Ribbentrop, was still on his official visit to the British capital. Indeed, during those same two hours when Schuschnigg, without a thought of food, was parrying and then bowing to Hitler's first ultimatum, Ribbentrop and his wife were sitting down to a lunch given in their honour at 10 Downing Street by the British Prime Minister, Neville Chamberlain. The story of that meal, even as recorded in a dry memorandum of Lord Halifax's, makes interesting reading.[14]

The lunch was over and the guests were on the point of leaving when two telegrams on the Austrian crisis were brought over from the Foreign Office. These were two more urgent messages just received from the British Legation in Vienna, in which Palairet, following up his dawn despatch on the frontier situation, was trying to keep pace with events.[15] The first reported the German demand, with threats, for the abandonment of the plebiscite, and Schuschnigg's refusal. The second described how the Chancellor, having made a complete *volte-face* by abandoning the poll, had now apparently been confronted with yet another ultimatum from Berlin, calling on him to resign himself within the hour. (Someone in the Foreign Office must have arrived rather out of breath at No. 10 with this second message, for the time-log shows that it was not received in London until 3 P.M.)

Lord Halifax looked at the two telegrams and passed them without a word to Chamberlain. The Prime Minister immediately called on Herr Ribbentrop to leave the party and come to his study 'for a private word'. The genial host had turned into the stern headmaster, and Ribbentrop's own account of what followed showed that he came in for some fairly severe handling.[16] Chamberlain read out the gist of both messages, said that 'an exceedingly serious situation' had now arisen, and demanded an explanation. Halifax, who appeared to Ribbentrop to be the 'more excited' of the two, interjected that the German threat of force, if confirmed, was 'intolerable'. As an impromptu suggestion, he asked, might not an impartial and internationally-policed poll on the Saar pattern be held in Austria to solve the problem ?

At this, Chamberlain stepped in to overrule his Foreign Secretary, remarking that, in his personal view, it would now be better if the plebiscite were not held at all. A minute or two later, when Lord Halifax spoke of Schuschnigg being 'threatened with invasion', the Prime Minister once again toned down his colleague's language, and agreed with Ribbentrop that there was nothing to support such a drastic view in the two messages they were discussing.

This marked desire of Chamberlain's to keep Austro-German relations on an even emotional keel, notwithstanding the disturbing news from Vienna, was to be one of the major keys to Hitler's triumph and Austria's tragedy in the next 24 hours. It cannot have surprised the German Foreign Minister, even at this awkward moment. Barely half an hour before, as Ribbentrop had sat with his host over coffee in the nearby drawing-room, Chamberlain had solemnly asked him to convey a personal message to Hitler. The guest had agreed with pleasure.

According to Ribbentrop's own report,[17] the British Prime Minister then declared that it had 'always been his desire to clear up German-British relations. He had now made up his mind to realize this aim. He requested me to tell the Führer that this was his sincere wish and firm determination.' When the Austrian plebiscite was briefly mentioned at this particular conversation, Chamberlain, despite the alarm signals from Vienna early that day, still dismissed it as a secondary and temporary obstacle to his plans. To quote Ribbentrop again, he said that 'once we had all got past this unpleasant affair and a reasonable solution had been found, it was to be hoped that we could begin working in earnest towards a German-British understanding'.

It was little wonder that, when Mr. Palairet's telegrams were thrust into his hands only a few minutes later, Chamberlain should have found them irritating as well as disturbing. For the plain fact of the matter was that they just didn't *fit*, and the Prime Minister had an orderly mind.

Despite all this, Ribbentrop clearly had to be taken to task over the Vienna mystery, and both Chamberlain and Halifax now pressed him hard for satisfaction. The German Foreign Minister extricated himself by declaring that the reports were just as big a mystery to him. He repeated his earlier attacks on Schuschnigg's 'provocations' and 'breaches of faith', but professed himself at a loss to comment on the telegrams. Perhaps, he hinted, they were only inventions put out by 'the dishonest Schuschnigg Government'. All he could promise, on taking his delayed leave, was to get in touch with Berlin straight away for an 'authentic report on the situation'. As he was due to meet Lord Halifax for another talk at tea-time, the three men agreed to let matters rest there for the moment.

For once, Ribbentrop was telling the truth. Though he knew of Hitler's determination to block the plebiscite, the really decisive blows had been delivered without any reference to him ; indeed, they had come at the very moment when he was amicably 'disposing' of the whole Austrian crisis over coffee with Mr. Chamberlain. Ribbentrop drove back to his Embassy and immediately telephoned his capital for news ; it is to Berlin that we must also now return for the explanation of Mr. Palairet's alarming messages.

For the second day in succession, the Führer was already up and about in his Chancellory at what was, for him, the unusually early hour of 9 A.M. Papen hurried there straight from his plane and found Hitler, 'in a state bordering on hysteria', surrounded by Göring, Himmler, Goebbels, the Generals Brauchitsch and Keitel, and with a gnat-like brown swarm of lesser ministers, party functionaries and officers buzzing about on the periphery. The Führer greeted his envoy from Vienna by shouting : 'The situation has become unbearable. . . . Schuschnigg has betrayed the Greater German ideal. . . . He cannot be allowed to succeed and he will not succeed.'[18] According to his own version of events — which is very probably accurate on this point — Papen urged moderation on his agitated master and recalled the personal pledge the Führer had given him after the Vienna *putsch* fiasco of 1934 to solve the Austrian problem from then onwards without recourse to violence.

Hitler's answer, after impatiently dismissing Papen, was to sign the famous 'Military Operation Instruction No. 1', which, as we have seen, he had discussed with General Beck the night before when ordering the first real invasion preparations against Austria to be launched. His next step was equally eloquent of his mood. He sat down and penned a long personal letter to Benito Mussolini, to ward off in advance any Italian interference with the blow he was now mounting. The message began by declaring a *fait accompli*. 'In a fateful hour', Hitler wrote, 'I am turning to your Excellency to inform you of a decision which appears necessary under the circumstances *and has already become irrevocable*' [19] [author's italics]. The letter went on to condemn poor Schuschnigg for arming his frontiers, preparing a Restoration, and plotting with Czechoslovakia 'to throw a mass of at least 20 million men against Germany if necessary'. But his real crime, of course, was the oppression 'of the national-minded majority in Austria by a negligible minority'. The plebiscite was yet another step in this campaign which Hitler had finally decided to crush. 'In my responsibility as Führer and Chancellor of the German Reich and likewise as a son of this soil. . . . I am now determined to restore law and order in my homeland. . . .'

The Führer was delicate enough not to mention military measures by name. But he left the Duce in little doubt about what was looming with his final 'solemn pledge'. This ran : 'Whatever the consequences of the coming events may be, I have drawn a definite boundary between Germany and France and now draw one just as definite between Italy and us. It is the Brenner.' The message ended on the unctuous note : 'I deeply regret not being able to talk to you personally at this time to tell you everything I feel.' It was signed 'Always in friendship, Yours, Adolf Hitler'.

This was an extraordinary document, reflecting the clash between fear and anger that was going on in the Führer's mind. The decision to use force against Schuschnigg was crystallizing steadily. Yet it by no means had the clarity and confidence at this stage that the message implied. The almost pleading note at the end of the letter belied its rather over-emphatic beginning. Mussolini's intentions were still unsure and had to be probed. The task was given to Prince Philip of Hessen, who as a son-in-law of the Italian King, enjoyed great favour in Rome. The Prince was summoned to the

Führer, given a brief résumé of the Austrian crisis, and bundled off to Rome in a special plane straight away with the letter.

Such then was the position in Berlin over lunch-time : concrete and detailed preparations for the invasion of Austria were in hand before Schuschnigg's reply to the ultimatum despatched overnight had been received. Nothing but encouraging messages had so far come out of Ribbentrop in London (the day before, Hitler had received a telegram from him which minimized British concern for Austria and actually recommended a solution by force, provided it was 'very quick'.[20]) Mussolini was the uncertain factor, yet everything had now been done to keep him both happy and passive. The Führer was clearly bracing himself for another 'summons from destiny', and the mood of his lieutenants was more of expectation than of anxiety.

It was in this general atmosphere that, at 2.45 P.M., Göring was called to the telephone. Seyss-Inquart was on the line from Vienna with the splendid news that Schuschnigg, after conferring with the Austrian President, had just announced to his colleagues that he would bow to Hitler's demands and call off the plebiscite. The Austrian crisis, which seemed to be ended by this news, now began in earnest.

Göring's own words at Nuremberg give the most vivid description of this new turning-point. As he told his judges : 'At this moment, I had an instinctive feeling that the situation had begun to slide and that here at last was that opportunity — so long and passionately awaited — to bring about a complete and clear-cut solution. And, from this time onwards, I must take the responsibility for what now happened 100 per cent on my shoulders, for it was not so much the Führer as I myself who set the pace here and forced things to a decision even against his doubts.'[21]

Göring looked back on the *Anschluss* without a trace of remorse ; indeed, he died proud at least of this part of his life's work and, by his own standards, perhaps justifiably so.

It was quite natural therefore that he tended to over-dramatize the part he played in events on the afternoon and evening of March 11, considerable though this was. As we have seen, Hitler's mind had been steadily veering round to violence again for the past 36 hours ; he had ordered actual invasion preparations the previous night and had signed the necessary instructions that same morning. With Schuschnigg showing no fight in Vienna, and nobody else showing fight for him in Europe, the odds are that those German troops would have marched anyway within the next few days. What Göring now did was to take the safety-catch off the pistol that Hitler was already drawing, and help to aim it for him.

It was still the Führer, however, who pressed the trigger. The misleading impression has arisen that Göring not only took executive control of the Austrian operation from now on but that he also acted quite independently of his master. This nobody did in the Berlin of 1938, least of all on a life-or-death decision over Austria, which Hitler had always reserved for himself. In fact, Göring made it plain elsewhere in the same Nuremberg testimony that, after receiving Seyss's telephone message, he conferred with Hitler and received his approval for the next decisive move. But whereas the Führer, though authorizing this drastic new step, still seemed to have the option of non-violence somewhere in his calculations, Göring banished all thought of 'evolution' from his mind and steered deliberately for a collision.[22]

At five-past three, twenty minutes after hearing the news of Schuschnigg's first retreat, Göring telephoned Seyss-Inquart again in the Vienna Chancellory. He passed him the following message, which Austria's Minister of Interior was told to take down in writing :

'Berlin cannot accept the decision of Chancellor Schuschnigg's in any form. In view of his breach of the Berchtesgaden Agreement, Schuschnigg no longer enjoys our confidence. . . . The national (*i.e.* pan-German) Ministers in Austria are to

Off with the old love!—
Schuschnigg and his 'pro-
tector' Mussolini in 1935

And on with the new!—Mussolini
with Hitler at Munich six months
before the fall of Austria

Seyss-Inquart, Chancellor of Austria for three days in succession to Schuschnigg, and his token 'Cabinet', formed a few hours before the German invasion

Herr von Ribbentrop, Hitler's Foreign Minister, who happened to be in London during the *Anschluss* crisis, leaving the German Embassy for Berlin on March 13, 1938

hand in their resignations at once to the Chancellor and to demand that he resigns as well.' Seyss was given 'at the most one hour' in which to report success, and told to send off in addition 'that agreed telegram to the Führer' with the request for German military aid. Finally, he found himself taking down like a stenographer from Göring his own appointment as Schuschnigg's successor. 'Obviously', the Field-Marshal concluded, 'Schuschnigg's resignation can only be followed with your own nomination by the Federal President to form a new Cabinet.'[23]

It was a bold and ruthless step forward. Once again — and now for the last time — Schuschnigg was to learn that he could not meet his opponents halfway, and that the Austro-German dilemma itself could not be resolved by half-measures.

With Göring's telephone call, the centre of the crisis moved back once more to the Vienna Chancellory. Seyss-Inquart returned to his Cabinet colleagues waiting in the so-called Hall of Columns and, 'white in the face and agitated',[24] read out the message from Berlin. For a moment there was silence. Then, from all sides, the Ministers started plying him with questions. Seyss's reaction gave a first foretaste of the bitterness and brevity of the triumph now approaching him. 'Don't ask me', he replied with a shrug, 'I'm nothing more than a historic telephone girl.'

That other well-meaning Austrian tool of Hitler's, Glaise-Horstenau, had also been chastened by Berlin's sudden display of brutality. His pained comment on the news was : 'I really don't know whether, under the circumstances, one can continue as a gentleman'. For these reasons of 'delicacy', Glaise then refused to accompany Seyss-Inquart into the Chancellor's private office and break the bombshell to him. It was a bit late in the day for that sort of compunction, but Seyss seems to have been too distraught to press the point. Leaving his fellow crypto-Nazi with the agitated group in the ante-chamber, he went in alone.[25]

Everything now depended on Schuschnigg. For the second time that day, the Austrian Chancellor was faced with the choice between outright defiance and complete surrender and, for the second time, he decided almost immediately for the latter. The motivation was the same : defiance would lead to the spilling of 'German blood', whereas surrender might preserve the shadow, if not the substance, of 'German Austria'. It is hard to judge his decision by its wisdom or folly, toughness or weakness, since, for his own inner self, the choice was simply not there.

It is, however, important to record, as a matter of historical fact, that Schuschnigg gave up the fight in Vienna shortly before either the Western Powers or Italy told Austria in so many words that they would not fight for her, and some twelve hours before the first German troops crossed her borders.

It was about 3.30 P.M., soon after receiving Göring's ultimatum from Seyss's hands, that the Chancellor announced he would place the resignation of his entire Government in the President's hands. By 3.55 Seyss-Inquart was already telephoning Berlin again to say that Schuschnigg was now with Dr. Miklas to announce his decision.[26] The Chancellor himself has described how Mussolini's first evasive reaction to all his pleas was brought in to him while he was actually with the President.[27] The British Foreign Office records show that a similarly lukewarm message from Lord Halifax did not reach the Legation in Vienna until 4.30 P.M.[28] While, therefore, it is true to say that Schuschnigg would have gained nothing by holding out for one extra hour, it is perhaps a pity for the Austrian record that he did not do so. As it was, surrender came just before abandonment — in confident anticipation of it.

Despite his action, however, throughout that afternoon and evening the red-white-red flag still flew from the Hofburg. For though the Chancellor had thrown in his hand, the President now defiantly struggled on without him. Dr. Miklas had yielded only reluctantly to Schuschnigg's insistence on his immediate resignation and had refused point-blank to fulfil the second and more important part of Göring's ultimatum by appointing Seyss-Inquart to succeed him. The President's argument was simple and irrefutable, though fast becoming irrelevant : it was just no business of Germany's who governed Austria, and whether the country should hold a plebiscite or not.[29] This was to have been the public verdict of the nation on the coming Sunday, and, up to lunch-time on that same day, it had still been the private language of the Government. Yet now it had a dreamlike quality in a world abruptly turned inside out by one message bellowed down the telephone from Berlin.

Though conscious of his growing isolation, Miklas was also conscious of his remaining power. Nothing that the Germans undertook could have the stamp of legality without his signature, and he seems to have sensed, more acutely than Schuschnigg, that the Führer was in fact psychologically dependent on such 'legality'. At all events, from now until midnight, the stubbornness of Miklas was the real voice of Austria, as it had been four years before when the capital lay temporarily paralysed under a Nazi *putsch*. Schuschnigg was persuaded to remain on, at least in a caretaker capacity, and the search for a suitable alternative to Seyss-Inquart as his successor began.

No one could be found to shoulder the deadly burden. In the next hour or two, a dozen names were canvassed and three men were formally offered the post by the President : Dr. Skubl, Schuschnigg's loyal Secretary of State for the Interior ; Dr. Ender, an authority on constitutional questions and head of a former Christian-Social government ; and General Schilhawsky, the Inspector-General of the Armed Forces. The background of these men — security, law and army respectively — showed the resolute lines along which Miklas was thinking. Had any one of them taken on the job and shown the old President's same spirit of defiance, Hitler and the world would have had much more to think about on that 11th of March, even if Austria herself might have had more to mourn.

There were, however, no takers. Skubl, whose personal courage cannot be questioned, knew that, as Vienna Police President, he had been on Hitler's black list for years and pointed out that his nomination as Chancellor could only act as an unnecessary provocation ; moreover, like Schuschnigg, he sincerely believed in Seyss-Inquart's basically Austrian loyalties and therefore held him to be 'the lesser evil in the circumstances'.[30] The other candidates were briefer with their arguments. Dr. Ender's reaction to Miklas was that 'his personal needs for the office of Chancellor had been more than adequately satisfied already'.[31] General Schilhawsky replied that he was an officer, not a politician, and that he anyway 'felt too poorly' for the task.[32]

At least once during all these depressing comings and goings, the President appealed again to Schuschnigg to stand by his post, complaining bitterly that, in this decisive hour, he was being 'deserted by everyone'. But the ex-Chancellor would still only consent to being a sort of acting Chancellor, going through the mechanical motions of government until someone could be found to fill his place. There was no sudden surrender here, but only the logical emergence of that hidden surrender implicit in his position all along. As he wrote afterwards of this anguishing afternoon : 'My task was finished. I had done my duty to the best of my knowledge, and I refused to be instrumental — directly or indirectly — in the preparations of Cain to slay his brother Abel.' [33] And, at another point, 'I saw no other possibility than Seyss-Inquart. With the little hope I had left, I clung to all the promises he had made me ; I clung to his personal reputation as a practising Catholic and a man of honour.' [34]

There is something of the pathos of Greek tragedy about

the last hours in office of this upright and well-meaning man who had governed Austria for the past four years. For, to the very end, he still clung to the beliefs and promises that had first blinded him and that were now to betray him and destroy his country. While Austria was in a political limbo — neither with a government nor without, neither captive nor free — Schuschnigg wandered around the Chancellory like a ghost, gazing at the gilt panelled offices and the oil portraits that made up its history. Schwarzenberg and Beust, Andrássy and Kálnoky, Berchtold and Aehrenthal, the massive picture of the Empress Maria Theresa and the little carved wood Madonna for the murdered Dollfuss — they were themselves a silent gallery of the Austrian dilemma : with Germany or against her ?

Seyss-Inquart was in no better shape during this time himself. He was plagued by what was essentially the same problem, and he tackled it in the same fatalistic fashion. Though informed by Göring that he was to be the next Chancellor of Austria, he refused to go and demand his 'rights' from the President. On the other hand, he could not simply do nothing, for there were the fruits of office to tempt him and the wrath of Berlin to spur him on. So, with help and advice from all and sundry, he sat down and tried to draw up Ministerial lists for a possible Seyss-Inquart Cabinet. He was still trying to devise an *Austrian* Cabinet out of all the combinations proposed ; up to this point, Schuschnigg's personal faith in him appeared justified. In fact, Seyss later described as his guiding principle the belief that 'the crisis would have purely internal repercussions, and would not affect the relationship between Austria and the Reich'.[35]

Though the hope was certainly naïve, it seems to have been sincere. In pursuing it, he rejected Kaltenbrunner, a nominee of the Austrian Nazi extremists, as head of security, and held out for Skubl instead. He also turned down a proposal to appoint Göring's Austrian brother-in-law, Dr. Hueber, as the new Foreign Minister, and pressed Schmidt to stay on at his post. Skubl, true to the advice he had given the President, agreed to serve under Seyss-Inquart. Schmidt, on the other hand, declined, saying that he had 'gone through thick and thin with Schuschnigg and would now resign with him'.[36] This, at least, was one true note struck among all the discords of Guido Schmidt's controversial career.

These events are interesting only for the light they throw on Seyss-Inquart's delusions and on Schuschnigg's faith in those delusions. Politically, they achieved nothing. Seyss still had no Austrian mandate for his negotiations and the conqueror's mandate had so far only arrived by telephone. What was technically to be Austria's last pre-war Government thus began, very fittingly, as a game of charades in the Chancellor's ante-chambers.

The scene certainly had something theatrical about it as the agitated Ministers, generals, Ballhausplatz officials and diplomats, 'Fatherland Front' leaders and Austrian Nazi spokesmen grouped and re-grouped aimlessly in the great 'Hall of Columns', as clouds of flies do on a summer's day. 'Over the whole building', one eye-witness later wrote from exile, 'an atmosphere of tension arose like a column of air shimmering in the heat. . . . One had the feeling that something frightful was about to happen. A spark was enough to send the mighty flame of events leaping up to heaven — a shout could do it, a stone, a shot. . . .' [37] By dusk, the hat-stands had become shapeless mountains of coats and uniforms, and the telephones never stopped shrilling. Amidst all the bedlam, one senior member of the Cabinet was observed sitting quietly by himself in a corner, a book in his hand. This admirable Stoic (unfortunately unidentified) was finishing off a 'History of the Renaissance in Italy' as long as there was still time.

All this while, Göring was relentlessly increasing the pressure. From 3.30 until midnight, though he never once spoke to the Austrian Head of State, it was President Miklas who was his sole target. The verbatim records which have survived of Göring's telephone calls to his Austrian minions during those hours give a vivid picture of the steady pursuit from Berlin and the utter confusion of the retreat in Vienna. The muddle at the Ballhausplatz became so great that once, at 5 o'clock, Göring even received a false victory message from Globocnig, who seems to have been as big a blockhead as he was a fanatic. For reasons which remain obscure, the Austrian Nazi leader reported to Berlin that Seyss-Inquart was already installed as Chancellor. On hearing this, Göring graciously extended the time-limit for the formation of the new Cabinet until 7.30 that evening, and telephoned what he fondly believed were his final instructions concerning the list of Ministers.

His illusions lasted less than half an hour. At 5.26 Seyss-Inquart got on the line again to Berlin himself and explained the true position : Miklas was still holding out and a successor to Schuschnigg had still not been appointed. At this, Göring exploded. It is quite plain from the record of the conversation that the particular action he now ordered was his own improvised decision, taken without the Führer's explicit authority.

After only a few seconds for reflection, he ordered Seyss-Inquart to mobilize the German Military Attaché in Vienna, Lt.-General Muff, and descend with him on Dr. Miklas to deliver the following fresh ultimatum : 'If he does not immediately accept the demands . . . then, this very night, the troops massed against and moving towards the whole length of the border will march in, and Austria's existence will be at an end'. Göring repeated his 7.30 deadline for the formation of a Seyss-Inquart Cabinet and then shouted, just before slamming down the receiver, 'If Miklas hasn't grasped that in four hours, he will have to get it into his head now, in four minutes.' [38]

The orders that Göring telephoned separately to General Muff a few minutes later were still more precise. The German Military Attaché was told to present the following message : 'If by 7.30 P.M. Field-Marshal Göring has not received the report that Seyss-Inquart has become Chancellor, 200,000 men standing in readiness at the border will march in.' [39] The General hastened round to the Ballhausplatz to execute his mission. Yet even these details of the threatened invasion force, delivered personally by a senior officer of the *Wehrmacht*, failed to budge Miklas. Muff was on good personal terms with the President, and his account of the interview, for all its restrained official language, shows he was not unmoved himself. 'After I had presented the ultimatum to the President . . . in the form ordered,' he wrote, 'I further asked him whether I might speak to him as one German to another and I then urgently requested him to proceed with the appointment of Seyss-Inquart. The President resolutely, and at times pathetically, refused to make the appointment under the threat of force.' [40]

By this time Keppler was back in Vienna again with his special instructions from the Führer and, probably just before Muff's interview with Miklas (the actual sequence at this point is not quite clear), he made an attempt of his own to bring the President round. Keppler's language seems to have been more temperate than Muff's, for he was carrying out orders issued to him by Hitler early that afternoon in Berlin, before anyone there had had cause to lose their temper with Miklas. Keppler's less savage approach may also have reflected Hitler's own oscillations between political pressure and naked force, which were certainly not evident in Göring's attitude to the crisis.

Yet even if Keppler used fewer threats than Göring's emissary, the music in this case was more important than the tone, for his basic demands were the same : the resignation of Schuschnigg and the creation of a Nazi Cabinet under Seyss-Inquart.

At all events, Miklas met him with the same firm refusal, using language which showed that at least the Austrian President could still distinguish between state and race. As he testified later : 'I stood by the unalterable standpoint that, as a free and independent country — even if of Germanic stamp — Austria could have her own government, not subject to the dictates of the German Reich'.[41]

At twenty-eight minutes past six, Muff and Keppler duly telephoned Göring in Berlin to report, in a somewhat crest-fallen manner, the failure of both their missions. The Field-Marshal replied with another angry explosion and another spontaneous decision. Keppler was told to present himself to Miklas yet again and inform him that, unless he yielded immediately, Nazi storm troops would be called out in the streets of Vienna and the German Army would cross the border 'in five minutes from now'.[42] Before the five minutes had ticked away, Keppler was back on the telephone to say that, once more, the Austrian President had 'rejected everything'.

Göring clearly had no express authority from Hitler for this fresh 'five-minute ultimatum' ; indeed, nearly two hours were to pass before the Führer finally ordered his army to march. The impatient Field-Marshal had in fact been bluffing, and Miklas had calmly called his bluff. Göring thereupon backed out of the conversation with a series of fierce but meaningless instructions, fired like ragged salvoes on the retreat. For once, he seemed almost as much at a loss as his Vienna henchmen.

The defiance of an almost isolated President, whose only strength was stubbornness and whose only weapon was legality, still stood between Hitler and his homeland. It was Schusch-nigg, to whom we must now return, who again broke the deadlock for Berlin with another of his deliberate, despairing steps backwards.

* * *

Throughout this long battle of wills between Göring and Miklas, the acting Chancellor of Austria had been addressing himself to two related problems : what help could Austria expect from abroad in the emergency and what, if anything, could be gained if she fought Hitler by herself ? He had in fact made up his mind in advance that the answers to these questions were 'None' and 'Nothing' respectively. But he was as conscientious as he was pessimistic, and all the motions of enquiry and debate were gone through during the afternoon and early evening of this nightmarish day.

Perhaps the best way to approach the tangled flurry of diplomatic activity touched off throughout Europe by the successive German ultimata is to return, in the first place, to London. Here, it will be remembered, we left Mr. Chamberlain and Lord Halifax seeing off their luncheon guest, Herr von Ribbentrop, on the steps of 10 Downing Street, after their confrontation over the suddenly worsening crisis in Vienna. We must now take a closer look at those two telegrams from Mr. Palairet which had caused all the excitement, for there was at least one sentence in them that Mr. Chamberlain had not read out to his visitor. This was a passage in the second of the two messages where the British envoy, after stating that Schuschnigg had been given one hour to resign, went on : 'Dr. Schuschnigg asks for the *immediate* advice of His Majesty's Government as to what he should do'.[43] It was curious that now, as after Berchtesgaden, the Austrian Chancellor avoided any outright appeal to Britain for help, or even a direct invocation of the Stresa Pact obligations, such as they were. No doubt he considered all this to be a waste of breath. The first reaction from London certainly bore him out.

At 4.30 P.M. the following reply from Lord Halifax arrived at the British Legation in Vienna for Schuschnigg : 'His Majesty's Government cannot take the responsibility of advising the Chancellor to take any course of action which might expose his country to dangers against which His

Majesty's Government are unable to guarantee protection'.[44] If Schuschnigg had phrased his question rather lamely, the response he got was as bad as anything he could have imagined. Britannia seemed to be wiping her skirts clean of the whole affair.

The truth was not quite as bad as that. The timing of the British reply shows that it must have been sent off as a prompt stalling operation, before any proper attempts had been made to sound out feeling and co-ordinate action in Paris and Rome. Though Schuschnigg was not told of them, these efforts were in fact launched with the utmost vigour in the next few hours. The aim was to dissolve the crisis quietly, by diplomatic pressure on Hitler, exerted by Britain alone and also, if possible, in concert with France and Italy. This aim was inadequate for the emergency, and it anyway proved futile. In pursuing it, Britain merely fulfilled her formal treaty obligations of 1935 to consult with her Stresa Front partners 'as to the measures to be taken in case of threats to the independence and integrity of Austria'. She did not take one step more, and never looked like doing so. Yet Schuschnigg, who had not even asked her point-blank to go as far as that, certainly helped her in not going further.

The British Government soon had the ideal chance to try direct persuasion on Germany, though, by an odd quirk of fate, the chance was spoilt. As we have seen, Lord Halifax was due to call on Herr Ribbentrop for tea, less than an hour and a half after the Downing Street lunch had broken up. At 5.15 he duly presented himself at the German Embassy, armed with another batch of telegrams from Vienna which confirmed beyond all doubt that Schuschnigg's resignation had been demanded by Berlin under the threat of an immediate invasion. And here, it seems, that blunder of Globocnig's in giving Göring a premature victory report from Vienna un-wittingly helped the Nazi cause.

Halifax describes [45] how Ribbentrop was still loudly

protesting innocence when, at about 5.30, his Embassy Coun-
sellor burst into the room with the urgent message from Berlin
that Schuschnigg had resigned and that Seyss-Inquart was now
Chancellor of Austria. This report, which can only have
been based on the totally misleading picture received in Berlin
half an hour before, turned the tables in London completely
in Ribbentrop's favour. He stopped apologizing on the
instant, and delivered a little homily instead on the necessity
imposed upon all nations from time to time 'of acting with
decision in a manner that others might consider hard'. He
recovered his bounce so quickly as to suggest that the 'settlement of the Austrian problem' just announced to them was,
after all, only what Britain had done in Ireland.

Halifax angrily rejected this parallel, but was rather at a
loss how to go on from there. Believing that Hitler had
already won a bloodless battle in Vienna, he could only utter
post-mortem warnings that this 'exhibition of naked force'
would 'put back for a long time the growth of friendly
understanding' between the British and the German peoples.
Half an hour later, both the Foreign Office and the German
Embassy knew that the message from Berlin was false. By
then, however, Halifax and Ribbentrop had parted, and were
not to meet again until Hitler's victory was genuinely secured
and past all challenge.

This intermezzo in London is not without significance,
since it was only in the British capital that Austria's potential
helpers had a Nazi leader at their continuous disposal as the
crisis developed on March 11. Not that London alone could
have saved the day; indeed, the only thing Hitler really
bothered about during these hours of pressure and counter-
pressure was not what Britain did by herself in the diplomatic
field, but what she did in common with France and Italy.
And on this broader front, absolutely nothing could be
achieved. Despite some honest efforts by both the British
and French Governments to prod Mussolini into joint action,

the Duce adopted an attitude which can only be described as aggressively passive.

With that, he blocked any effective restraint on Berlin, for, of the three Stresa partners, Italy was the only one who had a common frontier with Austria and the only one who, as in 1934, could give her immediate military support. Stresa without Mussolini was like Hamlet without the Prince of Denmark. It would have taken a lot to push him onto the stage in March 1938, and, thanks to Schuschnigg's costly policy of silence, nothing had been done to remind the prince, before the world audience, of his rôle.

The British approach to Italy left the Foreign Office at 5.40 P.M., after hurried consultation with Paris. The British Ambassador in Rome, the Earl of Perth, was ordered to seek 'an immediate interview' with Mussolini, inform him of the warnings issued to Ribbentrop in London over lunch, and to 'invite him to give his views'. The tail of the telegram wagged very weakly. Lord Perth was authorized, if pressed by Mussolini about Britain's actions so far, to reveal the negative attitude Lord Halifax had communicated to Schuschnigg an hour before.[46] All in all, it was not a very strong case to put before the Duce, and the British envoy must have been rather relieved to learn from his French colleague that he would never get a chance to put it.

France had been quicker off the mark than Britain in sounding the Italian Government. The French Chargé d'Affaires in Rome, M. Blondel, had already fixed one appointment with Count Ciano to discuss the overnight reports of German troop concentrations against Austria when, at 5 P.M., he was rung up again by Paris and told to speed things up in view of the deepening political crisis in Vienna. It was the answer that the French diplomat now received from the Palazzo Chigi that really sealed Austria's fate. He was curtly told by Ciano's private secretary that, if the subject of his visit was Austria, he could spare himself the trouble of coming, for the Italian Foreign Minister had 'rien à concerter ni avec la France ni avec l'Angleterre au sujet de la situation autrichienne'.[47]

As Count Ciano noted in his diary that night, M. Blondel, on hearing this, did not venture to call. The French envoy evidently saw no point in knocking at a door that had just been slammed in his face. Ciano added an angry reproach against both France and Britain for even attempting to secure common action at this time over Austria's plight. 'After sanctions, the non-recognition of our Empire and all the other miseries inflicted on us since 1935,' he wrote, 'do they expect to rebuild Stresa in an hour, with Hannibal at the gates?'[48]

Italy's savage refusal undermined whatever resolve there was in London and Paris for joint pressure on Hitler. The two capitals consulted again and finally agreed to make similar but *separate* protests in Berlin. These were duly delivered in writing that evening to Baron von Neurath, who had been pulled back to the German Foreign Office to stand in for the absent Ribbentrop. Referring to the reported threats against Schuschnigg, the two notes 'protested most emphatically against the use of coercion backed by force against an independent state'. Such behaviour, they concluded, 'is bound to produce the gravest reactions of which it is impossible to foretell the results'.

Britain kept almost exactly to the agreed text, but managed to blunt the tip of her arrow by the manner of shooting. Whereas the French note was a cold and formal one, beginning with 'M. le Ministre' and ending 'I have the honour etc.', the letter from the British Embassy was, considering the contents, ludicrously chatty. It started 'Dear Reichsminister' and was signed, like an invitation to a tennis party, 'Yours sincerely'. It is no mean achievement to smile and put your tongue out at one and the same time, but His Majesty's Government succeeded on this occasion.

To be fair, it should be added that the 'softness' of the British Embassy in Berlin throughout the crisis, which directly reflected the pro-German and anti-Austrian sympathies of the Ambassador, Sir Nevile Henderson, went beyond anything approved of in London. Indeed, at one point, the contrast grew so glaring as to produce a direct clash. In the early hours of Saturday morning Henderson reported to the Foreign Office that, in a discussion he had just had with Göring, he (Henderson) had 'reluctantly agreed that Dr. Schuschnigg had acted with precipitate folly'.[49] This was too much even for Lord Halifax, who replied with one of the sharpest rebukes Henderson can ever have received in his career. The envoy was told that this unauthorized remark had 'diminished the force' of the official protest and was ordered in future to keep his personal views either to himself, or else in line with His Lordship's own policy.[50] All this does something, in retrospect, to salvage the British Government's name. It came far too late at the time to be of the slightest help to Schuschnigg.

The Austrian Chancellor was not told in detail what France and Britain were trying and failing to achieve in Rome on the afternoon and early evening of the crisis. The information was not strictly necessary. He realized well enough from his own enquiries between 4.30 and 7.30 that whatever was being attempted on his behalf had collapsed, and that it was the short Roman sword of Mussolini, on which he had relied since 1934 for protection, that had now been plunged into his back. During those critical four hours, both the Chancellor and the Political Director of his Foreign Office, Dr. Hornbostel, had made further repeated efforts to get in touch with the Duce — always in vain. The only message to reach Vienna from Rome during the afternoon was ice-cold : 'As the Italian Government does not dispose of the evidence necessary to judge the situation, it is obliged to refrain from any opinion'.[51]

Hornbostel made one last attempt after General Muff had

done his sabre-rattling with Dr. Miklas ; he could only get Ciano on the line, and the Duce's son-in-law had nothing but excuses to offer. That was that, for earlier telephone calls to London and Paris had made it quite clear that though the Western democracies would act behind Mussolini, or at his side, they were not prepared, over Austria, to march ahead of him. The despair that now fell over the Ballhausplatz had a certain poetic justice about it. The Austrian leaders stood as alone in the world as they had left their own President alone in Vienna.

It was against this background that Schuschnigg turned to face his last and, in some ways, his most far-reaching decision as Chancellor : should Austria fight or not against the return of her unwanted Prodigal Son ?

Deep down in his own mind there was also no argument on this point, yet argument was forced upon him by some of his bolder colleagues. In purely military terms, the Austrian Army of March 1938 was of course no match in any extended campaign for Hitler's motorized *Wehrmacht* (appallingly inefficient though this turned out to be on its triumphal procession from Munich to Vienna). It could, however, have acted as a most awkward and embarrassing trip-wire, particularly if Austria's emergency defence measures had been adequately stepped up after Berchtesgaden a month before. As it was, only 5000 troops stood fully mobilized and ready for action along the German border at a few hours' notice when the final crisis broke. Field-Marshal-Lieutenant Jansa, who, as Austrian Chief of Staff until February 18, had planned the defensive campaign against Germany, reckoned that a further $6\frac{1}{2}$ divisions, numbering some 25,000 men, could have been thrown into the battle within 48 hours, followed by another 50,000 trained troops 'in the five days following'.[52]

The equipment position was mixed, and, on the whole, parlous. Artillery was old but adequate, thanks largely to the Austrian guns captured by the Italians in the First World

War and handed back by Mussolini in 1935-37 as part of his now-abandoned 'Watch on the Brenner'. One hundred and fifty of these now faced Hitler along the River Enns defence line. On the other hand, there were no tanks beyond a few light models (also Italian) ; no anti-aircraft defences beyond two light batteries recently delivered from Sweden ; and no air force to speak of.[53] The state of ammunition supplies summed up the whole situation. There was enough 'for two full days' battle' ; [54] after that the troops would have had to count every bullet.

In contrast to these material deficiencies, the morale of the Austrian Army was held by all contemporary observers (Germans included) to be high. One authoritative estimate, based on lists discovered later, put the number of Nazi sympathizers in its ranks at 5 per cent,[55] a figure well below the national average. Nor did anyone, Schuschnigg included, have any doubt that, despite all the racial links and the memories of a wartime comradeship of arms, the Austrian troops were quite willing to defend their frontiers against a German invasion, if firmly ordered and firmly led in the attempt. True, they would have fired with greater natural gusto at any of their five other neighbours (excluding perhaps the pacific Swiss but quite definitely including their Italian 'protectors'). The Austro-German military relationship itself had been placed by all the hysterical pros and cons of the Nazi debate on a razor's-edge balance of love and hate. Duty and emotion could push it to either side with equal force, provided the clear lead were given. And so — for the army as for the nation — everything rested on Schuschnigg's own decision.

His answer to those who urged him to consider resistance on this March 11 (and they included President Miklas, Bürgermeister Schmitz and, at times, Guido Zernatto) was calm and consistent : without any apparent prospect of immediate outside military aid, a one- or two-day fight alone against the powerful invader would be but a useless sacrifice. It was pressed upon him -- and he agreed — that the para-military forces of the 'Fatherland Front', the armed bands of Revolutionary Socialists, and thousands of the nation at large were ready to join the Army in the struggle, and that a guerrilla war could thus be touched off which would smoulder on in the forests and mountains of Austria long after any main battle front had collapsed in the plains. Yet, to this too, he had a swift retort. As he put it later : 'The result, at least for Vienna, would have been an immediate air bombardment, which simply could not be risked in view of the utter defencelessness of the people. . . . And had the entire population of Austria ranged itself with unanimous determination against the aggressor, this, in my opinion, would not have changed the hopelessness of resistance, even from the viewpoint of foreign affairs.' [56]

It is difficult not to sympathize fully with these arguments of a Chancellor asked to take the blood of his own countrymen on his head. It is equally difficult to agree with them fully, either in the short term or the long term. As regards the March crisis itself, it seems highly doubtful — in the light of all we now know about Hitler's political hesitancies and complexes towards the land of his birth — whether he would in fact have risked an aerial bombardment of its capital. Vienna in 1938 was neither a Guernica nor a Rotterdam ; there was no Civil War and no World War to 'justify' the *Luftwaffe's* attacks. The city was to be spared nothing in the end and, ironically, it was German SS flame-throwers which started the destruction of St. Stephen's Cathedral in April 1945. Yet had that symbol of the Holy Roman Empire been shattered by German bombs in peace-time seven years before, the explosions would have been rude enough to mobilize the conscience of the world, including the new Roman Empire of Mussolini.

A land attack directed purely against the armed forces of Austria was, on the other hand, very much in Hitler's calculations from the start. Though Schuschnigg might conceivably have warded it off by giving public notice *in advance* of his intention to defend his country, resistance once Hitler had crossed the border would probably have done little to help the country in its immediate plight. There would, however, have been some longer-term dividends all round had little Austria fought back at the German invader even for a few hopeless hours in March 1938, as an even smaller Denmark did two years later.

To begin with, Austria herself would have enjoyed full co-belligerent status with those Allies who eventually won the war that followed. The four-power occupation of Austria would not have begun on the terms it did in 1945, and even the Russians would have had trouble in spinning it out for the ten years it then lasted. Perhaps more important were the wider aspects. Had Hitler been greeted with even a few ineffective bullets at the Austrian border instead of bouquets of flowers, and had some blood been spilled instead of wine, the Western democracies, including an inward-looking America, would have been shaken out of their apathy there and then. The piecemeal abandonment of Czechoslovakia could scarcely have happened as it did in the next twelve months, for Hitler would not have embarked so soon on 'liberating' the Sudeten-Germans if the Austrian-Germans had not given such apparently convincing proof of his racial policies. Indeed, the Führer might even have been pushed back in the sequence of his conquests towards that tentative deadline of 1942–43 he had warned his own generals against.

In short, by ordering his troops to fight in March 1938, Schuschnigg could neither have saved Austria from being overrun nor have prevented the World War from breaking out. What he might well have done was delay that war, unite and strengthen the Allies more rapidly before it arrived, and help the case of his own country after it ended. He would have been a remarkable prophet to have seen all this at the time. In fact, his decision then was determined not so much by any calculation of profit and loss as by that part-idealistic and part-fatalistic way in which he regarded Austria's 'German mission'. As he wrote nearly twenty-five years later : 'I am convinced that the 11th of March 1938 was really decided already in November 1918'.[57]

* * *

This feeling of Schuschnigg's that what was about to happen in Vienna was somehow written in the stars underlay the next vital steps he took, now that the last hope of foreign intervention had been written off. The first was an executive order he issued to General Schilhawsky to pass down to all units of the Austrian Army. These were withdrawn from the border areas to behind the River Enns, leaving the frontiers wide open, and were commanded to offer no resistance against any German forces which might march in.[58] The die was thus cast on that military front where such stern preparations for action had been ordered less than six hours before. The Chancellor then proceeded to make public his similar *volte-face* on the political front. At 7 P.M. Radio Vienna was authorized to reveal the postponement of the plebiscite ; a few minutes later, the resignation was announced of the entire Cabinet, with the significant exception of Seyss-Inquart who, it was said, was 'remaining in office as Minister of Interior'.

This broadcast finally pulled the carpet from under the feet of President Miklas and anyone else who was still contemplating organized resistance to Hitler. Until then, the surrender had been known for certain only to the swarm of Ministers and officials inside the Vienna Chancellory and to the Foreign Offices in three or four capitals abroad. Everyone else had been fed on rumour or hope. Now the truth was announced to the world, and not least to those groups of Nazi 'activists' who were waiting, glued to their radio receivers, all over Austria. A series of miniature *putsches* followed in provincial centres throughout the country in which the local Nazis — following the good example already set by their Styrian comrades in the afternoon — seized control of government buildings and ran amok in the streets.

For want of a lead of any sort from the capital, the provinces capitulated without a shot and almost without a murmur. In Salzburg and in Linz, for example, the regional 'Gauleiters' of the illegal Nazi party simply demanded and were given the seals of office in the name of Seyss-Inquart. The Provincial Governors acted technically within their rights, since, according to Vienna Radio and all that they could learn over the telephone, the Minister of Interior was indeed the only remnant of legal authority left in the total vacuum. Yet this bloodless surrender, one after the other, of Austrian cities which had been freshly plastered again that same morning with Schuschnigg's slogans of patriotic defiance remains a wretched display of mass paralysis — and a most revealing one.

Vienna itself was now fast approaching the same condition. Swastikas began to unfurl like war pennants from the windows of both Ministries and private houses and, despite the strong guard encircling the Chancellory, the first handfuls of Austrian Nazi youths had managed to slip into the building, where they wandered insolently around with their close-cropped hair and their white stockings — incongruous, yet somehow already at home.[59] These symbols of the new age seemed to have moved about quite unchallenged ; the very seat of government by now had no more dignity and discipline than a crowded railway platform.

There was muddle to the end. At 7.30 Göring's ultimatum had expired and, though the Vienna radio announcement half an hour before had covered most of the Field-Marshal's demands, Seyss-Inquart — thanks to Miklas — was still not Chancellor of Austria. The threatened invasion was therefore due to begin. Sure enough, a few minutes later, a report was telephoned through that the advance guard of the German

Army had just crossed the border.[60] The message was completely unfounded. In fact, the *Wehrmacht* did not march until dawn of the following day, and then not to enforce Austria's capitulation but merely to solemnize it.

Yet this false alarm, which sounded only too real, was enough to prompt Schuschnigg into making his final act of withdrawal. In an attempt to stop the bloodshed which he now thought imminent, despite his earlier orders to the Austrian Army, he determined to broadcast to the nation immediately himself. The President was told of this decision, though there is some doubt whether he gave it his blessing. There is even more doubt whether he approved of all the resigned language his Chancellor used, dignified and moving as it was.

Arrangements for the transmission were quickly made in the so-called Corner Room, which adjoins the grand staircase on the first floor of the Ballhausplatz building. Four years before, these same cream-and-gold walls had witnessed another violent scene in the Austro-German drama. Indeed, the microphone was set up only a few feet from the spot where Dollfuss had fallen under the Nazi assassin's bullets on July 25, 1934. This time, Hitler was to strike down a whole country, not just its Chancellor, and without a shot being fired.

It was ten minutes to eight when Schuschnigg, surrounded by a hushed group of colleagues, stepped forward to take leave of his people. Now, at last, they were to learn the truth about the famous 'German peace'.

He began by telling them of the German ultimatum, delivered under threats of invasion earlier that day, to appoint a Chancellor and a Government nominated by Berlin (he mentioned no names, though Seyss-Inquart and Glaise-Horstenau were standing at his elbow). All reports that the Austrian authorities were no longer in control of events due to workers' riots breaking out all over the country were, he

declared, 'invented from A to Z'. Schuschnigg then announced, in the President's name, that Austria was 'yielding
to force'. The Austrian Army had been ordered to withdraw
without resistance before the invaders because 'we are resolved
that, on no account, and not even at this grave hour, shall
German blood be spilled'. He ended with what he called, in a
choking voice, 'a German word and a heartfelt wish — God
protect Austria'.

It was an odd speech of farewell, all sorrow and no anger,
not even reproach. And it was followed by an episode just as
remarkable. A few minutes before Schuschnigg had begun to
speak, his Commissioner for Cultural Propaganda, Hammer-
stein-Equord, who was crippled in both legs, had hobbled
into the room with the latest reports of Berlin's radio attacks.
The oppressive silence which descended after the Chancellor
had finished speaking proved too much for this doughty old
fellow, whose heart was stouter than his legs. He lurched
forward, brandished one of his crutches and, before the
technicians could pull out the contact, shouted into the live
microphone : 'Long live Austria ! Today I am ashamed to
be a German.' [61]

However unrehearsed, this little coda was really all of a
piece with the broadcast. Schuschnigg simply wanted his
speech to make plain to the world what he had been con-
cealing from the world all along — that Austria was capitulat-
ing before blackmail and violence. But, unwittingly, the
words he chose added something just as significant for the
historian — the innermost reason for that capitulation. It was
not foreign blood that would have flowed in a battle, but
'German blood', and the 'heartfelt wish' for Austria at the
end was also a 'German word'. Similarly with that outraged
cripple : the height of his patriotic fervour was shame at
sharing the invader's race.

Today — a generation and a World War later — an
Austrian Chancellor could be called on to resign for preaching

the sanctity of common Teutonic blood, while no official in the public service would think of himself, much less proclaim himself, as a German *tout court*. But this was 1938, and the hypnosis of race still prevented Austria's state-consciousness from stretching its limbs, let alone clenching its fists.

* * *

Schuschnigg's broadcast had announced a capitulation, but not a solution. Indeed, in the political field, it left confusion worse confounded. He had not mentioned his own resignation nor given any hint about his successor. Thanks to her President's defiance and the hesitations of her two crypto-Nazi Ministers, Austria was still drifting along in a constitutional limbo — unable to make up her own mind and virtually waiting for Berlin to make it up for her. Such, in fact, was to be the real importance of Schuschnigg's radio speech in the development of the crisis. For at least the second time that day, a step back by the Austrian Chancellor prompted an immediate lunge forward by his German adversaries. And, on this occasion, the lunge was to be absolutely decisive for Austria's fate.

Schuschnigg had spoken under the mistaken impression that German troops were already streaming across his frontiers. Yet, ironically, it seems to have been his own broadcast which finally brought Hitler round to signing the invasion order. This is what emerges if we now reconstruct what followed in the next twenty minutes from the captured Berlin-Vienna telephone log-books and the testimony of eye-witnesses in both capitals.

Schuschnigg's speech took a bare four to five minutes. Even so, Seyss-Inquart must have streaked out of that Corner Room as soon as he decently could and put through another immediate priority call to Göring, for the records of the Reich Chancellory show that, at 19.57 P.M., the two men had already begun talking to each other once more. Göring indicated with his opening remarks that he had just heard Schuschnigg's broadcast himself. The exchange that followed is worth re-producing. It brings out once again, and in the actual language of the actors, how the passivity of Vienna on that day served to provoke German violence far more surely than any defiance could have done.

> *Seyss-Inquart :* The Government has put itself out of office. General Schilhawsky has command over the military and will withdraw. They take the attitude here that they are now waiting for the march-in.
>
> *Göring :* So you haven't been appointed to succeed ?
>
> *Seyss-Inquart :* No !
>
> *Göring :* Removed from your office then ?
>
> *Seyss-Inquart :* No ! Absolutely no one has been removed from office. Instead the Government has, so to say, withdrawn from its duties and is just letting things take their course.
>
> *Göring :* And you are not nominated ? That has been refused ?
>
> *Seyss-Inquart :* That's been refused just as before. The idea is that one should now simply wait for the march-in to take place and then, as that happens, the executive power will anyway pass to other people.[62]

In view of this picture painted from Vienna — and it was certainly not an exaggerated one — Göring's reaction was not just predictable ; it was inevitable. Without a moment's hesitation, he declared that he would now issue the necessary invasion orders from Berlin and told Seyss to make it clear at his end that any Austrian who lifted a finger would be dealt with by German military courts. This, he specified to Seyss's obvious discomfiture, included President Miklas.

In fact, of course, it had to be Hitler who gave the invasion command, and the Führer was still hesitating between just waving the pistol at Austria's head or actually firing it. Ever since 4.30 in the afternoon, he had been holding a continuous conference on the crisis in the so-called Smoking Room of the Chancellory. Hess, Bormann, von Papen, the Press Chief Dietrich and the Generals Keitel and Brauchitsch were among those in attendance, as well as Göring, who kept on jumping up to make his Vienna calls from the main switchboard in the building. (On this, of all days, the instrument in the Smoking Room was out of order.)

Though full-scale preparations for the attack had been underfoot ever since lunch-time, when Hitler signed the 'Operational Instruction No. 1', their tempo had ebbed and flowed with the Führer's moods and with the news from Vienna itself. At one point, soon after Globocnig's premature victory report at 5 o'clock, they were cancelled altogether, only to be restarted and extended to the Air Force when the report turned out to be false.[63] Throughout the afternoon and early evening, Papen, backed up by the *ex-officio* Foreign Minister, von Neurath, had been urging Hitler to call off the invasion for fear of possible complications all round with Italy, Czechoslovakia and the Western democracies. An account received from London at tea-time of Chamberlain's stern language to Ribbentrop seemed to support their case ; so, for all their shortcomings, did the French and British protests in the early evening. Meanwhile, though the first reactions from Rome were fairly encouraging,[64] Mussolini's vital reply to the Führer's personal appeal had still not arrived.

Despite these risks and uncertainties, which he had to concede, Göring was constantly pressing Hitler from his other elbow to march, whatever the cost,[65] and regardless of whether Seyss had sent his prefabricated appeal for assistance or not. It was the telephone call from Vienna immediately after Schuschnigg's broadcast which seems finally to have tipped the trembling balance of the Führer's mind. A German Major-General of police called Grolmann, who was present in the Chancellory on that historic evening, is our witness of the

decisive moment. He describes seeing Hitler walking slowly
back with Göring to the Smoking Room from the telephone
exchange, listening reflectively as the Field-Marshal renewed
his pleas. Suddenly, the Führer was seen to slap his thigh,
jerk back his head, and exclaim 'Jetzt geht's los',[66] which can
roughly be rendered as 'Off we go!'

The time must have been around 8.15, for, by 8.30,
Göring had already issued the order to march, 'in the name
of the Führer', through his own personal adjutant, Boden-
schatz. A quarter of an hour later, at 8.45, Hitler himself
signed the 'Instruction Number 2 for Operation Otto'. This
single-page document [67] made no bones about the issue whatsoever. It stated flatly that, as the 'demands of the German
ultimatum to the Austrian Government' had not been fulfilled,
the *Wehrmacht* would march into Austria at dawn the following
day, 'in order to prevent further bloodshed in Austrian towns'.
The pretext of 'preserving the German peace', which had
been used to cripple Austria, was now also used to bury her.

This grotesque pursuit of 'legality' went on even after the
assault had been ordered. The German Foreign Office archives
for March 11 contain two copies of a telegram addressed to
'The Führer and Chancellor in Berlin' in which a body
described as 'The Provisional Austrian Government' requests
the immediate aid of German troops in 'restoring law and
order'. The origin of this telegram is as suspect as its text.
Though it bears Seyss-Inquart's name at the bottom, there
seems little doubt that this hesitant henchman of the Führer's,
with a typically belated pang of his Austrian conscience, had
refused to have anything to do with it ; at all events, he was
cleared of this particular charge at Nuremberg.

It is possible that Hitler's special Commissioner for Austria,
Dr. Keppler, sent off the message in Seyss's name, for it follows
word for word a draft that Göring dictated over the telephone
to Keppler in Vienna at about ten minutes to nine.[68] It is, in
any case, the precise timing that damns the 'appeal' more than

the disputed sender. Both copies in the German archives —
one on strips of telegraph tape and one typed on a telegram
form — give the time of despatch from Vienna as 9.10 P.M.,
and the time of receipt in Berlin 9.40 P.M.[69] As the *Wehrmacht*
Supreme Command files for that night show, the final invasion
order had by then been signed by Hitler for nearly an hour.

Yet — and this again speaks volumes for the complexes
the Führer had towards his native land and for the limitless
powers of his self-delusion — he positively beamed with delight
and magnanimity when told that this post-factum 'appeal'
from Vienna was on its way.[70] On the strength of it, he even
ordered all units of his invasion forces to muster their military
bands and collect their regimental colours during the night, so
that the march-in at dawn should appear ceremonial rather
than warlike.[71] It is impossible to say how much this command was prompted by cynical shrewdness in manipulating
world reaction, and how much by a genuine conviction that
6½ million Austrians now awaited him with love and impatience across the frontier. Both motives were probably
present. Both were made to look justified in the days that
followed.

At a quarter to eleven that night, a second and even more
exciting piece of good news reached the Berlin Chancellory.
Prince Philipp of Hessen rang through from Rome to say
that the Duce, whom he had just left at the Palazzo Venezia,
had received Hitler's letter 'in a very friendly way'. Mussolini sent his warm personal greetings and indicated that,
from the moment Schuschnigg had determined to go ahead
with the plebiscite against his advice, Italy had been forced to
'write Austria off'.

Then followed that extraordinary conversation in which
the Führer, beside himself with joy and relief in Berlin,
promised Mussolini heaven and earth over the telephone,
while in Rome, all that the overawed Prince could do was to
interject a 'Jawohl' here and there into the receiver. Hitler's

spontaneous outburst — which, incidentally, casts strong doubts on any suggestion of a pre-arranged Axis 'bargain' over Austria — culminated in the following pledge, which the Prince was asked to convey :

'I will never forget that he has done this, no matter what comes. If he is ever in need or in any danger, he can rest assured that I will stand by him through thick and thin — whatever happens and even if the whole world were raised up against him. . . .' [72]

On Sunday, September 12, 1943, Hitler was, for once, to live up to his solemn word : early that morning, ninety paratroops plucked the fallen Duce from his mountain prison in the Abruzzi and carried him off like eagles to Munich, where his rescuer was proudly and affectionately waiting. Thus, when the end finally came for him before a partisans' execution squad at the village of Dongo on April 28, 1945, Mussolini could reflect that his abandonment of Austria seven years before had at least earned him an extra eighteen months of liberty.

* * *

Back in Vienna, the last act of the long day's tragedy was meanwhile being played out. By 9 P.M. it became clear that Skubl's invasion report had been a false alarm and that the German troops were still poised on their side of the frontier. Seyss-Inquart, who had hoped that events would place him in office unaided, was now forced, somewhat reluctantly, to take the initiative himself. He drew up yet another Cabinet list whose composition amounted to moderate Austrian Nazidom tempered with pan-German Austrian Catholicism. Dr. Wolf, the new Foreign Secretary, Professor Menghin, the new Minister of Culture, and the indestructible Glaise-Horstenau as Vice-Chancellor, all represented the latter camp — if that is not too precise a term for such an assorted band of well-meaning muddlers.

The whole concept was an odd partnership of God and

the Devil ; but, for all its faults, and for all his own, Seyss-Inquart earnestly believed in it. With this sort of compromise he hoped to make of Austria a second and more privileged Bavaria within the Reich — integrated in the military, economic and diplomatic spheres with Germany, yet retaining wide domestic freedoms. As administration had, for centuries past, been judged more important in Vienna than government, the vision was perhaps understandable.

Before it could be tried out on Hitler, however, it still had to be got past Miklas. Seyss had his revised list ready before 10 P.M. Yet it was not until after midnight — with the Austrian army withdrawn, the last of the provinces in Nazi hands, the outside world silent, and forty thugs from the same SS Standarte 89 which had murdered Dollfuss gathered in the courtyard below — that the President, after his ten hours of solitary resistance, finally gave way.

Shortly before 1 o'clock in the morning, the last and most short-lived Cabinet of the First Republic came into being over his signature. Seyss-Inquart, of course, headed it as Chancellor, and the three fellow pan-German Catholics he had proposed were all in at their appointed posts. On the other hand, to balance this 'moderate' trend, Göring was personally represented by his Austrian brother-in-law Dr. Hueber, as the new Minister of Justice, while two leaders of the extremist Nazi SS wing — Kaltenbrunner and Klausner — were nominated as State Secretaries for the Interior and 'Political Education' respectively.

They and their ilk were the real heirs to power in Austria, as the fate of Dr. Skubl was to show. The Police President of Vienna had agreed to remain in office as the last loyal executive link with the now vanished era of Schuschnigg. Himmler took one astonished, icy look on the tarmac at this servant of the 'Fatherland Front' when he landed at Vienna airport the next morning to take over the Austrian security apparatus, and immediately demanded his resignation. Seyss-Inquart spluttered indignantly that he 'would not allow himself to be dictated to from outside',[73] but Skubl went none the less as the Berlin Gestapo moved in.

Soon after becoming Chancellor in the early hours of Saturday morning, Seyss had made another and equally vain attempt to keep the grip of Germany from tightening on his throat. With the stubborn Miklas bludgeoned at last into despair, and a régime of Austrian Nazis or crypto-Nazis installed in effortless triumph throughout the country, there now seemed little point in the *Wehrmacht* marching in. The political victory was won, and any military action could only serve to knock down that precious screen of 'spontaneity' which the Nazis in both Vienna and Berlin wanted to erect before the outside world.

Between 1 and 2 o'clock in the morning therefore, in his first hour of office, the new Austrian Chancellor tried to turn back the very tides that had carried him to power. He secured the co-operation of Keppler — whose last direct order from the Führer had been, after all, to establish a Seyss-Inquart Government and nothing more — and, for the second time, Lt.-General Muff found himself called upon to play the middleman. A minute in the German Foreign Office archives records that, at 2.10 A.M., the General called up from Vienna on the Chancellor's instructions to request that 'the alerted troops should stay in their positions and not cross the border'. Keppler, who followed General Muff at the receiver, backed up the appeal.[74]

A long argument now ensued in Berlin between the Foreign Office, the War Office and the Reich Chancellory as to whether this surprising about-turn in Vienna was genuine and, if so, what should be done about it. Finally, SS Obergruppenführer Brückner, Hitler's personal adjutant, agreed to wake his master up and put the problem to him (further proof that, whereas Göring expostulated, only Hitler decided).

The Führer had retired happily to bed before midnight,

after receiving Mussolini's sanctimonious blessing and Seyss-Inquart's bogus appeal. Hitler may well have been both puzzled and irritated that his satrap in Vienna should have tried, and tried so quickly, to shake off the arm that held him up ; nor was 2.30 A.M. an agreeable hour at which to be aroused from sweet dreams of conquest. But if the Führer threw one of his tantrums, we are not told of it. After very brief consideration, he ruled that 'the entry could no longer be stopped' and ten minutes later, a disappointed General Muff was informed of this in Vienna.[75] So Hitler went back to his bed, and Seyss-Inquart was sent back to his kennel.

One last painful task faced the new Chancellor of Austria that night — to dispose of his predecessor. Schuschnigg, officially a private citizen since midnight, had lingered on in the Chancellory, watching the new era explode into life under his eyes. He had seen Hitler salutes given from the graceful little stone balcony of the building to a yelling crowd below ; he had watched torchlight processions of triumphant Nazis converge through the Inner City on the Ballhausplatz ; and, whenever he listened to what, four hours before, had been the Austrian radio, he had heard shouts of 'One people, One Reich, One Führer' coming over between repeat performances of the 'Badenweiler' and the 'Hohenfriedberger', two very German military marches. The music had reached Vienna ahead of the troops.

That this new era spelt danger and perhaps death to the leaders of the old was ominously likely. The ex-Chancellor's closest colleague, Guido Zernatto, had already drawn the necessary conclusions for himself : some two hours after Schuschnigg's resignation broadcast, he crammed a few clothes in a suitcase, slipped out of Vienna by car, and fled across the border to safety and exile. He was not the only one whose patriotism was combined with discretion that night. Fifty miles east of the capital, where both the Czech and Hungarian frontiers enclosed Austrian soil, long queues of fugitives had piled up by midnight at the customs posts — Monarchists and 'Austro-Fascists', Jews and Catholics, most of them members of that 'Fatherland Front' whose four years of defiance to Hitler had now been blown away like a puff of smoke.

Yet Schuschnigg himself refused to flee. Some of his staff now tried to press him to drive to Aspern airfield — the scene of so many momentous comings and goings that day — where a plane and a pilot could still be found to put him out of Hitler's reach. Even Seyss-Inquart was moved to suggest that he might like the protection of the Hungarian Legation, which was only a few hundred yards behind the Chancellory.[76] The ex-Chancellor declined all offers. He had committed no crime and he would therefore stand his ground.

This was courage. It was also logic, for he still believed in the good faith of those around him. The new Chancellor of Austria was, after all, a Catholic gentleman, and Hitler was a fellow German statesman. That same moral rectitude that had so handicapped Schuschnigg during his long struggle with the Nazis now helped to immobilize him in defeat.

At about 2 A.M., after 21 hours of crippling and incessant tension, he left his office under the protective escort of his successor. Schuschnigg's own words are the most moving description of his last moments in the Chancellory from where he had governed Austria, to the best of his abilities and convictions, for nearly four years :

'Outside the room, the sentries snapped smartly to attention as on any other day. I walked over to shake hands with one of them. As I looked up into the stony face of the six-foot soldier, I saw that his teeth were clenched and slow tears were rolling down his face.

'We walked along the corridor and came to the grand staircase. There, two lines of civilians, with swastika armbands lined the steps. For the first time, I realized that the Government building had been occupied. We descended without taking notice of the arms raised in the Nazi salute.

Downstairs the military guard presented arms for the last time. In a flawless line, they seemed to be the wall that separated yesterday from the morrow. I said a few words of thanks and farewell. Then I got into the car together with Seyss-Inquart. . . . Outside, the yelling crowd was still thick. In the street, the taxis sounded their horns continuously ; the trams were decorated with swastika flags. . . . I only knew that we had come to the closing of a chapter. . . .' 77

Seyss-Inquart's car took Schuschnigg to ten weeks of house arrest at his own home, followed by seven years in Hitler's prisons and concentration camps. As for the new Chancellor, he began his butterfly reign over a country no longer free, but still that night called Austria. This final anomaly was soon to be removed by the Führer. For the First Republic, it was the whole book, and not just a chapter, that was now closing.

NOTES

1. See Schuschnigg, *Requiem, op. cit.* p. 44.

2. Documents on British Foreign Policy, *op. cit.* Third Series, Vol. I, No. 10.

3. See testimony of Dr. Hoffinger, Schmidt Trial Protocols, *op. cit,* p. 140.

4. *Ibid.* Papen Memorandum, p. 381.

5. Documents on British Foreign Policy, *op. cit.* Third Series, Vol. I No. 11.

6. For an account of these events, see the Nuremberg testimonies of Seyss-Inquart (I.M.T., Vol. 16, p. 109) and Glaise-Horstenau (I.M.T., Vol. 16, pp. 132 *et seq.*).

7. See Schmidt Trial Protocols, *op. cit.* p. 63.

8. Documents on German Foreign Policy, *op. cit.* Series D, Vol. I. No. 345.

9. See on this Zernatto, *Die Wahrheit über Oesterreich, op. cit.* pp. 296-304. Also Raab, Reither and Skubl in Schmidt Trial Protocols (pp. 117 ; 238-239 ; and 325).

10. Letter to the author, 16.2.62.

11. Schuschnigg, *Requiem, op. cit.* p. 46. (It should be noted that the actual timing given by Schuschnigg in his account of the March 11 events — written, of course, from memory — is out, sometimes by as much as two hours.)

March 11, 1938 : Austria's Longest Day

12. See Glaise-Horstenau at Nuremberg, I.M.T., Vol. 16, p. 133.

13. *Ciano's Diary 1937–38*, p. 87.

14. See Documents on British Foreign Policy, *op. cit.* Third Series, Vol. I, No. 44.

15. From internal evidence it seems clear that the two telegrams in question here are Nos. 17 and 19 of Documents on British Foreign Policy, *op. cit.* Third Series, Vol. I.

16. See Ribbentrop's Memorandum in Documents on German Foreign Policy, *op. cit.* Series D, Vol. I, No. 150.

17. *Ibid.* No. 151.

18. See Papen Memorandum, Schmidt Trial Protocols, *op. cit.* p. 381.

19. For the full text, including all passages omitted from the later published version, see Documents on German Foreign Policy, *op. cit.* Series D, Vol. I, No. 352.

20. *Ibid.* No. 146.

21. Göring's testimony at Nuremberg, I.M.T., Vol. 9, pp. 333 *et seq.*

22. *Ibid.*

23. This and all following telephone extracts are from the original transcripts seized in the Berlin Chancellory files in 1945. They are reproduced in the Schmidt Trial Protocols, *op. cit.* pp. 459-467.

24. The following eye-witness description is based on Zernatto, *Die Wahrheit über Oesterreich*, *op. cit.* pp. 308 *et seq.* Other details from Schuschnigg's *Requiem*, pp. 48 *et seq.*, though his times, as stated above, are often well out.

25. Testimony of Seyss-Inquart, I.M.T. Vol. 15 p. 681.

26. *Ibid.* and Berlin telephone log for March 11 (quoted in Schmidt Trial Protocols p. 459).

27. See *Requiem*, *op. cit.* p. 48.

28. Documents on British Foreign Policy, *op. cit.* Third Series, Vol. I, No. 25.

29. See testimony of Miklas, Schmidt Trial Protocols, *op. cit.* p. 261.

30. See Schmidt Trial Protocols, *op. cit.* p. 325.

31. *Ibid.* p. 113.

32. *Ibid.* p. 262. Also, for the whole episode, *Requiem*, *op. cit.* pp. 49-54.

33. *Requiem*, *op. cit.* p. 50.

34. *Ibid.* pp. 51-52.

35. Schmidt Trial Protocols, *op. cit.* p. 338.

36. *Ibid.* p. 253.

37. Zernatto, *Die Wahrheit über Oesterreich*, *op. cit.* p. 306.

38. For text of telephone conversation, see Schmidt Trial Protocols, *op. cit.* p. 462.

39. Documents on German Foreign Policy, *op. cit.* Series D, Vol. I, No. 371.

40. *Ibid.*

41. Schmidt Trial Protocols, *op. cit.* p. 261.

42. *Ibid.* p. 463.

43. Documents on British Foreign Policy, *op. cit.* Third Series, Vol. I, No. 19.

44. *Ibid.* No. 25.

45. *Ibid.* No. 44.

46. *Ibid.* No. 28.

47. *Ibid.* No. 43.

48. *Ciano's Diary, op. cit.*, entry for March 11, 1938.

49. Documents on British Foreign Policy, *op. cit.* Third Series, Vol. I, No. 46.

50. *Ibid.* No. 54.

51. See Schmidt Trial Protocols, *op. cit.* p. 140 and p. 172.

52. *Ibid.* p. 220.

53. *Ibid.* p. 589 (Schuschnigg's own survey).

54. *Ibid.* p. 220.

55. *Ibid.* p. 223.

56. *Ibid.* p. 589.

57. Letter to the author, 16.2.1962.

58. See Schuschnigg's *Requiem, op. cit.* p. 51.

59. *Ibid.* and eye-witness account of Zernatto, *op. cit.*

60. See I.M.T., Vol. 15, p. 685 and Vol. 16, p. 199.

61. Schmidt Trial Protocols, p. 290.

62. *Ibid.* pp. 463-464.

63. See Jodl's Diary, *op. cit.* for 11.3.1938 ; also Papen in Schmidt Trial Protocols, pp. 381-382 ; also Göring, *ibid.* p. 301.

64. See Documents on German Foreign Policy, *op. cit.* Series D, Vol. I, Nos. 348 and 349.

65. Göring's testimony, I.M.T., Vol. 9, pp. 335 *et seq.*

66. Grolmann's Affidavit, quoted in Eichstaedt, *Von Dollfuss zu Hitler*, Wiesbaden, 1955, p. 411.

67. Reproduced in Schmidt Trial Protocols, *op. cit.* p. 577.

68. *Ibid.* p. 464.

69. See Documents on German Foreign Policy, Series D, Vol. I, footnote to p. 580.

70. See Papen in Schmidt Trial Protocols, *op. cit.* p. 382.

71. Affidavit of Gen. Weichs, quoted in Eichstaedt, *op. cit.* p. 416.

72. See text in Schmidt Trial Protocols, *op. cit.* pp. 466-467.

73. *Ibid.* p. 327.

74. Documents on German Foreign Policy, *op. cit.* Series D, Vol. I, No. 364.

75. *Ibid.*

76. See *Requiem, op. cit.* p. 54.

77. *Ibid.* p. 55.

CHAPTER EIGHT

Hitler comes Home

THE German advance patrols had slipped over the deserted Austrian border shortly before dawn and, at first light, the mass of the 8th Army, with the 27th Infantry Division as its spearhead, poured across after them. 'Operation Otto', which the *Wehrmacht* had treated as among the least urgent of all its plans, thus came into action before any of them, with a crestfallen Chancellor, instead of a triumphant Emperor, as its target in Vienna.

General Bock's troops found themselves pushing at an open door. At many crossing-points, the frontier barriers had been obligingly dismantled before they arrived ; at the remaining posts, the Austrian custom guards helped willingly with their removal. The key areas of Passau, Salzburg and Kiefersfelden — where, only a month before, Austrian Army engineers had laboured away at the Inn Valley flood defence line — were all in German hands by breakfast. With that, the last chance had passed of even an unauthorized delaying action in the border area, launched by some ultra-patriotic local commander in defiance of his orders from Vienna.

Here and there, senior Austrian officers of this stamp certainly existed : at the Wiener Neustadt Military Academy, for example, Major-General Towarek had issued live ammunition to his 400 cadets, in confident expectation of a Thermopylae that never came. March 12, 1938, was just not the day for sentimental die-hards, and it says much for the pliable character of the Austrians, as well as for their dazed and desperate mood, that not one single gesture of military defiance was reported from the length and breadth of the entire country.

As the invader advanced, the swastikas went up on the buildings, the hands went up in salute, and the rifles were silent. For reasons we can examine later, the capitulation that Schuschnigg had ordered was also a voluntary one.

Towards noon, Hitler, accompanied by General Keitel, arrived by air at the 8th Army Headquarters in Munich to take personal charge of the operation. Before leaving Berlin, where Göring was now installed as acting Head of Government, the Führer had signed a proclamation to the German people. This message, read out over the radio for him by Dr. Goebbels, combined Hitler's worship of race with his respect for 'legality' and his contempt for facts.

There was a long historical prologue in which the Austria of the 'Fatherland Front' was described as 'the oppression of more than six million people of our own extraction by a numerically small minority'. Schuschnigg was presented as a usurper of power, in contrast to Hitler, who reminded his listeners that they had always 'confirmed the legality' of *his* existence and *his* actions. The Austrian plebiscite was, on the other hand, a fraud, and the culmination of a long campaign of injustice against which 'the German people in Austria have finally risen'.

Hitler's message ended : 'The Reich will not permit Germans to be persecuted any longer in this territory because of their membership of our nation or their loyalty to certain views. . . . I have, therefore, decided to place the assistance of the Reich at the disposal of the millions of Germans in Austria. Since early today, the soldiers of the German armed forces have been marching across the entire border of German Austria. . . . [They] will be the guarantee that the Austrian people will shortly be given the opportunity to decide their future and their destiny by means of a genuine plebiscite. . . . I, myself, as Führer and Chancellor of the German people, shall be happy, as a German and a free citizen, once more to enter the country which is my homeland.'

It would be difficult to think of a more delirious confusion of the words 'German' and 'Austrian', or of the concepts of race and state, liberty and oppression. Yet, since all these definitions were so blurred on both sides of the frontier, the portrait was not so much a forgery as a caricature of the truth, and a caricature in which even Schuschnigg could have recognized some distorted features of his own philosophy. Hitler's arguments may have been rubbish, but they were unanswerable rubbish.

The Führer's reference to entering Austria 'as a German and a free citizen' summed up the odd situation in which he now found himself. By the time he reached Munich, Goebbels was already on the air, and the War Ministry had confirmed from Berlin both the successful launching of 'Operation Otto' and the complete lack of military reaction, either in Austria or anywhere else in Europe.[1] Clearly, Hitler would soon have to follow his troops across the border ; but what as ?

He could not enter as the C.-in-C. of an invading army, for no war had been declared and, technically, no invasion was taking place. He could not go on an official visit, for he had not been invited. He could not appear as the ruler of the Austrian people, for they still had a President of their own whom, as yet, Hitler had not decided to supplant. Nor could he arrive on party business, for Austria was still sovereign in name and the Austrian Nazis were still an illegal movement there. So, as far as the outside world was concerned, Adolf Hitler went home as a tourist, 'to visit the grave of his mother'. This, at least, was what Göring had told Sir Nevile Henderson in Berlin during the early hours of the morning.[2]

According to the official German account,[3] it was not until ten minutes to four in the afternoon that the Führer finally crossed the border at his birthplace, Braunau-am-Inn. If the delay had been caused to any extent by lingering doubts about the reception awaiting him, these were swept away the moment his open Mercedes-Benz car reached the frontier bridge which, until that morning, had linked two independent countries. The troop columns that had entered before him had marched — brass bands out at the front and ammunition trains left far behind in Germany — along roads lined with cheering crowds. The arrival of Hitler himself turned this enthusiasm into frenzy, and the frenzy mounted to a fateful climax as the procession of cars made its way from Braunau across the rolling countryside of Upper Austria, through Ried and Wels and so into the streets of the provincial capital.

At Linz, as everywhere along the route, there were also some who stayed, silent and bitter, in their homes. As everywhere, not every uplifted arm meant an uplifted heart. But of the 120,000 people that the city numbered at the time, 100,000 must have been out to watch the Führer arrive at 8 o'clock in the evening, and neither Hitler nor the photographers needed to look beyond the outstretched arms. Driven partly by genuine Nazi and pan-German fanaticism and partly by the mass hysteria of this dramatic moment, the town went wild and produced a welcome that was more Oriental than European in flavour. On this part of the story, the descriptions circulated by Goebbels' team of propaganda writers tallied for once with the accounts of all foreign observers present.

Hitler rose to the occasion with his oratory. In a short and moving speech from the balcony of the Town Hall, he referred to the 'solemn vow' that he had carried away with him when leaving Linz for Germany as a ragged cast-out a generation before. 'Try and measure my innermost emotions', he shouted, 'at having fulfilled this solemn vow after so many long years. . . . I have believed in my task, I have lived for it and I have fought for it, and you are all my witnesses that I have now accomplished it, my witnesses and my guarantors.'

The hints for the future were exciting, if vague. 'I do not know', the Führer went on, 'on which day you will be called. I hope the day is not far distant. And then you will have to pledge your own vow and I believe I shall be able to point with pride to my homeland before the whole of the other German people.'

It was a stirring performance, and it duly earned fresh storms of applause which the Nazi cheer-leaders in the crowd scarcely needed to prompt. But it gave no hint as to what decisions those tides of emotion were shaping in the Führer's mind. He was still behaving as the simple 'German and free citizen' of his midday proclamation. Indeed, his balcony speech had begun with the threefold greeting : 'Germans, German racial comrades, Herr Bundeskanzler'.

This was a curious, but, in the circumstances, a correct piece of protocol. The Germans were those who had marched in with him and, by implication, the whole audience. The German 'racial comrades' were the Austrians in the old-fashioned sense, and the 'Herr Bundeskanzler' was, of course, their last Head of Government, Artur von Seyss-Inquart, who had flown to Linz that afternoon to greet the Führer, in the company of Himmler and Keppler. Seyss was also sticking to the same ghostly protocol. He had welcomed his distinguished guest 'in the name of all Austrians', taking care to hail him as 'the leader of the German nation' but not as the ruler of any new 'Reich'.

Seyss-Inquart had been going through similar empty motions of independence all day, attempts to assert himself which were so earnestly pathetic that any severity with which he is judged must be blended with a certain compassion. His first thought on waking up as Austrian Chancellor that morning, for example, had been a renewed effort to prevent the occupation from taking place at all. This request was brushed aside by Berlin, but a comical compromise was agreed to in its place : units of the Austrian Army were to be allowed a simultaneous 'invasion' of Germany in order, presumably, to symbolize Austria's 'independence'.⁴ And so, in fact, it came about. While the German 8th Army fanned out triumphantly all over Austria, a company of the 15th Austrian Infantry Regiment was put on show in Berlin, and the famous 'Deutschmeister' of Vienna were paraded in the streets of Munich. Thus Seyss-Inquart tried to save his country's face when he had already bartered away its soul.

All that night in Linz, this bitter farce continued. The 'two German Chancellors', as technically they still were, conferred for several hours together in the Hotel Weinzinger, where the Führer was staying, apparently without the word '*Anschluss*' being even mentioned. Finally Seyss-Inquart, no wiser and no less troubled, drove back through the darkness to 'his' capital, having invited Hitler to follow him there the next morning. When Sunday, March 13, came, however, the Führer stayed on at Linz, to fulfil his duties both as the returned Prodigal Son and as the conqueror. It was on that day that he paid the promised visit to his parents' grave, and it was on that day that he also resolved to bury his homeland as an independent state.

The evidence that this decision was improvised, and that it was prompted by the rapturous welcome he had received, is as conclusive as can be. Schuschnigg later maintained that, in his view, Hitler's immediate objective after Berchtesgaden went no further than forcing Austria into 'some kind of voluntary acceptance of a Protectorate'.[5] Göring declared at Nuremberg that the Führer's initial aim when he crossed the frontier on March 12 was a sort of merger or *Zusammenschluss* between the two countries, a personal union with Hitler as the titular head of both states but with a measure of domestic autonomy preserved by Vienna.[6] Dr. Stuckart, Secretary of State in the German Ministry of Interior, testified that a draft law to implement such a union had in fact been drawn up shortly before the invasion.[7] This corresponded with the proposals Göring had made to his Austrian guests in Berlin the the previous November, and with Hitler's own demeanour when he had entered Linz the previous day. Both men seem to have changed their minds simultaneously on the night of March 12-13, and for the same reason. Our best witness of this is Dr. Schwarzenberg, secretary of the Austrian Legation in Berlin, who was present when Göring was explaining, a day or two after the event, how the *Anschluss* had come about.

Göring described how, after listening on the wireless to the 'joyous welcome' in Linz, he had sent off a messenger by special plane to the Führer with the query : 'If the enthusiasm is so great, why don't we go the whole hog ?' At almost the same hour, Hitler had despatched a courier of his own to Berlin to ask Göring what he thought of the idea of a total annexation. Göring concluded his account : 'The two messengers crossed each other in the air. The decision to wipe out Austria was taken after the reception in Linz.' [8]

Clearly, therefore, the citizens of Linz had done the Austrian cause severe damage on the night of March 12 ; indeed, few bursts of cheering in history can have achieved so much by themselves. Yet it would be unrealistic to press the point so far. A score of other towns on the road to Vienna — and, for that matter, the capital itself — might well have performed the same service. And even if the Austrians had been a little more restrained all round with their welcome, their fate in the long run would probably have been no different. Hitler had crossed the border with a plan for a merger of sorts already in his pocket, and the fusion within the Greater German Reich would surely have become a complete one as the emergency of his total war developed. The essential difference was that, instead of taking two bites at the cherry, as he did later with Czechoslovakia, the Führer had now been tempted into swallowing Austria all at once.

As always when he had taken a decision, the execution was performed at breathless speed. Stuckart was summoned in person to Linz and, by midday on the Sunday, he had already produced the drafts of two *Anschluss* laws — the first for

Austria, and the second complementary one for Germany. The régime of Seyss-Inquart now collapsed like the pack of jokers it really was. Seyss himself had been warned by telephone from Linz during the morning of what was in store. He seemed to have been half-expecting the news. At all events, when Stuckart arrived in Vienna by air that same afternoon to hand over the proposed 'Law for the Re-unification of Austria with the German Reich', the Chancellor immediately summoned his Cabinet and urged them to accept it. His argument was the same as Hitler's : the *Anschluss* was obviously 'the will of the people'.

There was one last nostalgic echo of the 'Austrian mission' on which, until that week-end, Seyss-Inquart had built his entire political philosophy. He admitted to his colleagues that he would have preferred to see 'a certain measure of independence' preserved for Austria ; however, as real power was now in German hands, it was better that the Reich should also carry the full responsibility towards the outside world.[9] There had never been much stuffing in either Seyss-Inquart or his escapist doctrine, and the Nazi steamroller had promptly squashed both of them flat.

The assembled Ministers — Nazi, crypto-Nazi, pan-German and ex-Fatherland Front alike — all assented like rabbits and, once again, it was left to Wilhelm Miklas to make a solitary gesture for the history books in Austria's name. The President refused point-blank to sign away the independence of his country when Seyss-Inquart, flanked by two colleagues, presented Stuckart's 'Re-unification Law' to him in the early evening. He was still Head of State and he could still take his stand on that constitutional ground of strict legality which even Hitler approached with caution. Such a law, Miklas pointed out, could only be passed after direct sanction by the people, and he asked his Chancellor, with ironic formality, whether such a poll had already been held.[10]

Miklas realized, of course, that the battle was by now

irretrievably lost ; his main concern, whatever the personal dangers involved, was to dissociate himself in public from the actual deed of surrender. As the ground of the 1934 Constitution he stood upon was full of cracks, a compromise was eventually found. The President declared himself 'hindered in the exercise of his office' and, according to Article 77 of that Constitution, which provided for such an eventuality, he transferred his functions 'with effect from the present day' to the Federal Chancellor.

The First Republic thus ended, just as the Empire had ended twenty years before, with a face-saving formula for the Head of State. The Emperor Charles had 'renounced participation' ; Miklas had been 'hindered'. Austria's reluctance to call a spade a spade, which helped to cause her successive political catastrophes, also survived them. Yet at least it could be said of 1938 that Miklas's final half-measure of defiance was 50 per cent better than anyone else's.

The last legal obstacle to the *Anschluss* was now removed and, at 8 o'clock that same evening, this was proclaimed to the world. Article 1 of the Re-unification Law announced the facts : 'Austria is a province of the German Reich'. Article 2 gave the retrospective sanction : 'On Sunday, April 10, 1938, a free and secret plebiscite of the German men and women of Austria over 20 years of age shall be held on reunion with the German Reich'.

The niceties of protocol were preserved to the end. Seyss-Inquart returned again to Linz to report, in his last act as Chancellor, the extinction of his country. Soon after midnight, Hitler put his signature to a document which declared the Austrian decree to be also 'the law of the German Reich'. The final scene was very typical. The Führer was weeping for joy, but taking snap decisions all the time. Seyss-Inquart, feeling there must be *something* he could extract out of all this shipwreck for Austria, got him to promise a better exchange rate for the schilling.

The issue of the *Wiener Zeitung*, the official Austrian gazette, for that March 13, is an interesting historical curiosity. It records, in a series of formal communiqués, the country's swift slide into legalized disaster that week-end. There is Miklas's letter to Schuschnigg relieving him at his request of the office of Chancellor (according to Article 86 of the Constitution). Then follows the appointment of Seyss-Inquart (according to Article 82, para. 1, of the Constitution) and of the whole of his crypto-Nazi Cabinet (according to Article 91, para. 3, of the Constitution). True, there also appears on the front page the text of Hitler's invasion proclamation, and an anonymous article ending with the words: 'The German people are awakened; the springtime of the German nation has begun; the Greater German Reich yearned for by all National Socialists has risen up'. Yet, somehow, printed alongside all the official announcements, and coming right underneath the Austrian coat-of-arms which, at that time, had got the traditional second head back on its eagle, the Hitler speech and the Nazi propaganda appear like some monstrous practical joke of the Government printers.

And, as if to reassure us that the normal life of the Austrian Republic was, of course, continuing quite untroubled, the foot of the same page displays a list of Austrian decorations gazetted for all and sundry that day. The Federal President had bestowed the Officers Cross of the Austrian Order of Merit on a provincial government official at Innsbruck, the Golden Badge of Honour on a forester near Linz, and the Large Silver Medal of Honour on the Director of the Savings Bank at Strasswalchen. One cannot help but feel sorry for these worthy citizens who had been given their honours just too late ever to wear them. But the significance of this last official Gazette of the Republic is the aura of authority which pervades it. The Federal President in office still appeared as the living symbol of his country's sovereignty, and the symbol was one for which even Hitler had a superstitious respect. It was a thousand pities that almost the only Austrian to have seen this clearly was Miklas himself.

*   *   *

That stately requiem for Austria in the columns of the *Wiener Zeitung* was not the only irony of the moment. The supreme paradox was that Austrian independence should have been extinguished on the very day — March 13, 1938 — chosen by Schuschnigg a week before to proclaim the country's freedom in a nation-wide poll. A dramatist would have been accused of seeking cheap effect had he invented this authentic trick of history.

Preparations were started instead for another Sunday plebiscite, the vote ordered by Hitler four weeks hence to give the tragi-comedy its legal sanction in front of the world. The first steps towards this had been taken before the 'Re-unification Law' was even promulgated, as the Nazi police machine spent its first week-end in Vienna destroying both the labels and the leadership of the Austrian Republic. The Red-White-Red colours, if flown at all among the sea of swastikas, now appeared only with the Nazi symbol stitched hastily in the middle. 'Obelisks of liberation' replaced the placard columns of the 'Fatherland Front', and the statues of its founder, Engelbert Dollfuss, were among the first Austrian symbols to fall under the pickaxes. Physically, the capital seemed to have been swept clean of its past like the soggy leaflets announcing Schuschnigg's poll that were swept out of the gutters.

The arrests and deportations carried out by Himmler's agents that week-end of all Austrians suspected of the crime of patriotism were a far heavier blow against any independent spirit that survived. The case of Austria in March 1938 was, indeed, unique in the history of modern Europe, though Hitler soon repeated the experiment elsewhere : almost the entire leadership of the nation was neutralized or destroyed by the conquerors within the space of a few days.

The first wave of arrests in Vienna alone were said to number 76,000,[11] and though many of these were subsequently released from detention, they remained semi-prisoners in the community, their place of residence prescribed and their every movement under Gestapo surveillance. The victims made up the known élite of that Austrian patriotic movement which had flickered into painful life during the five-year struggle against Nazism. They ranged from ex-Chancellor Schuschnigg himself and members of his various Cabinets down through the staffs of provincial governments to the smallest cells of his followers in the villages. A number of Left-Wing leaders who had opposed Schuschnigg and who might be resolute enough to oppose Hitler as well, followed the 'Fatherland Front' into the police vans. None of these people had actually resisted the German occupation. They were seized for what they represented, not for what they did.

An administrative purge went hand-in-hand with the police terror. Even the incomplete dossiers which have survived show, for example, nearly 6000 immediate dismissals of Austrian officials from the key Ministries of Public Safety and Education. The provincial government of Lower Austria, a traditional stronghold of patriotism, promptly lost 395 members of its staff, nearly half of them in senior positions.[12] The Austrian diplomatic service was wound up by the last Foreign Minister, Dr. Wolf, after he had been barely forty-eight hours in office ; its prominent anti-Nazi figures, like Dr. Hornbostel in Vienna or Dr. Vollgruber in Paris, followed the Catholic Right Wing and the 'revolutionary' Left, the Monarchists, the scholars and the Jews into exile or the concentration camps.

As for the Austrian Army, this had been absorbed into the *Wehrmacht* by yet another of Hitler's decrees signed at Linz on March 13, and all its officers ordered to take a personal

Mass welcome for the Führer on the Heldenplatz in Vienna, March 15, 1938

Even Austrian gypsies gave their version of the Hitler salute, hoping (as it turned out wrongly) for better treatment

Hitler's homecoming: the Führer's procession advances on Vienna Town Hall
with the Burgtheater behind

And what it meant for some : a Jewish child in
Vienna being forced to paint the word 'Jud' on
a Jewish-owned shop

Viennese Jews and other 'undesirables' que
for exit visas at a local Vienna police stat

oath of allegiance to him. That the Führer was not satisfied merely with the lip-service of the Austrian officers' corps was shown by what happened next. General Zehner, the last Austrian Defence Minister, was murdered ; the Commander-in-Chief and some twenty generals were dismissed ; one-third of the general staff was pensioned off and the remainder dispersed throughout the Reich. This was the reverse side of the glittering '*Anschluss*' medal. It portrayed a Hitler recoiling in fright from an Austria that had not lifted a finger against him.

Such nervous suspicion, which all the cheering in Upper Austria could not entirely banish, was the reason why Hitler had tarried in Linz while Himmler was making Vienna a perfectly safe place for dictators to visit. The cavalcade that, at last, brought the Führer into the capital of his new province, summed up this picture of massive force displaying itself somewhat unnecessarily to a passive or smiling population. Light tanks rattled sternly ahead of the civilian cars and a pair of field guns closed off the long column at the rear.

It was soon after five o'clock on the afternoon of Monday, March 14, that the Führer entered Vienna — a tense unsmiling figure in the brown overcoat of the Storm Troopers, standing bolt upright in his open car, the right hand outstretched in salute, the left gripping the top of the windscreen. The 120-mile journey from Linz had taken over six hours, a snail's procession caused partly by the loyal addresses and the cascades of flowers *en route*, but partly by the traffic chaos on the road as SS vehicles tried to leap-frog the broken-down lorries of General Bock's mechanized regiments. The first dress rehearsal of the new *Wehrmacht* had not, in fact, gone at all smoothly, and this accounted for the mixed temper in which the Führer arrived.

Vienna's welcome was perhaps less concentrated than that of Linz, for the cosmopolitan capital, with its large Jewish colony, harboured many more of Hitler's natural enemies than the pan-German citadel of Upper Austria. Yet the sheer numbers involved made the setting even more spectacular, and the thousands of 'activists' Himmler had rushed into the capital had an easy time of it. The climax came at the Heldenplatz on the morning of March 15, when a wildly cheering crowd over 200,000 strong jammed the historic square and the surrounding streets to watch Hitler take up his Austrian crown. In doing so, he could not resist one final sneer at that other crown of the Holy Roman Empire still resting in the Hofburg behind him. (It was soon transferred to Germany, together with all the other Habsburg regalia of Vienna.)

'A Legitimist leader', he declared scornfully, 'once described the task of Austria's so-called independence as that of hindering the construction of a really great German Reich. I now proclaim for this land its new mission. The oldest eastern province of the German people shall be from now on the youngest bulwark of the German nation.' He ended : 'I can in this hour report before history the conclusion of the greatest aim in my life : the entry of my homeland into the German Reich'.

That same day, special maps of Europe were already on display in Vienna showing the 'German nation' as a solid red block stretching from the Baltic to the South Tyrol and from Alsace-Lorraine to the Sudeten lands of Czechoslovakia. That same night, the formula was announced by which the Austrians were to confirm their position in this prefabricated geography. The plebiscite question read : 'Do you acknowledge Adolf Hitler as our Führer and the reunion of Austria with the German Reich which was effected on March 13, 1938 ?'

The campaign for the poll was immediately launched, and it soon became clear that the almost total vacuum in Austrian patriotic leadership created by the Gestapo would give Goebbels' propaganda machine a clear run to the ballotbox. Indeed, with the whole of the non-Nazi Right Wing and the uncompromising part of the Left Wing muzzled or jailed, there were only two effective centres of influence left to inspire even passive resistance among the people. These were the Catholic Church and the moderate Socialist faction — both still intact and both now intensely courted by the Nazis. It would have been too much to have expected open defiance from either side ; the call for martyrs had gone unsounded and unanswered over the week-end, and the time for heroics was now passed. Yet, considering what both of these forces stood for ideologically, they can hardly be congratulated for bowing so swiftly to Hitler, or so deeply.

Cardinal Innitzer, the Catholic primate of Austria, was first off the mark. Indeed, he literally met Hitler half-way by sending out a greetings message to the Führer as he was advancing on the capital, with the news that the churches had been ordered to hoist swastikas and ring their bells in honour of the event.[13] Chime they duly did, to give Hitler an Emperor's welcome all the way from Schönbrunn Palace to the Hotel Imperial, where the crowds called him again and again to the balcony.

At this point, Papen makes his final appearance on the Vienna stage. That same morning, 'in honour of his valuable services', the envoy had been made a member of the Nazi party and given one of its highest awards, the Golden Badge of Honour.[14] He now tried to square his Nazi status with his Catholic conscience and, in his own sincere if ironic-sounding phrase, to 'perform one last service for Austria'.[15] Just before Hitler flew out of Vienna on the Tuesday evening, Papen brought Cardinal Innitzer to the Führer's hotel suite, to discuss the place of Austrian Catholicism in the New Order. Considering what the participants represented, the confrontation that followed was surprisingly harmonious.

The Cardinal declared that 'German thoughts and German feelings had never lacked in Austria'. He promised that Austria's Catholics would become 'the truest sons of the great

Reich into whose arms they had been brought back on this momentous day', provided that the liberties of the Church were respected and its rôle in educating the young guaranteed. It was the age-old market talk between Pope and Caesar, and, on this occasion, Caesar raised no objections. In Papen's words : 'Hitler was delighted with the Cardinal's patriotic words, shook his hand warmly, and promised him everything'.[16]

From here on, it was a short and logical step to the letter that Cardinal Innitzer addressed three days later, on March 18, to Gauleiter Buerckel, Hitler's newly appointed pro-consul in Vienna. The letter enclosed a 'solemn declaration of the Austrian bishops', signed by Innitzer and five other prelates, in which Austria's Catholics were given this firm prod with the crosier about how to behave on polling day : 'On the day of the plebiscite, it is the obvious national duty of us bishops to declare ourselves as Germans for the German Reich, and we expect of all faithful Christians that they know what their duty to the people is.'

Exactly one week before, on March 11, the same Archdiocese of Vienna had issued the following glowing appeal in support of Schuschnigg's abortive anti-Hitler poll : 'As Austrian citizens, we stand and we fight for a free and independent Austria !' The somersault had been as nimble as it was unqualified. Too late, the Vatican reached out in alarm to stiffen the back of its over-pliant Cardinal. In Vienna, the Papal Nuntius, Cicognani, tried, without much success, to tone down the terms of the capitulation. Three weeks later, Innitzer was summoned in person to Rome to explain his behaviour. By then Buerckel had his promise, Goebbels had his headlines, the priests had their orders, and the damage was done.

On April 3, after weeks of pressure and persuasion, the Nazis trapped their second quarry ; Karl Renner, first Chancellor of the 'German-Austrian Republic' of 1918 and, ever since, the dominant personality of the moderate Socialist wing, added his personal support for the plebiscite. Renner's approval had been longer delayed, and may have been partly extorted by blackmail over his colleagues held by the Gestapo. In any case, it reflected more restraint than the Cardinal's head-long surrender.

Renner's declaration [17] made it quite clear that the methods used to bring about the union with Germany had not been those to which he subscribed. 'But', the statement went on, 'the *Anschluss* has none the less been achieved ; it is a historical fact, and I regard this as satisfaction indeed for the humiliations of Saint-Germain and Versailles. . . . The twenty years' stray wandering of the Austrian people is now ended and it returns united to the starting-point set out in its solemn declaration of November 12, 1918.' [18]

Many echoes could be heard here, both personal and political : the pan-German student of Imperial Moravia ; the Socialist Chancellor of the infant Republic, seeking protection in an '*Anschluss* with Socialism' ; the embittered and defeated leader of Austria's delegation to the Peace Conference ; the historian, seeing the continuity of his people above the tumults of war and peace ; and, above all, the pragmatist who tried, like Innitzer, to fit in the harsh needs of the moment with the larger perspectives of past and future.

Of all this, Hitler and Goebbels needed and used only the one word 'Yes !' Just as Innitzer's blessing had made the coming plebiscite acceptable in the remotest mountain village that could boast a Catholic priest, so now, the more measured support of Karl Renner made it palatable in the workers' factory cells and tenement flats of the towns. To the ordinary Austrian, the *Anschluss* began to appear not only as an inevitable act of history but as an event almost sanctified by the joint blessing of two rivals who rarely agreed upon anything.

It was not surprising therefore that, when the urns were emptied late on April 10, a majority of 99·73 per cent in favour of Hitler could be claimed. According to the official figures, 4,453,000 of the 4,484,000 eligible electorate had voted 'Yes'; a bare 11,929 had voted 'No'; while another 5776 hardy souls had spoiled their ballot papers. Most foreign observers present in Vienna on the day accepted that the polling had been free from any open intimidations. Well it might have been; by then, the most effective pressures were all non-physical.

Papen was indulging in some more of his wishful thinking when he claimed that 'any other plebiscite under neutral supervision would have produced the same result'.[19] Yet a plain majority of some sort would probably have emerged in Hitler's favour on that day, even if the stifled opposition had been given more freedom to air its views. The basic reason was psychological rather than political. By April 1938 Austria had written herself off as a free country, and had been written off as such by the world. Some voted out of fanaticism, some out of fear; some out of opportunism and some out of sheer relief.

This last factor should not be underestimated. The Republic had lived through two decades of political strife and economic hardship, ending with five years of the smouldering Nazi crisis which had themselves culminated in five weeks of unbearable tensions. Many of those to whom Hitler was either anathema or suspect now wearily accepted him as the bad solution that is better than no solution at all. The emotional fibre of the nation had snapped with exhaustion as a constantly vibrating machine suddenly breaks apart with metal fatigue.

In the nation, as in the metal, the worst stress had been hidden — that all-pervading mental conflict between the German race and the Austrian state. It was only small opposing minorities at the fringes who both saw their loyalties quite clearly and followed them consistently. Such, on the Nazi side, were Leopold, Rainer, Globocnig and their fellow-spirits in the illegal movement, men who, one and all, acted and *felt* as subjects of Hitler's 'Reich' and not as citizens of Schuschnigg's Republic. Such, on the ultra-Austrian side, were men like the Catholic Monarchist intellectual and deputy-Mayor of Vienna, Ernst Karl Winter, who wrote after Hitler's seizure of power : 'Who is for Austria must be against Germany, for Germany and the National-Socialist state are today identical'.

Everyone in between these two uncompromising camps wobbled to some degree or other, and this great intermediate mass, numbering 40 per cent of the people or more, always tipped the political balance. In early March Schuschnigg could have won them over ; by early April they were all Hitler's. All factions appealed to them for support, yet only deepened their confusion by holding up the same German racial ties before them in rival contexts. Just as Schuschnigg had his 'German peace', so Cardinal Innitzer had his 'Christian German East Mark', Seyss-Inquart his 'German cultural heritage', and Renner his Socialist 'German Austria'. By 1938 the word 'German' had come to stand for almost everything and to mean practically nothing.

This factor lay at the root of Austria's meek surrender to Hitler, for it compounded and enlarged all the other factors, of which the most important was the yearning for a quieter and more prosperous existence in a grander political framework. The Republic had not enough will to resist by itself because it had not enough will to live by itself. It did not fight for its image because it could not recognize that image. Nobody else in Europe was prepared to perform these services for it.

*   *   *

Abroad, everyone had been taken aback by the suddenness and completeness of Austria's collapse — even Göring in Berlin, for whom nothing could go fast enough. The Field-Marshal had spent the week-end sweeping up, on the Führer's behalf, all the diplomatic porcelain broken by the German invasion. He arranged with von Neurath for a formal rejection of the French and British protest notes on the haughty grounds that 'the relations between the Reich and Austria were an internal concern of the German people which were no concern of third powers'.[20] This general line was repeated to the principal German diplomatic missions in a guidance telegram circulated on March 12, with the fairy-tale of Seyss-Inquart's 'appeal for help' thrown in for good measure.[21]

Göring's only serious concern seems to have been to keep the Czechs quiet. Their turn had not come yet, and a panic reaction from Prague at this juncture might have proven a fatal stimulus to the restive Western Powers. He succeeded with a mixture of threats and blandishments conveyed through Mastny, the Czech Minister in Berlin. As the invasion was being launched, Mastny was told to inform Beneš that, if he lifted a finger, 'one thousand bombers would reduce the Hradcin to ashes'.[22] Throughout the next day, Göring then proceeded to shower the Czech envoy with promises and, as 'proof' of his good faith, had the German invasion forces moving on Vienna north of the Danube reduced to a single battalion which kept itself nine miles from the Czech border.[23] These tactics removed the last diplomatic hurdle. The Czechs relaxed just long enough to let Hitler ride smoothly home.

An appeal from Prague — and, still more, a dramatic Czech military move such as general mobilization — would have acutely embarrassed France and Britain and prolonged the tension all round. Yet it is questionable whether even this would have roused the Western democracies to drastic action, once the suddenness and completeness of the German victory had been established. In London, for example, with Eden out of office, the 'anti-appeasement' faction had lost its only powerful voice in the Cabinet. Chamberlain stood at the helm unchallenged and, despite its ugliness, the *Anschluss* was, for him, essentially a reef which had to be circumnavigated in that course of general agreement with the Axis powers he was still determined to steer.

None the less, his initial reaction had been one of anger as well as sorrow, and both moods were reflected in the speech he made to the House of Commons on March 14. The tenor of this statement was that, though the Austrian affair could no longer be remedied, it could also not be quickly forgotten. After a factual account of the crisis, which rebutted the German propaganda version, the Prime Minister declared : 'It seems to us that the methods adopted throughout these events call for the severest condemnation and have administered a profound shock to all who are interested in the preservation of European peace'.[24] He re-emphasized that Britain's formal obligations in the matter did not go beyond the consultation provided for in the Stresa Pacts and maintained that these obligations had been 'fully discharged'. Then came the admission which put the whole Western case in a nutshell : 'The hard fact is that nothing could have arrested this action by Germany unless we, and others with us, had been prepared to use force against it'.

In his speech, Chamberlain had recognized the 'special interest' Germany always claimed in Austrian affairs, and it was indeed the method by which Austria had been killed, rather than the fact that she was dead, that now preoccupied the British Government the most. Assurances from Göring that German troops would be withdrawn from Austria 'as soon as the situation was stable'[25] were requested and received ; hopes were expressed through the Foreign Office in Berlin that the April plebiscite would be genuinely free from intimidation ; and a fanfare of trumpets was sounded in Parliament about securing protection for Hitler's racial and political enemies in Austria.

Even this concern proved difficult to sustain in view of the apparent rapture with which Austria was sinking into the Führer's arms, and a week after the *Anschluss*, most (though not all) of the British press had come round to the conclusions already jumped at in Vienna by Cardinal Innitzer. Finally, on April 2, there followed Britain's formal acceptance of the *fait accompli*. Appropriately, it was Sir Nevile Henderson — who had always, at heart, considered the *Anschluss* to be inevitable or desirable or both — who performed the act that ended centuries of diplomatic relations between London and Vienna. On that day, he handed Ribbentrop notes which, with immaterial reservations, acknowledged 'the union of Austria with the German Reich' and announced that, as from April 15, the British Legation in Vienna would be replaced by a Consulate-General.

The British Ambassador went on to ask Ribbentrop 'whether he might sometime write privately about certain persons in Austria who had found themselves in personal difficulties there after the reunion'. Henderson emphasized that he was not making an official appeal 'as he had no authority whatever for so doing'.[26] That was, in fact, about all that came of his Government's assurances, given in the House of Commons a fortnight before, that 'stern and solemn' representations were being made in Berlin about political persecution in Austria. The conversation then turned to a project of quite a different sort already discussed between Lord Halifax and Ribbentrop in London : the transfer to Germany of a British colony in the Congo Basin, 'subject to certain restrictions'. The *Anschluss*, it seemed, had been tucked away into its political and geographical perspective.

Whereas France, overshadowed by the fall of the Chautemps Government, could produce nothing but sympathy for Austria, Italy, the third Stresa partner, did not offer as much as that. This icy detachment reflected the cynical resignation of Mussolini himself rather than the unanimous opinion of his advisers. The Italian Army was particularly restive at a *coup* that had brought the *Wehrmacht* face to face with it at last along the Brenner ; as for public opinion, even the German

Embassy in Rome had to admit that 'in many Italian circles, one meets with lack of understanding, not to say criticism, of Mussolini's stand'.[27]

Yet Austria's self-appointed 'protector' had little trouble in riding the opposition down. Even if it is true, as one witness claimed,[28] that the Duce was 'floored' ('*atterrato*') by the news of the *Anschluss*, and raged at the '*maledetto tedesco*', he soon found his composure and his new bearings. On March 12, the day after getting Hitler's letter, and while the invasion of Austria was in full flood, Mussolini was already defending the Führer's action — as well as his own — before the Fascist Grand Council. According to Ciano,[29] he told them: 'If we had eight million Italians on our frontiers, we should do the same'. And, referring presumably to the Italian annexation of Fiume, he added: 'I have, in fact, already done it'.

This was his capitulation to his colleagues. The next day, March 13, came the capitulation to the Germans. A telegram was despatched to the Führer in Austria in which the Duce proclaimed: 'My attitude has been determined by the friendship sealed in the Axis pact between our two countries'. There was really no need for the conqueror to read the text. The address on the telegram — 'Hitler, Vienna' — told him everything.

That same evening, in Rome, Mussolini was already philosophizing over the blow. 'One ambiguity', he told Ciano, 'has been removed from the map of Europe'. He then listed three others that would, in his opinion, 'go the same way, one after the other, and in this order: Czechoslovakia, Switzerland, and Belgium'.[30] The Duce was only a little more reliable as a prophet than as an ally.

It is interesting to note that though the *Anschluss* was not, as Hitler had claimed, exclusively an Austro-German concern, it was almost exclusively a European concern. The United States and Russia, whose dialogue as the world's two superpowers was to determine every aspect of diplomatic relations after Hitler's war, were almost silent in this great crisis that preceded it.

In Washington, for example, the German Ambassador Dieckhoff got a completely passive and almost approving reception from the Secretary of State, Cordell Hull, when he called on March 12 to present the official German version of events. He found Mr. Hull studying the text of Hitler's noontime proclamation, with which he was 'obviously still thoroughly impressed'.[31] The envoy ended his account of this surprisingly smooth interview : 'From a few questions which he asked, it was apparent that Mr. Hull thoroughly understands our action'.[32]

However, when Dr. Dieckhoff called at the State Department again three days later to hand over, on instructions from Berlin, the text of the 'Re-unification Law', he found a very different atmosphere. The Secretary of State was now 'reserved', and accepted his note 'without a word', while the Under-Secretary, Mr. Sumner Welles, whom the envoy saw later, 'even gave expression to a sort of malevolent bitterness'.[33] This reflected a similar change in the tone of the American press, which, by this time, was almost unanimous in attacking the *Anschluss* as a brutal example of power politics.

Dieckhoff puzzled for weeks over what exactly had caused this violent transformation of official opinion, unique in any Western capital at the time, and we may well puzzle with him. Finally, in a long analysis sent to Berlin on April 18, he presented his conclusions.[34]

In the Ambassador's view, it was a personal intervention by President Roosevelt that had caused America to think aloud again, in private and in public. The President's own convictions as a democrat were anyway such that he could 'hardly welcome the fact that an authoritarian state should acquire such increased power and heightened prestige as Germany has through its annexation (*sic*) of Austria'. Dr. Dieckhoff still had to explain why these convictions, so dormant on

March 12, should have suddenly become so active on March 14.

He advanced three reasons for this. The first was the hostile reaction of American public opinion to the detailed reports of racial and political persecution which had come from Vienna over the week-end. The second was a desire to 'speak up and deter the Germans in time' from any further aggression against Czechoslovakia. The third was a general tendency that Dieckhoff claimed to have noted in Washington for the State Department to follow Britain's lead in such matters. Mr. Sumner Welles, for example, had attacked him in words 'which to a large extent tallied with the Chamberlain address in the House of Commons, received by cable a few hours earlier'.

As for the ups and downs of American newspaper comment towards the crisis, 'the British watchword is of considerable, if not decisive significance to the American press, at least in matters of European policy'. The subsequent calming-down of American public opinion and America's formal recognition of the *Anschluss* in April were, Dieckhoff claimed, part of this same 'follow-my-leader' process. The envoy may well have coloured his account highly in order to present his own difficulties to Berlin in the best light. But the basic picture was a correct one : in March 1938 Washington still regarded Hitler's depredations in Europe as no great concern of hers, and even less of her responsibility.

Ironically enough, in view of what happened after the war, it was from the other flank of Europe that the only long-range support for Austria's cause now came, in the form of renewed Russian attacks on the Fascists. As early as March 27, 1938, the Soviet Foreign Minister Litvinov had used the *Anschluss* to plead for 'a common front against aggression', and he renewed his demand for collective measures against Germany when the League of Nations discussed the implications of Hitler's *coup* the following September. But the League had met to bury Austria, not to praise it, and the Soviet Union had to content itself at Geneva with the rôle of solitary public mourner.

*   *   *

God did not save Austria, as Schuschnigg had prayed into a non-committal microphone. Providence seemed on the side of the big battalions that week-end, or perhaps heaven was just following the French motto of only helping those who helped themselves. At all events, the deed was done : Hitler, who spoke of 'reuniting Austria with the German Reich', had, in fact, welded them together for the first time in history. A new situation arose for all concerned, and for all — aggressor, victim and bystanders alike — the world would never be the same place again. The *Anschluss* marked the end of the Europe of the Peace Treaties and the beginning of the Europe of the Nazi war.

To Germany herself, it meant, in the first place, a welcome strengthening of economic and military sinews. Göring got the Austrian ore and timber he had coveted so long for his Five-Year Plan, with a substantial treasure in gold and foreign exchange thrown in. Hitler, with his $6\frac{1}{2}$ million new citizens, nearly 6 million of whom were of acceptable Teuton stock, got a human reservoir for eight new *Wehrmacht* divisions as well as a shortened frontier for that *Wehrmacht* to defend. His troops now stood at the Brenner, gateway to the Mediterranean, and in Vienna, the crossroads of the Danube Basin. The Bohemian Diamond, that other strategic key to the continent, was already enclosed and soon to be crushed.

Neumann had dreamt of 'Mitteleuropa' before the First World War and, in the last months of that war, at Spa on May 12, 1918, the two German Emperors had signed a treaty which might have realized the dream, if the Central Powers had won the day. Now the slogan had become an accomplished fact ; Hitler had out-dared even Bismarck by joining two capitals — Vienna and Berlin — which the Iron

Chancellor was wise enough to keep apart, in both their interests. True, the *Wehrmacht* had restored to Austria one historic rôle she had not filled effectively since the days of Prince Eugene : a stronger German arm than ever now shielded Western Europe along the Danube from 'Slav invasion'. Yet this was small consolation once that same arm started to strike down the whole continent into subjugation. In 1918, and, for that matter, again in 1945, the powers that had defeated Germany gave Austria her independence as much in their own interests as in hers. The wisdom of both decisions was shown by March 1938 and what came after it, when the 'Mitteleuropa' dream became a European nightmare.

Of even greater importance than all these military and strategic aspects of the *Anschluss* was, however, its psychological impact on all sides. It was not simply that the territorial *status quo* of Versailles had been changed for the first time, so that what the Western democracies had long written off in their hearts was now also written off on the map. It was the method of the change which set an even graver precedent. Blackmail backed by naked force had proved a paying policy, not in far away Abyssinia but in the heart of Europe. The balance of power had not only been altered on the continent ; it had been shifted in such an effortless manner as to make further blows against it inevitable.

This was the decisive circumstance, for it could not be explained away by all Hitler's talk of racial unity and all the 'self-determination' of the April plebiscite. Both sides went on talking of peace for nearly eighteen months after the *Anschluss*, but both began to prepare in earnest for war. That last fatal risk which Hitler took in September 1939, and the dismayed defiance with which France and Britain responded to it, were both pre-conditioned mentally in March 1938. There was a straight line, psychologically as well as geographically, from Austria through Czechoslovakia into Poland.

All this only became clear later when the line had already

been drawn. Yet the military and political steps taken in all the principal European capitals immediately after the *Anschluss* showed the path that had now opened up. In London, in that same speech to Parliament on March 14 by which Mr. Chamberlain had accepted the *Anschluss* as a *fait accompli*, the British Prime Minister went on to call for 'a fresh review' of Britain's defence programme ; [35] a quickened impetus was indeed given to British rearmament during the following months, particularly in the air. That same day in Paris, the new Government of M. Blum asked for urgent supplementary credits to expand its own armed forces, 'in view of the gravity of the present situation', and categoric assurances were sent to Prague that France was now more than ever resolved to uphold the independence of Czechoslovakia. The extra credits were put to good use, even if the assurances melted away at Munich six months later.

Even more important for the broad course of world history was the impact made by the *Anschluss* and its aftermath in Washington. Once the initial passivity there had disappeared, the rape of Austria took its place as the first of a series of blows which Hitler unwittingly struck at American isolationism, and therefore at his own 'Thousand Year Reich'. The Führer's shrewd envoy in Washington, Dr. Dieckhoff, is again one of our best witnesses of this. In a telegram sent to Berlin ten days after the German invasion he wrote :

'The President [Roosevelt] who for a long time has not been very well-disposed towards us, is said to be greatly upset by the Austrian *coup* and to believe that the moment when the "democracies" must fight the "dictatorships" is not far off. He is very systematically getting this country ready both in sentiment and in armament for that moment ; the present Navy Bill, which was passed yesterday by a big majority of the House of Representatives . . . is the first step in this direction.'

Dieckhoff, after apologizing in case he was 'becoming a

The plebiscite that *did* take place : part of the massive propaganda display in
Vienna for the post-*Anschluss* poll

One who was carried to vote in the 99 per cent 'yes' poll

And one who walked : the Austrian Cardinal Innitzer, whose public support for the *Anschluss* swayed many of the country's Catholics

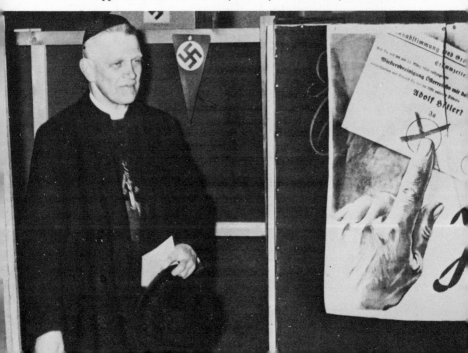

bore in Berlin' on the subject, then repeated earlier warnings that Germany 'could no longer count on America's isolation' and should be prepared, in case of a world conflict, 'to see the Americans throw their weight into the British scale'.[36] Hitler, of course, ignored all pessimistic prophecies except his own; yet, as on this occasion, he usually helped them to come true.

On the Axis side, the *Anschluss* brought about a similar closing of the ranks — though it was far less subtle than that slow and diffuse process of ideological polarization which had now started up, across the Channel and the Atlantic, between the Western democracies. After March 1938, Italy was delivered up to Germany just as surely as Austria had delivered herself up to Italy by the Rome Pact Protocols four years before. For all Hitler's 'undying gratitude', it took Mussolini two months of tough negotiation before he could salvage in Berlin something of the substantial economic stake which Italy, as the 'protecting power', had invested in her Austrian connection. Finally, on May 28, 1938, a series of agreements were signed with Germany which covered the whole complex of former Austro-Italian interests, and, with them, the new protector paid off the old.

Of more significance was something that took place in Rome early that same month, while Hitler was paying an official visit there to the ally who had now become his neighbour. Count Ciano records that, on May 5, he was approached by Ribbentrop, who was with the Führer's party, and offered a military assistance treaty, 'secret or public', to perpetuate and strengthen the new frontier across the Brenner.[37] This was the first link in that 'Pact of Steel' which the dictators took into war with them a year later.

Finally, the victim itself. If the *Anschluss* had reminded both the dictatorships and the democracies of their rival affinities, it reminded the Austrians, quite simply, of themselves. Something cataclysmic was needed to rouse them out of that racial trance in which their confused ideas of nation-hood had drifted for a good fifty years, and the healing shock had now come. 1938 succeeded where even 1918 had failed in forcing the Austrians to find their own roots in the modern world.

For one thing, the change itself was still more drastic. Twenty years before, with the collapse of the Habsburg Empire, the Austrians had lost at one blow their world power status, their way of life and their apparent justification for living. But, in 1918, at least the name had remained, together with the sovereignty and the capital. Now, all this too was swept away. Overnight, Vienna became to Berlin what Graz had for centuries been to Vienna — a provincial centre in a unified German-speaking state. For a while, the concept of the 'Ostmark' was allowed to linger on, to recall for the Austrians the philosophy of that 'special German mission' which had led them straight into Hitler's arms. Then even this disappeared from the official vocabularies and Austria became instead simply the 'Danube and Alpine Gaue' of the Third Reich. In April 1939 these two new 'Gaue' were formally absorbed under the central administration of Berlin ; a fortnight later Seyss-Inquart's shadowy authority as 'Reichs-staathalter', or provincial Viceroy of the Führer's, was wound up accordingly. The wheel had turned full circle for Austria's last Chancellor, crushing him underneath it.

Yet for the Austrians as a whole, this same grinding process of Nazi assimilation brought an unexpected new life. By seeking to abolish all differences between the two peoples, Hitler only succeeded in emphasizing them. Tens of thousands of those psychological 'wobblers' among his new subjects became, for the first time, proper Austrians when the Führer tried to convert them, also for the first time, into proper Germans.

The symbol and the breeding-ground of this process was the Austrian resistance movement, which began to stir into life a matter of days after the German march-in.[38] This too had its built-in contradictions. Hitherto, loyalty to the common German race meant treason to Austria; now, loyalty to the submerged Austrian state meant still more clearly treason to the common Reich. But the second antithesis proved easier to solve than the first had been, even for those Austrians who, until the end, went on regarding the *Anschluss* as a family disaster rather than a foreign invasion. In the active resistance movement inside Austria, and in that equally important passive resistance movement in the concentration camps outside, the leaders of the First Republic managed to come to terms emotionally with themselves as well as with their German captors. It was only in emigration that the Austrian Civil War continued. For the millions absorbed in the Reich, seven years under the swastika brought tolerance, in addition to patriotism. In a roundabout way that was typically Austrian, they began to find their country from the moment it had ceased to exist.

There is a saying that 'Austria is the little world in which the big world holds rehearsal'. Both worlds failed their test in March 1938. Yet, in that failure, both learned what their true values were ; and, so far, neither has forgotten the lesson.

NOTES

1. Documents on German Foreign Policy, *op. cit.* Series D, Vol. I, No. 368.

2. Documents on British Foreign Policy, *op. cit.* Third Series, Vol. I, No. 46.

3. Hartlieb, *Parole : Das Reich*, Leipzig 1939, p. 509.

4. See Seyss-Inquart's testimony at Nuremberg, I.M.T., Vol. 15, p. 686.

5. Letter to the author, 12.12.1961.

6. See Göring at Nuremberg, I.M.T., Vol. 9, pp. 505 *et seq.*

7. Affidavit of Stuckart, quoted in Eichstaedt, *op. cit.* p. 429.

8. Schmidt Trial Protocols, *op. cit.* p. 201. (The author is also grateful to Dr. Schwarzenberg for a personal account of the incident, and other happenings at the time in Berlin.)

9. See I.M.T., Vol. 15, p. 690.

10. See Miklas in Schmidt Trial Protocols, *op. cit.* p. 263.

11. See *Red-White-Red ; Justice for Austria*, Part One, Vienna, 1946.

12. *Ibid.*

13. See Keppler's evidence at the so-called 'Wilhelmstrasse Trial', Nuremberg, Case 11, p. 12928.

14. See the *Reichspost* for March 14, 1938.

15. See Papen in Schmidt Trial Protocols, *op. cit.* p. 383, for this incident.

16. *Ibid.*

17. Carried, in interview form, in the Vienna *Tagblatt*, 3.4.1938.

18. When the new Austrian Republic had declared itself, in a resolution promptly vetoed by the victorious allies, to be 'an integral part' of the new Germany.

19. Schmidt Trial Protocols, *op. cit.* p. 384.

20. See Neurath, I.M.T., Vol. 16, p. 703.

21. See Documents on German Foreign Policy, *op. cit.* Series D, Vol. I, No. 366.

22. See Schmidt Trial Protocols, *op. cit.* p. 133.

23. See Göring, I.M.T., Vol. 9, p. 336.

24. Text in Hansard for 14.3.1938 ; reproduced in Documents on British Foreign Policy, *op. cit.* Third Series, Vol. I, No. 79.

25. Documents on German Foreign Policy, *op. cit.* Series D, Vol. I, No. 376.

26. *Ibid.* No. 400.

27. *Ibid.* No. 399.

28. Col. Liebitsky in Schmidt Trial Protocols, *op. cit.*

29. *Ciano Diaries*, *op. cit.* Entry for 12.3.1938.

30. *Ibid.* 13.3.1938.

31. Documents on German Foreign Policy, *op. cit.* Series D, Vol. I, No. 362.

32. *Ibid.*

33. *Ibid.* No. 391.

34. *Ibid.* No. 401.

35. See Hansard, *Parliamentary Debates*, Fifth Series, Vol. 333.

36. Documents on German Foreign Policy, *op. cit.* Series D, Vol. I, No. 445.

37. *Ciano Diaries*, *op. cit.* Entry for 5.5.1938.

38. For a detailed account of the movement, see Brook-Shepherd, *The Austrian Odyssey*, *op. cit.* pp. 141-172.

INDEX

Adam, Col., 54, 56
Anschluss: origin of the idea, xiv-xviii ; Hitler decides on, 192-4 ; terms of, 195 ; effects of, 212-17
anti-Comintern pact, 22
Attlee, Clement (later 1st Earl), 87, 92
Austrian Army : strength, 166-7 ; absorption in *Wehrmacht*, 198-9
Austrian attitudes to Germany, xv-xvi ; bait of cultural leadership in Greater Reich, 6, 27 ; wobble between race and state, 6, 25, 102-103, 204-5
Austrian Civil War (1934), xviii
'Austrian Legion', 47
Austrian Nazis, xv ; H.Q. raided, 13 ; Schuschnigg's plan to exploit split in, 26-9, 34-5 ; reaction to Schuschnigg's Diet speech, 104-5, and Innsbruck speech, 123 ; take over provincial capitals, 171 ; *and see* 'Committee of Seven' ; Fatherland Front ; Leopold, Capt.
Austrian pan-Germanism, xvii, 6 ; *and see* 'Committee of Seven'
Austrian youth, 29, 119, 126
Austro-German Pact (1936), xxi-xxiii, 25, 32-3, 67, 70, 115
'Austro-Marxists' and 'Austro-Fascists', 108-11, 114, 125-6

Beck, Gen., 133
Berchtesgaden meeting (1938): Schuschnigg prepares for, 22-40 ; arrives at Berchtesgaden, 42 ; interviews with Hitler, 44-9, 57-8, 60-62 ; first ultimatum, 53-5 ; Pact signed, 62 ; aftermath, 65 ff.; reactions of Miklas, 66-9 ; decision to play down at home, 72, and abroad, 73-7 ; reactions of

Vatican, 73, Mussolini, 77-9, 94, France, 79-83 and Britain, 84-94 ; 'implementation' by Germany, 97-100
Blomberg, F.-M. von, 8, 10, 12 ; fall of, 30, 32, 131-2
Böhme, Gen., 57
Britain : Göring's assessment of, 4, and Hitler's, 9 ; Austrian hopes of, 22 ; reactions to Berchtesgaden Pact, 84-94, of the Press, 84, Socialist opposition, 87, and Foreign Affairs Committee, 87 ; not asked for help, 90-2 ; supports plebiscite, 129-30 ; fails to help, 160-2, or to get Stresa Front to help, 162-165 ; accepts *Anschluss*, 208 ; *and see* Chamberlain, Neville ; Eden, Anthony ; Halifax, Earl of ; Henderson, Nevile
Bürckel, Josef, 38, 202

Canaris, Admiral, 68-9
Chamberlain, Neville, 25, 85 ; passivity criticized, 87-8 ; protests to Ribbentrop, 145-7 ; reaction to *Anschluss*, 207, 214
Christian-Socialist Party, xvii
Churchill, (later Sir)Winston, 87-8, 94
Ciano, Count, 78-9 ; rebuffs French *démarche*, 163-4
'Committee of Seven', 15 ; H.Q. raided, 15-16 ; 'Tavs' Plan, 16-19
Coudenhove-Kalergi, Count, 50
Cranborne, Lord (later 5th Marquess of Salisbury), 93
Czechoslovakia, 4, 9, 206

Delbos, Yvon, 81-2, 103, 144
Dieckhoff, Dr., 210-11, 214-15
Dollfuss, Engelbert, xviii, xix-xx, 39, 103

Index

Hofer, Andreas, 120-1
Hornbostel, Dr. T. von, 137, 165-6, 198
Horthy, Admiral, 117
Hossbach Memorandum, 8-12
Hueber, Dr., 139, 180
Hull, Cordell, 210

Innitzer, Cardinal, 123, 201-3, 205
'Instruction No. 1', see Operation Otto
International Sporting Exhibition, Berlin (1937), 2-7
Italy : Göring's assessment, 2, 4, and Hitler's, 10 ; no longer Austria's champion, 22, 77-9 ; popular resentment at *Anschluss*, 208-9 ; under German domination, 215 ; *and see* Mussolini ; Rome Protocols ; Stresa Front

Jansa, F.-M.-Lt. Alfred, 1, 57, 166
Jodl, Col., 133

Kaltenbrunner (Nazi extremist), 100, 155, 180
Karwinsky, Baron Erwin, 115
Keitel, Gen., 42, 58-9, 68, 132-3
Keppler (Nazi Commissioner for Austrian Affairs), 36, 52-3, 98-100 ; advises Miklas to yield, 158-9 ; forged telegram asking for troops? 177-8 ; fails to stop invasion, 181-2
Kienböck, Dr., 67
Klausner, Maj. Franz, 98-100, 180
Königgrätz (Sadowa, 1866), xiv, 114-15

Legitimists, see Monarchists
Leopold, Capt., 13-14, 17, 28, 36-7, 98-100
Liebitzky, Col., 118
Linz, 106, 190
Ludwig, Eduard, 54, 56

Margesson, David, 88
Menghin, Prof., 179
Miklas, Dr. Wilhem : relations with Schuschnigg, 39, 66 ; reaction to

Berchtesgaden Pact, 66-9 ; refuses to make Seyss Chancellor, 152-4, 157-60, 180 ; counsels resistance, 167 ; refuses to sign Re-unification Law, 194-5 ; hands over to Seyss, 195-7
Mittler, Karl, 122-3
Monarchists, xv, 16 ; attitude to : of Schuschnigg, 111-17, Hitler, 112-13, Göring, 113, and Mussolini, 114 ; anti-Nazis *par excellence*, 114-15 ; *and see* Otto, Archduke
Muckermann, Father, 49-50
Muff, Lt.-Gen., 127, 157-8, 181
Mühlmann, Dr. Kajetan, 36-8, 39, 60
Mussolini : warned off by Göring, 2 ; reaction to Berchtesgaden Pact, 77-9 ; urges Anglo-Italian settlement, 94 ; advises against plebiscite, 118 ; 'unavailable', 141-142, 144 ; letter from Hitler, 147-9, 178 ; refuses to rebuild Stresa Front, 162-6 ; defends *Anschluss*, 208-9 ; *and see* Italy

'National Opposition', xxii, 29
Neurath, Baron von, 8, 11, 23 ; replaced by Ribbentrop, 30, 32 ; Schuschnigg sounds him on Restoration, 113-14 ; advises against invasion, 176
Nicolson, (later Sir) Harold, 87

'Operation Otto', 16, 113, 132-3, 187 ; 'Instruction No. 1', 133-4 ; 'No. 2', 177
Otto, Archduke, 115-17 ; *and see* Monarchists

Palairet (British Ambassador at Vienna), 137
Papen, Franz von, xxi, 13-14 ; plot to kill, 16-17 ; woos Schuschnigg, 23, 32-3 ; summoned to Berlin, 30-1 ; at Berchtesgaden, 52-3 ; obtains one concession from Hitler, 67, 70 ; reproaches Schuschnigg,

THE END